Sustainable Gardening for Florida

UNIVERSITY PRESS OF FLORIDA

Florida A&M University, Tallahassee
Florida Atlantic University, Boca Raton
Florida Gulf Coast University, Ft. Myers
Florida International University, Miami
Florida State University, Tallahassee
New College of Florida, Sarasota
University of Central Florida, Orlando
University of Florida, Gainesville
University of North Florida, Jacksonville
University of South Florida, Tampa
University of West Florida, Pensacola

Sustainable Gardening for Florida

Ginny Stibolt

Illustrated by John Markowski

University Press of Florida
Gainesville · Tallahassee · Tampa · Boca Raton
Pensacola · Orlando · Miami · Jacksonville · Ft. Myers · Sarasota

Library of Congress Cataloging-in-Publication Data
Stibolt, Ginny.
Sustainable gardening for Florida / Ginny Stibolt ; illustrated
by John Markowski.
p. cm.
Includes index.
ISBN 978-0-8130-3392-1 (alk. paper)
1. Sustainable horticulture—Florida. 2. Natural landscaping—Florida.
I. Markowski, John. II. Title.
SB319.95.S75 2009
635.09759—dc22   2009008374

The University Press of Florida is the scholarly publishing agency for the
State University System of Florida, comprising Florida A&M Univer-
sity, Florida Atlantic University, Florida Gulf Coast University, Florida
International University, Florida State University, New College of Florida,
University of Central Florida, University of Florida, University of North
Florida, University of South Florida, and University of West Florida.

University Press of Florida
15 Northwest 15th Street
Gainesville, FL 32611-2079
http://www.upf.com

I dedicate this book to Dean Avery—my husband
and my partner in green living.
He has supported this endeavor in countless ways.

Contents

Preface

This is not an armchair or coffee table gardening book; it's a let's-work-together action book—similar to a cookbook with recipes that provide guidance for creating tasty treats. While beginning cooks tend to follow the recipes exactly, more experienced cooks may adjust the recipes to suit their own needs. Enough detail has been included in this book to provide beginners with recipes to follow, but more experienced property managers may use the instructions as guidelines and adjust them to suit their own situations.

When working with Mother Nature, there are no guarantees; she adds a fifth dimension of chance to the three dimensions of space and the fourth dimension of time. Gardeners embrace this element of chance; it makes gardening as much an art as a science. The science of providing the best possible situations greatly improves the probability of success, but Mother Nature always has the ultimate say-so.

I came to write this book after a chance meeting with John Byram of University Press of Florida in March 2006. He was looking for an organic gardening book for Florida, but after some discussion we settled on sustainable gardening as a broader topic. I appreciate his confidence in my ability to write this book and his continuing guidance throughout the process. And I'm grateful for the expert pre-readers who went over the manuscript or parts of the manuscript to check for errors and clarity: Gil Nelson, Steve Christman, Kristina Serbesoff-King, Trish Gramajo, Ann Stodola, Rose Broome, Amy Baldwin, and Peter Colverson. Helen Marshall helped with her sharp editor's eye. Their insights, suggestions, and numerous corrections were most helpful, but any errors remaining in the final version are my own.

The wonderful illustrations by John Markowski—architect, artist, gardener, and good friend—help to clarify the text. My instructions for various projects are made much clearer with his drawings.

I am pleased to share the royalties from this book with The Nature Conservancy of Florida. Their ability to preserve some of our most significant wild places in the state becomes more critical as our population increases. I'd like to think that this book's message, if applied by a large number of Floridians, would also play a part in slowing the destruction of habitat and improving the water quality in our waterways.

If I May Get up on My Soapbox for a Moment . . .

The environment is not something that is separate from us. We are all participants in it. Our actions, lifestyles, consumption are all part of the mix. We won't make much progress if we just talk about "the environment" or if we fund yet another study. No matter how much we pay for it, talk is cheap. There are many other lifestyle changes that we may make, outside of the scope of this book, that will further reduce our footprints on Florida:

- Recycle more. Fill up the curbside recycling bins with aluminum cans, bottles, and paper; reduce what you throw away. Recycle your old computers. Donate old cars, used clothing, and other useable items to charities.
- Handle hazardous material correctly, and report anyone pouring hazardous waste into the streets or storm drains. Clear debris from the storm drains in your neighborhood, so less organic material enters our waterways.
- Drive less and drive fuel-efficient cars. Walk or ride your bikes more, and lobby for bike paths and village centers so people can find more of what they need close to home.
- Eat lower in the food chain. Eat more vegetables and fruits and less meat—it's better for your health and the health of our environment and reduces the amount of energy required to put food on your table. Of course, if you raise some of your own vegetables

and fruit, you're using even less manufactured energy to sustain you and your family.

- Drink filtered (not bottled) water, if tap water offends your taste buds. This will reduce the amount of plastic waste that goes into our landfills and especially into our waterways.
- Install solar panels to augment or replace your hot water heater or to generate some of your own electricity. Use solar powered outside lights, too. Install fluorescent bulbs or LED (light-emitting diode) lights all around. Cut back on extraneous outdoor lighting—it's better for plants and wildlife to experience darkness at night.
- Insulate your house, use double-glazed windows, install ceiling fans, and then set the thermostat higher in the summer and lower in the winter. You may find that 82 or 83 degrees is quite tolerable in the summer if you use fans to move the air. In the winter, set the thermostat lower and dress warmly. Encourage businesses to turn up their air conditioning—it's ridiculous that we have to carry sweaters in the summer.
- Consume less and buy items with the least amount of packaging.
- Get involved in neighborhood and local politics to change unsustainable policies concerning lawns, community lands, development, and other environmental issues.
- Support and vote for public officials who will make greener choices for Florida and the country.

This book is a call to action on a wide assortment of sustainable practices and techniques to use in your gardens and landscapes. But I suspect that you (like most folks) will start with just a few items that make the most sense for your situation. This is fine because when you find that you're saving time and money, you'll include a few more sustainable landscaping practices each season—it's better for the environment and it's addictive.

And while you're at it, pass the word. Involve youth groups, community associations, and local governments in sustainable landscape management, and see if you can get the local press interested. Please send me your experiences and results along with before-and-after photos and links to any press coverage, and I'll post your story on this book's Web site.

ℒ

A companion Web site for this book can be found at www.Sustainable Gardening4Florida.com. It includes updated references for each of the chapters and other current topics on sustainable gardening in Florida.

Sustainable Florida

Moving toward sustainability in managing your landscape can happen with bold, sweeping changes or with small steps, but it does need to happen. Florida's warm climate and beautiful natural resources attract a steady stream of new residents every day. As the population increases, those same natural resources are being strained—especially the waterways, the water supply, and the land's wild places.

There's a lot of advice out there on how to go "green" and live more lightly on the planet. These are not new ideas. The Native American Iroquois Confederacy Chiefs and their people were charged with bearing in mind the effects of their actions for seven generations. These days, the need is more urgent, and many people and companies seem more generally aware that they should do their part. There are recycling programs, low impact development regulations, smart growth initiatives, water saving devices, and **carbon-offset organizations**. Even events like the Super Bowl buy carbon-offsetting certificates. As a result, thousands of trees are planted and the stadium is powered by renewable energy sources during the game. The Nature Conservancy has details on how to calculate your carbon footprint on its Web site (search under "carbon footprint"): http://www.tnc.org.

The purpose of this book is to provide ideas to reduce your ecological footprint by making changes in your landscape management. Homeown-

Organization of This Book

There are two appendices: the glossary and the plant list. Terms defined in the glossary are shown in **bold** the first time they appear in the text. The plant list, arranged alphabetically by common name, provides additional details on plants mentioned in the text.

The chapters are written in a way that allows you to skip around the book to learn about specific topics. Because of the overlapping nature of the material, you may find that reading several aligned chapters will provide a more complete coverage of the topic.

Resources listed at the end of each chapter provide more information on the subjects covered. Many of the references are Internet Web sites. Because only the main URL is given for each Web site, you may have to search sites for specific topics. All of the referenced Web sites were current as of January 2009. This book's Web site, http://www.SustainableGardening4Florida. com, will be updated with new and updated resources as information becomes available.

ers, families, schools, municipalities, community groups, churches, businesses, and other landscape managers will find interesting, money-saving action items to help them become better stewards of their individual properties and of our shared lands and waterways. While Florida's environmental challenges are huge, each of us can take responsibility to make our own landscape management greener. Added together, our efforts do make a difference.

Defining Sustainable Gardening

Without the continuing hand of the gardener, Mother Nature works to equalize any gardened space to its surroundings and starts the slow process of **succession** toward a wild state for that particular environment. By definition then, a garden is not self-sustaining. So then, what is sustainable gardening?

Sustainable gardening and sustainable landscape management are wide-ranging collections of techniques that reduce your gardening footprint on the planet. They can be summarized into eight categories.

1. Having minimal impact on the environment—from using little or no artificially produced chemicals, (pesticides, herbicides, quick-release fertilizers) to reducing the use of powered devices in the care of the landscape. All those string trimmers, leaf blowers, and lawnmowers not only pollute the air and use unsustainable fuel, they also cause noise pollution. (Electric or propane powered tools are greener than gas-driven ones, though.)

2. Making the best use of available resources: using rain barrels to collect rainwater, for example; arranging garden areas to make use of rainwater overflow; mulching bare soil to preserve moisture, and enriching soil with compost that you make with waste vegetation.

3. Saving time and money. For example, by using good gardening techniques when planting so you don't have to replace plants later; by reducing the size of your lawn and managing what's left in a more natural manner; by replacing lawn in hard-to-mow drainage ditches with easy-to-maintain rain gardens.

4. Reducing carbon dioxide and increase oxygen in the air by promoting installation of many large plants. Greater plant **biomass** increases the amount of **photosynthesis**—that magical chemical process whereby green plants absorb sunlight and transform carbon dioxide and water into sugar, with oxygen gas as a byproduct.

5. Offsetting some of the heat absorbed and stored by urban/suburban buildings, roads, and other hard objects. Landscapes with more trees, shrubs, and understory perennials will absorb more stormwater and increase **transpiration**. This puts water vapor into the atmosphere, reducing the air temperature in the immediate vicinity.

6. Increasing habitat for wildlife including birds, bees, butterflies, and other critters. The sustainable landscape supports an active ecosystem where plants, microbes, insects, and other animals all depend on one another.

7. Preventing damage to underground infrastructure. In other words, don't start digging until you know the location of underground utilities and pipes. Also look up to locate overhead wires, and plan your landscape to avoid them. It's definitely not sustainable to remove or top a tree because you didn't plan for its adult size.

8. Preparing for disasters such as hurricanes, fires, and drought. Designing your landscape to withstand or minimize damage when a disaster strikes is sustainable. After the disaster you may have fewer structural repairs to make and fewer plants to replace.

Florida Yards and Neighborhoods

Florida Yards and Neighborhoods is an outreach program sponsored by the University of Florida's IFAS (Institute of Food and Agricultural Sciences) extension service and other organizations. The program's nine principles align with the principles of sustainability. You can find more information about each of these topics in the chapters listed.

1. Right plant, right place: chapters 2 and 8
2. Water efficiently: chapter 10
3. Fertilize appropriately: chapters 3, 4, and 8
4. Mulch: chapter 3
5. Attract wildlife: chapter 5
6. Recycle: chapter 3
7. Control yard pests responsibly: chapter 9
8. Reduce stormwater runoff: chapters 10, 11, and 12
9. Protect the waterfront: chapter 13

Other Definitions of Sustainable Landscape Management

- National Wildlife Federation's list of sustainable gardening practices is part of their backyard and schoolyard wildlife habitat certification process. Their list includes various sustainable categories with specific activities that will contribute to the cause.
  - Water Conservation: creating vegetative buffer zones in front of or around water features; rain gardens; capturing rainwater from rooftops; xeriscaping, using drip or soaker hoses for irrigation; reducing lawn areas; reducing erosion; eliminating chemical pesticides; eliminating chemical fertilizers; and mulching.
  - Soil Conservation: mulching; reducing erosion; composting; eliminating chemical pesticides; and eliminating chemical fertilizers.
  - Control of Exotic Species: monitoring nesting boxes; keeping your cat indoors; removing invasive plants; restoring native plants; and reducing lawn areas.
  - Use of Organic Practices: eliminating chemical fertilizers and chemical pesticides; encouraging pest predators; and composting.
- The Army Corps of Engineers has its own definition of the terms "sustainable" and "sustainability": "A level and method of resource use that does not destroy the health and integrity of the systems that provide the resource; thus the long-term resource availability does not ever diminish due to such use."
- Sustainable Agriculture: While gardening and landscape management differ in theory and practice from agriculture, it may be useful to note that in 1990, the U.S. government defined sustainable agriculture as "an integrated system of plant and animal production practices having a site-specific application that will, over the long term, satisfy human food and fiber needs; enhance environmental quality and the natural resource base upon which the agricultural economy depends; make the most efficient use of nonrenewable resources and on-farm resources and integrate, where appropriate, natural biological cycles and controls; sustain

the economic viability of farm operations; and enhance the quality of life for farmers and society as a whole."

Sustainable Gardening versus Organic Gardening

The chemical definition of "organic" is a compound that includes carbon and hydrogen, along with other naturally occurring elements. With very few exceptions, anything that's alive or has been alive is made up of organic materials, because most life on our planet depends in some way on carbon-based sugars formed by green plants during photosynthesis.

J. I. Rodale coined another use of the word "organic" in the 1940s when he started *Organic Gardening Magazine* and wrote about farming without using artificial chemicals. The materials he used for fertilizer and pesticides were derived from plants and animals—they were organic. Organic farmers now face a rigorous process in order to become certified, so you can be assured that no synthetic pesticides or fertilizers have touched food that has been labeled "organically grown." For instance, if an organic farmer uses hay as a mulch, it must be free of any artificial chemical residues, and all the seeds must have come from organic gardens. If the local government sends a mosquito insecticide spraying truck near your garden, your pesticide-free environment will be compromised. Your local extension agent can provide the rules and regulations for certified organic farming.

Organic gardening is often defined by what you don't do—you don't use artificially produced chemicals for fertilizer or pesticides for insect control. Many (probably most) organic gardeners use sustainable gardening practices, but sustainable gardening covers a broader set of practices for ensuring that your garden has the smallest impact on the environment. For example, growing rice in the desert could be certified as organic if no artificial chemicals are used, but it's not sustainable because cultivating rice requires a huge amount of water—a rare resource in the desert.

Another point about organic products: if a product carries an organic label, this does not necessarily mean that it won't damage the environment; it only means that the product is derived from animals or plants. Poisons, organic or not, kill both beneficial and pesky bugs, and their use should be minimized or eliminated as you work on integrated pest management (IPM) as discussed in chapter 6.

Sustainable Gardening versus Permaculture

Sustainable gardening and sustainable landscape management are elements of permaculture. "Permaculture," a term coined in the 1970s by Australian ecologist Bill Mollison and one of his students, David Holmgren, is often described by the accompanying subtitle, "Sustainable Living." The practice of permaculture extends beyond gardening and agriculture to more politicized arenas, such as urban planning, sociology, ethics, and reducing people's reliance upon those industrial systems that adversely impact ecosystems and neighborhoods. Permaculture design begins with a set of ethics: first, "care for the Earth"; second, "care for the people"; and third, "set limits to population and consumption." This is an admirable but often controversial formula to push people to exchange wasteful ways for more sustainable lifestyle choices. Sustainable landscape management is one part of the permaculture movement.

Florida Is a Diverse State, Gardenwise

To manage your landscape in a sustainable manner, you need to be aware of the climate and other conditions found in your particular area. There are dramatic differences in temperatures, rainfall, and soils across the state.

Florida has five different climate zones, from north to south, each determined by the coldest average winter temperature within that range. The current USDA Plant Hardiness Zone Map, last updated in 1990, shows Florida's zones ranging from 8a, which dips into the panhandle near Pensacola, to 11 in the Keys. In 2006, the National Arbor Day Foundation updated the planting zones to include more recent temperature data—in Florida the old zone demarcations have slid significantly northward. Gardeners have been aware of this, as they've had success growing plants that were not formerly hardy enough for their gardens.

The American Horticulture Society (AHS) has produced another map that's based on high temperatures—the number of days per year above 86 degrees Fahrenheit. High temperatures can also be a limiting factor in how well a plant does in a certain environment. Florida's high temperatures range from zone 8 (with 90 to 120 days above 86 degrees) to zone 12

1990 USDA zone map

(with more than 210 days above 86 degrees). AHS has rated many plants for their heat tolerance, but their heat rating is not widely found on seed packets or other planting instructions. The 1990 USDA map is still the standard.

There's more to consider than just cold and hot temperatures. Soils have a huge impact on native and cultivated plants, from the Georgian red clay in the northwest to the alkaline limestone substrate in the southeast and the Keys. Each region has distinct environmental and gardening issues. Consider the regional recommendations as broad suggestions, because your property may have its own **microclimates** and special situations that will influence your decisions. It's best to find out about your property's conditions in a thorough and organized manner:

- Test soil from several separate areas on your lot and test your compost, too.
- Determine where impervious surfaces (such as driveways, roads, and sidewalks) drain. Observe where water collects after a hard rain and how long it sits before it soaks in.
- Find out what's going on in the soil. After a hard rain and after a drizzle, dig past the mulch and into the soil to see how far the moisture has soaked in. Another test is to dig a two-foot-deep hole and wait to see if water seeps into it. If it fills with water, your water table is just below the surface. If no water seeps in, fill it with water and see how long it takes to soak in. These tests will help you figure out your drainage characteristics. For more details on drainage see chapter 12.
- Note the plants that are doing well and those that are not. Further examine any additional conditions if plants are not successful:
  · Is the whole bed failing or just individual plants or a certain species of plant?
  · Is there a nearby physical structure such as fence or a building? If so, what is the exposure?
  · Is there wilting in the heat of the day? If so, do plants perk up each night?
- Examine the roots of weeds or dead plants that you pull from the soil to check for root rot or knobs due to damage from those tiny worms, root-knot **nematodes**. Examine the soil in the plant's hole to check for bugs, moisture, or other underground factors relating to the plant's failure, such as a surface root from a nearby tree.

Water, Water Everywhere, or Not

While Florida normally has its fair share of precipitation, with an average annual rainfall ranging from 39 to 64 inches, and despite the appearance of endless supply from North Florida's beautiful springs, there is a problem in paradise. As the human population increases with our demand for

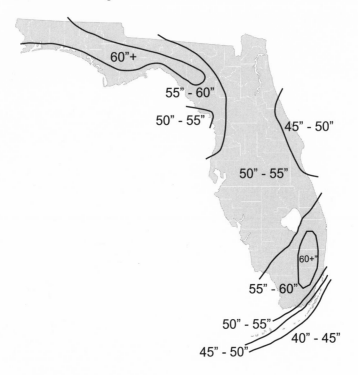

Florida's average annual rainfall.

more and more water, the groundwater and aquifers are being strained. We are using too much water and wasting a lot of it. Waterwise landscaping will reduce some of the strain.

Rain: too much or not enough. There are significant regional differences in rainfall in Florida as we see in the table below and the average rainfall map. What's important to note is that the seven dry-season months average only half the rain per month as the five months of our wet season. In contrast, New York City's rainfall ranges from three to four and a half inches per month, for a total of 49 inches per year—there is no pattern of wet or dry months. (This is one reason plants from temperate climates don't usually adjust well to our wet and dry seasons.)

When there's a drier-than-average dry season, the water table lowers, but people use more water than ever. Good landscape design and management practices should help the plants withstand those dry seasons with

Average monthly rainfall in inches—from 1971 to 2000

	Pensacola	Apalachicola	Jacksonville	Tampa	Miami	Key West	Avg./mo.
January	5.34	4.87	3.69	2.27	1.88	2.22	3.378
February	4.68	3.76	3.15	2.67	2.07	1.51	2.973
March	6.40	4.95	3.93	2.84	2.56	1.86	3.757
April	3.89	3.00	3.14	1.80	3.36	2.06	2.875
May	4.40	2.62	3.48	2.85	5.52	3.48	3.725
June[a]	6.39	4.30	5.37	5.50	8.54	4.57	5.778
July[a]	8.02	7.31	5.97	6.49	5.79	3.27	6.142
August[a]	6.85	7.29	6.87	7.60	8.63	5.40	7.107
September[a]	5.75	7.10	7.90	6.54	8.38	5.45	6.853
October[a]	4.13	4.18	3.86	2.29	6.19	4.34	4.165
November	4.46	3.62	2.34	1.62	3.43	2.64	3.018
December	3.97	3.51	2.64	2.30	2.18	2.14	2.790
Total	64.28	51.64	52.34	44.77	58.53	38.94	51.750

Source: http://www.noaa.gov.

a. Wet season (5 mos.), 6.01 inches/mo. Dry season (7 mos.), 3.22 inches/mo.

a minimum of irrigation. Using a good rain gauge will help you better manage the irrigation and water only when needed. This way, when water use restrictions are implemented, your plants will be prepared for lower water conditions. See chapter 10 for drought-proofing strategies. Drier-than-normal seasons often bring wildfires that scorch the land, threaten houses, and close down roads. Fires may be natural events in our state, but firewise property design provides fire-retarding buffers. This and other strategies are discussed in chapter 14.

Florida's wet season gains national attention when Atlantic and Caribbean tropical storms spin into hurricanes, but most of the time our wet seasons consist of many ordinary, frog-choking gully washer rainstorms. Stormwater can erode unstabilized soil and may wash nutrients and pollutants from landscapes and paved areas. This water, laden with debris, silt, and pollutants, surges down the storm drains. These pollutants include fertilizer and pesticides washed from landscapes, along with roadway runoff—a combination of vehicle drippage, microscopic pieces of rubber, and pieces of asphalt. If the stormwater system slows down the runoff in settling ponds, some of the debris and silt will sink, but the water-soluble pollutants may stay in the water and add to the nutrient overload plaguing Florida's waterways. Landscape managers can design water retention features such as rain gardens to filter the rainwater before it becomes part of the groundwater, as discussed in chapter 12.

Both floods and droughts led to the creation of the Water Resources Act of 1972. This legislation launched the water management districts that now divide Florida into five regions with similar water supplies and conditions. They are the Northwest Florida WMD (Water Management District), Suwannee River WMD, St. Johns River WMD, Southwest Florida WMD, and South Florida WMD. The WMDs monitor water quality and define policies pertaining to use or changes to wetlands, shorelines, and structures, such as bulkheads or docks. They acquire and manage conservation areas, usually near bodies of water, which serve to recharge groundwater. The WMDs work with local utilities to set water-use restrictions when the water supplied by groundwater and aquifers is low or if there are other conditions such as contamination or saltwater intrusion. The districts also work to educate the public about saving water and about waterwise landscaping practices.

Florida Is Special

Florida's warm temperatures and its wet and dry seasons don't necessarily work well for many plants native to temperate climate areas. You can save time, money, and frustration by choosing native and non-native plants that have proven themselves in your region. If you purchase bulbs, those produced in Holland or in other temperate climates may not be the best choice—you may wish to consider southern sources for plants and bulbs. Many bulbs, such as tulips, don't do well without an extended cold period each year. It's more sustainable to choose bulbs and other plants that thrive in our climate, not ones that need special treatment.

Just because a garden shop has plants, bulbs, or seeds for sale, it doesn't mean that they are appropriate for your climate in that season. Know what you're getting. Do some homework to find how appropriate that plant is for your region and for the season before you buy it. It's best to have a plan, avoid impulse purchases, and purchase plants that fill the niches of your planned landscape.

Sustainable Gardening Is Greener

You don't need a green thumb to become a "greener" gardener or landscaper, but by paying attention, making best use of available resources, and increasing the survival rate of your plants, you can become a more sustainable gardener.

Resources

Web Sites

Seven Generations Ahead is a nonprofit organization based on the Iroquois Seventh Generation Law on sustainability: http://www.sevengenerationsahead.org.

The Florida Natural Areas Inventory is a comprehensive database of the biological resources for Florida: http://www.fnai.org.

The University of Florida's Institute of Food and Agricultural Sciences (IFAS) has agricultural extension offices in 67 Florida counties. These host the Florida Yards and Neighborhoods program, which offers detailed information and plant lists for Florida: http://www.floridayards.org.

The Common Ground Alliance started an 811 "call before you dig" number in order to help people avoid hitting utility lines: http://www.commongroundalliance.com.

Florida's Department of Environmental Protection provides an overview of the five water management districts: http://www.dep.state.fl.us/.

The United States Environmental Protection Agency (EPA) Web site has information relating to regulations and environmentally friendly practices: http://www.epa.gov.

Books

Brower, Michael, and Warren Leon. *The Consumer's Guide to Effective Environmental Choices: Practical Advice from The Union of Concerned Scientists.* New York: Three Rivers, 1999.

Willey, Zach, and Bill Chameides, eds. *Harnessing Farms and Forests in the Low-Carbon Economy: How to Create, Measure, and Verify Greenhouse Gas Offsets.* Durham, N.C.: Environmental Defense, Duke University, 2007. (Available online at http://www.nicholas.duke.edu.)

Gardening Strategies, Mother Nature's Way

Gardeners are rearrangers. Flowerbeds, designed to present favorite plants in an attractive manner throughout the seasons, are a gardener's sometimes-elusive goal. If you use the most appropriate plants for your particular situation and use the best gardening techniques, your plants are more likely to be healthy and vigorous throughout their life cycle. Isn't this what we all want?

Enlist Experts to Help Create a Plan

An expert or two may save you money, time, and frustration over time, if you choose your experts carefully. Sound advice on plant selections and landscape features to fit your particular conditions on various sections of your property may greatly increase the survival of the plants. For general advice and plant identifications, your county extension agent is there to help. He or she will have data sheets on many plants with particular information as it relates to your county. A certified arborist can evaluate your trees for stormworthiness and suggest new trees suitable for your location. If you have frequent problems with stormwater on your site, you'll probably want the help of a civil engineer to map out a grading plan. The

Good Gardening Is Sustainable

Using the best gardening practices is sustainable because appropriately planted specimens live longer, need less care, and require less water. Using the best tools and methods for gardening helps sustain gardeners, too. When you reduce plant loss and make the best use of resources, it's better for the environment, and you'll have more time and money for other projects.

engineer will also know if you need permits for regrading your property. A landscape architect can help with the overall planning.

Be cautious of advice from landscaping companies that offer to install an instant landscape; they are in business to sell the plants in stock and may not be the best source of information. Although you may be anxious to finish the job, a more studied and deliberate approach over several seasons is usually the most prudent. You can fill in the blanks in your landscape with inexpensive annuals while you wait for growth or more permanent replacements. Whenever possible, choose native plants if you have a suitable location for them.

You can become more expert and learn what you need to become a more sustainable gardener. Go to garden fests and plant shows, take courses and attend workshops, go on guided field trips, or ask questions at reputable nurseries. Join your local garden club, your regional chapter of the Florida Native Plant Society, or another gardening group. Buy field guides so you can identify native plants and learn which invasive non-native plants may plague your part of Florida.

It's smart to keep a garden log or journal to keep track of your successes and failures. For each, record planting and harvesting (or picking) times, types of seeds or plants, and where you bought them. Having this personal reference will help you become a more sustainable gardener over time.

Design Considerations

When planning for sustainability in your garden spaces, there is more to consider than just buying pretty plants and creating interesting textures. Design for ease of care, water conservation, improved wildlife habitat, and the general appropriateness of plants for specific locations. Develop areas in your landscape that are compatible with various human activities, too.

Create a plan for your property. This plan can be a formal, scale drawing provided by a landscape architect, a copy of your plot with areas of concern highlighted and noted, or an informal sketch or series of sketches in your garden log. Whichever method you choose, note what's already in place and what projects you plan for the future. That way, when you're at a nursery or garden center, you'll be more likely to avoid impulse purchases and choose just the right plants to fill out your planned area and just the right supplies to meet your actual needs.

Ease of Care

While gardeners generally love to spend time in their gardens, planning for sustainability can help produce a better looking landscape, increase gardening successes, and reduce a few of the more tedious tasks. Implementing some of these strategies means that your garden time will be more enjoyable.

Work with odd numbers of plants with differing branching patterns arranged at different heights. Don't try to bookend areas in your landscape with matching plants. Even if you purchase plants that look similar at the nursery, they may not grow in the same way. Opt for more naturalistic groupings—maybe place one larger tree or shrub near one side of a building face and plant three smaller shrubs in a shallow triangle to offset it on the other side. When you select appropriate plants for specific places, you won't have to be heavy-handed with the pruning.

Shearing of shrubbery into artificial shapes is not sustainable, because every spurt of growth looks out of place. Create a hedgerow of different types of plants growing into their natural shapes instead of the boring, single-species sheared hedge. A variety of plants provides better habitat for birds and butterflies, too. If plants in a hedgerow require cutting back, prune individual branches back to a lower branch growing in the desired direction—this is called "**drop-crotch pruning**." There is more information on pruning in chapter 6.

Avoid sharp-angled, hard-to-mow-around corners in your landscape. Use sweeping curves and install pavers along the edges of mowed areas, so no extra trimming will be needed.

Use mulches to keep down the weeds, conserve moisture, and moderate soil temperatures. If weeds do grow (Of course weeds will grow—this is Florida!), try to get rid of them before they go to seed or before they crawl all over your gardens or meadows. It's much easier to handle weeds early in the season. Some of these volunteers may be attractive native plants, though. Work on identifying the invasive weeds, and let the others grow until you know what they are. Until you know, let them grow.

If your plans include plants that are not well suited to your local environment, it's generally not sustainable to attempt to adjust the total garden to provide good conditions for those plants. Use containers or raised beds to better control the soil and other growing conditions for special plants. For instance, if you live in the Keys where the soil (what there is of it) is alkaline, planting an acid-loving plant such as a tomato in the ground wouldn't be prudent. Tomatoes could thrive there in the microclimate of a pot or raised bed, though. Pay attention to the requirements or preferred habitat of each plant you acquire.

Microclimate Gardening

Unless your landscape is an open field, it will include various microclimates caused by proximity of planting sites to buildings, other plants, or bodies of water. The lay of the land can also influence the planting environment. Choosing plants suitable to a particular microclimate is part of planting the right plants in the right places, and it's also part of a waterwise landscape plan. It's usually not sustainable to modify the inherent conditions found in a specific location, so create garden or landscape features that will take good advantage of existing conditions.

Having a variety of habitats throughout the landscape creates more interest and is good for the environment as well. Here are some of the environmental situations that will influence the microclimates in your landscape:

Sun exposure: Areas on the north and east side of a building will not be exposed to strong afternoon sun. Plants on the south and west side of the house will receive intense afternoon sun in the summer if there are no trees to shade them, particularly with re-flected light from a white or light-colored wall. Terrain that slopes down to the south will intensify the solar heating, while terrain that slopes down to the north will be less affected. These tempera-ture contrasts remain in the winter, although the sun is lower in the sky and therefore less intense. You can build some shade by altering the sun exposure with pergolas, trellises, or arbors. Trees and shrubs can provide shade on the sunny sides of buildings to reduce the heat buildup and perhaps reduce your need for air conditioning.

Wind: If you live near the water, the prevailing winds tend to come from the ocean or from the Gulf, and these winds may carry salt. Inland, the winds can come from almost any direction as weather systems cross the state. Wind's effects on plants and trees will be greatest when there are no obstacles to block or reduce it. Wind speeds up and eddies as it passes around buildings, so wind dam-age may be more severe for plants located at the corners of build-ings.

Moisture: Sunny areas, raised areas, or areas with higher winds will naturally be drier than places with shade or wind protection. Places where the soil is usually damp or where it alternates be-tween dampness and dryness constitute different sets of microcli-mates. Choose plants according to their moisture requirements.

Traffic: Areas where the soil is compacted by foot and vehicular traffic are also microclimates in your landscape. Instead of fight-ing to keep turf or other groundcover growing in such unfriendly places, install stepping-stones, pavers, or mulched pathways. Plan for stepping areas within and between your garden beds so you have good access for working.

Vegetation: Existing plants in the landscape create microclimates, too. Turfgrass and many other plants don't do well under shallow-rooted shade trees. In the mulched beds around trees, use compatible plants that do well in shade and can compete or peacefully coexist with the trees' root systems. Some plants may have aggressive roots, send up new sprouts, or produce tubers that crowd out neighboring plants. Know what you grow. You can use containers, raised beds, or other methods to avoid adverse conditions. For instance, you may wish to plant monarda or other aggressive mints in a sunken pot so that their roots don't crowd out other plants in your herb garden.

Hedge your bets. Sometimes there will be aspects of a microclimate that aren't obvious to you, so watch your plants—they will react positively or negatively to a location. When you bring new plants into your landscape, plant them in a few locations, and then let the plants tell you where they belong. If you have enough plant material, trade with a neighbor so you'll each have a plant bank. That way if something happens to your populations in one spot, you can make a withdrawal from your plant bank and replant in a more appropriate space.

Appropriate Garden Spaces

Think about how your property will be used and design outside spaces with that in mind. A landscape should complement the style of the buildings it serves. Good landscape design is sustainable because planning ahead reduces the probability of having to replace inappropriate plants or redesign and replant what ended up being an awkward garden area.

Consider your schedule when designing garden spaces. If you work all day, don't spend your time and effort on plants that peak before noon; concentrate on evening bloomers instead. Landscapes in commercial spaces should provide for interest and shade during hours of operations and for staff break areas. If a property won't be used during certain, predictable time periods, plan for peak garden showiness when folks are there to enjoy it. For instance, if you're landscaping a school, summer vacation means that maybe you don't need to install a summer-blooming garden.

Plan instead for fall bloomers that can make it through the summer break without any help.

Work to your plan. Make sure when designing outdoor spaces that they will serve a purpose. If you don't have a specific need for a lawn, reduce its size or remove it entirely. Replace it with a combination of low-care habitat and sustainable, mulched beds. A sustainable landscape should be able to thrive without a gardener's hand for long periods of time.

The Waiting Game

If you've planted new trees and shrubs in your landscape and have followed the sustainable practice of planning for their adult sizes, you'll have some gaps to deal with. It's a waiting game, but you can create some quick shade and fill in some of those spaces while you wait.

Use a combination of trellises, arbors, or pergolas, and plant some fast-growing vines to climb them to create some temporary shade. The vines can be annuals that you replant each year, or you can plant some perennial vines, such as Virginia creeper, grape, trumpet creeper, and coral honeysuckle. In a few years, when your trees are larger, you can remove these vines and arbors or change their configuration to accommodate your growing trees. Using large pots to contain the vines and other temporary plants will make the transition easier.

Fast-growing, tall shrubs such as southern bayberry or elderberry could also fill in the gaps quickly. Plan to remove them or trim them back as the trees grow into their allocated spaces. If you plan to transplant them in a few years, **root prune** them once or twice a year to ease the transplant shock.

Transplanting and Division Ideas

The best time to transplant or divide plants will differ depending upon the plant and your location within the state. Transplant or divide perennials or bulbs just after their active growth or flowering period, because when they go into dormancy you may forget where they are. In North and Central Florida, transplant most deciduous woody plants in January or February—the end of dormancy. In South Florida, the recommended

Transplanting from the Wild

When transplanting from someone else's property, make sure you have permission. Removing plants from public lands is not allowed. Keep in mind that transplanting from wild areas is likely to fail for most plants, large and small, for several reasons. First, it's difficult to reproduce the exact conditions needed to grow wild plants, and also these plants have not been root pruned and roots from other plants may be entangled with them. You may kill not only the plant you are trying to transplant, but also others in the surrounding area.

Rescuing desirable or fragile native plants from areas that are to be developed is recommended but is best left to folks with the right tools. Some chapters of Florida's Native Plant Society and other groups sometimes set up rescue parties that you might join. Meanwhile, buy your wildflowers and native plants from the many reputable nurseries that specialize in Florida natives.

time is June—just before the rainy season. More details on handling trees and shrubs appear in chapter 6.

Dividing Perennials

Well-sited perennials are a joy in a sustainable garden, because they need so little ongoing care. Each year they continue to produce their wonderful textured leaves or reliable color while flowering, and if you're lucky, their fruits, too. In Florida we have a huge selection of native and non-native perennials, such as ferns, goldenrods, crinum lilies, asters, ornamental grasses, and many more.

When the perennial outgrows its spot, when it begins to lose its vigor, or when it's big enough that you can take some of it to plant in other places, then it's time for the mathematical oxymoron—multiply by dividing. If the plants form a wide mass, such as the net-veined chain fern or goldenrod, remove plants from the middle of an overcrowded area, then replace your divot like a golfer. Leave the border populations alone so that they may continue to expand naturally. The individuals that you've dug up should be planted in similar soil and in similar conditions, and for best success, prepare the soil in and around the planting site with some compost before transplanting. Plant them no deeper than they were before. Water well and add mulch. Hand water until the plants stop wilting each day, then water on a regular basis until you see new growth. During the first year, be sure to irrigate the transplants during long dry periods.

If the plants are clumpers, such as ornamental grasses, then you'll want to dig up the whole plant mass and pry apart the various sections or maybe even chop the clump into thirds or fourths. Wait until after their prime growing season before you dig them. The best tool for prying is a large garden fork, which makes it possible to have more roots stay with their growth nodes. Add some compost into the original hole and mix well with the soil before you replant one of the clumps back in the hole. Make sure it's not too deep. Then water deeply and mulch. Hand water on a regular basis until the plants stop wilting each day, then water on a regular basis until you see new growth.

For bulbs that multiply, after they've flowered and when most of the leaves have died down, dig up the whole bunch and gently separate the bulbs and bulblets by hand. Add some compost to the hole and mix well with surrounding soil, then replant three or five of the bulbs back in the

Protect bulbs from nibblers with a cage made from ½-inch gauge hardware cloth.

same hole. Choose some full-sized bulbs and some smaller ones for each hole. Take the remaining bulbs and plant them in odd numbered groups in well-prepared holes. Mulch the area over the bulbs and label them so you don't lose track of where they are. Water once—don't over water bulbs or they'll rot. If squirrels, voles, pocket gophers, or other bulb-eating critters populate your landscape, you can enclose each bulb in a hardware cloth basket built to impede the nibblers but not the plant.

Dealing with Seeds and Seedlings

Planting seeds and watching as they sprout and grow into robust plants is one of gardening's great pleasures. Starting plants from seed is sustainable because transporting seeds, rather than plants, takes much less energy and because you can control pesticide and fertilizer applications. Planting your own seeds gives you the peace of mind of controlling their environment, from seed to table. You can also participate in heritage seed programs, as discussed in chapter 8, to help promote crop diversity. It's disappointing when seeds don't sprout or when seedlings are chopped off by a cutworm, crowded out by a jungle of Florida weeds, or attacked by a damping-off **fungus**. Growing plants from seed is Mother Nature's miracle, but there are ways to increase your odds of success.

Planting Seeds in the Garden

When you plant seeds directly in the garden, Florida's weeds will also invite themselves to your nicely prepared soil. To increase the germination of your seeds, reduce problems with fungal infections, and suppress weeds, use a topdressing of a sterilized medium such as treated soil, **vermiculite**, or unfertilized potting mix. Follow the directions on the seed packet for pretreating the seeds for sprouting. On planting day, thoroughly moisten the soil so it's damp at least two inches deep, then add an inch-thick layer of your sterile topdressing. Plant only one to three seeds in each hole depending upon the seed size and the suggested spacing, and place labels by the holes. Moisten the topdressing with a fine spray. To reduce fungal problems, water only in the mornings so the leaves can dry out during day. This is particularly important when the seedlings are small.

Don't plant too many seeds: it's most sustainable to plant just slightly more than your estimated need. And don't plant too many in a row: even if you thin them to the proper density you'll have thrown away a lot of viable plants. On the other hand if you don't thin, all of your seedlings will be compromised by overcrowding. It's a good idea to prepare an area in the garden as if you were planting seeds but where you don't plant anything. This is your test area where only weeds will sprout. When you see these volunteers in your planted areas, you'll be able identify them as weeds to pull out. To avoid fungi, some folks advise not to plant seeds when it's hot and humid, but then we'd never get our seeds in the ground here in Florida!

Planting Seeds in a Controlled Environment

While some large-seeded plants like beans, sunflowers, zinnias, or squashes do best when they're planted right in the garden, others are more successful when they're handled with more care for a few weeks and then transplanted into your beds. If you're working a sustainable multicropped vegetable plot, starting seeds elsewhere gives the current crop up to eight more weeks in the soil. Older seedlings started in pots are often more likely to survive than tiny sprouts sown directly into the wilds of your garden.

There are any number of strategies for starting seeds in pots or flats, but whichever method you choose, keep the seedlings close at hand so you can see if they wilt or need other attention. Follow the directions for each seed type for planting depth and whether or not to presoak. Poke holes in the soil for each seed, or scatter the smaller seeds on top of the soil and cover them with vermiculite. Here are two different methods for starting seeds.

One method is to plant several seeds in each of several little starter pots. When the seeds sprout, save only the two or three best seedlings in the pot, and cut the rest off at the soil line. Continue to grow the seedlings in the pots until they are ready to set out in the garden.

Another method adds an extra step. Sow the seeds into a flat where they will sprout quite thickly. After one or two of their first real leaves grow, transplant the seedlings into starter pots, where they'll have more room to grow. Depending upon how big they are and how well they take

FOLDED NEWSPAPER SEED POT

Plant seeds in folded newspaper pots. They afford some protection from cutworms and reduce transplant shock.

to transplanting, you could plant them singly or in groups of two or three in a pot. This is a delicate transplant because the seedlings are so small. Handle each one as little as possible, and don't squeeze the stem: use the tough **cotyledon** (seed leaves) or root-ball as a handle. The advantage of the second method is that you eliminate the germination issue because you deal only with seeds that have sprouted.

Seedling pots can be four-inch plastic pots, recycled yogurt tubs, or other hard-sided containers. Wash them well. You can also use egg cartons or other fiber containers. Some folks make planting cups by folding several layers of newspaper and holding them together with a paperclip. When you're ready to plant, the newspaper cup can be sunk directly into the soil and the paperclip removed. Fill your containers with a thoroughly moistened seed starter soil mix—a combination of vermiculite, compost, and **coconut coir** (pronounced "core") in approximately equal amounts. You can also purchase a seed starter medium, but without chemical fertilizers added. Don't use **peat moss**, because it's not a sustainable product and because it may actually dry out your seedlings. Also, don't use garden soil unless it's been sterilized, because it may harbor injurious organisms and weed seeds.

The general rule of thumb is to provide gentle bottom heat to promote good germination. Here in Florida, we can set our seeds outside in the middle of the day during cooler months. Morning is probably best time during the hotter months. Outside light is best for good growth. Put your seeds in the morning sunlight, but move them into the shade for the afternoon. If you're working inside, set them under and close to white florescent bulbs. If the seedlings become spindly, they probably need more light.

To water, place your containers in a pan of water for 20 minutes once a day. Don't let your seeds sit there all day. You can also use a soft mist to water from the top, but test to make sure the water soaks into the soil or that you've watered enough to leave a layer of water in the bottom of the tray. You want to train the roots to grow down, not come to the surface.

Two or three weeks after they sprout, fertilize the seedlings weekly with diluted compost extract or a gentle organic fertilizer such as highly diluted fish emulsion. Don't use harsh chemical fertilizers on seedlings. Once they have one or two real leaves, start **hardening them off** by setting them outside in the vicinity of where they will be planted and tapering off their watering. This way, their stems will build up strength to endure the breezes and their leaves will become accustomed to sun exposure.

Choosing Plants from a Nursery

You could, of course, let someone else do the work of nurturing seedlings and purchase them when they are ready to plant. To be sustainable, you have to be aware of how much work you can accomplish, and buying seedlings is one way to save on labor. There are some disadvantages, though. The selection of cultivars will be limited to only the most popular ones. You also won't know how the plants have been treated—obviously, they've survived if they are on the shelf, but they may have been over fertilized or over watered.

Look for plants with thick top growth with good green color. Blooms or fruits on edible plants are not usually an advantage. It means that they've probably been forced. A more telling way to judge their health and potential growth is by their roots. Slip a plant or two out of its pot to see what's happening below the soil. If the roots are white and just beginning to fill out the bottom of the pot, then the seedling is ready to plant. If the roots form a solid mass inside the pot, then the plant has been in the pot for too long. If the roots are still white, purchase it and spread the roots out upon planting. If they are tan or mushy, don't buy the plant.

Planting Seedlings

The day before transplanting, soak the plants in their pots. Prepare the garden beds where they'll be planted. Remove weeds, especially the deep-rooted ones. Work in the compost and other organic matter and measure out the positions for planting. Soak the beds so they are moist down to a depth of two or three inches. Have some mulch ready to place on the bed to moderate the temperature and the moisture. Choose a cloudy day to plant or do it in the early evening so the seedlings won't be baked in Florida's hot sun right away.

Turn the pots upside down or sideways, depending upon the plant size, and urge the root-ball out by squeezing the pot, poking your finger into a drainage hole, or by slicing around the inside of the pot with an old table knife. Put two fingers across the top of the pot with the plant between them and tip the pot up so the plant falls into your hand. Handle the plant by the root-ball. It's important not to pull the plants out by their stems, because you could damage the flow of water up the stems if you squash the cell walls.

If there are two or three plants in the pot, carefully separate them. Your seedlings should each have a healthy mass of roots. Dig a hole that's deep enough for the roots to stretch down. Fill in the hole with soil and provide support for the stems. Unlike with trees and shrubs, you can pack soil up higher on the stems of seedlings. In the case of tomatoes, it increases the number of roots. Water the seedlings thoroughly to eliminate the air pockets around the roots. Prop up the plants again so they are upright and not stuck in the mud. Mulch around (but not touching) the seedlings.

For the next week or two you'll need to check your seedlings every day and water as needed to prevent drying, because as soon as they've wilted, there's only a short window of opportunity to revive them. If the seedlings aren't rehydrated quickly, they'll die. Once they adjust and really start growing, you won't need to be so vigilant.

Sustaining the Gardener

Being outside with Mother Nature and watching your plants grow lowers the stresses of the day and makes every gardener smile. As gardeners know, gardening also provides good exercise with its bending, digging, shoveling, hoeing, weeding, and hauling. Beware of Florida's hot sun— plan your gardening time so you don't get heatstroke. For your comfort, early in the morning or evening are usually the best gardening times during warm weather. Bring drinking water with you. During winter months, though, the middle of the day might be best.

By using the right tools and **ergonomically** correcting your gardening techniques, you can prevent some of the usual aches and pains. Then you can work just as hard the next day. It's most efficient to keep your body in neutral positions while working. This lessens the amount of stress on joints and muscles and allows you to work longer and use less energy. The neutral position for your wrist is the position it's in when you're not using your hand. If your wrist is bent in any other direction, you have less strength and are more prone to injury.

Hand tools are often easier to work with if they have extended or long handles. This keeps your wrist in the neutral position and reduces the chance of repetitive motion injury in the garden. There are specially designed ergonomic hand tools that strap to your arm just below the elbow and extend like a light brace down to rubber grips that stick up perpendicular to the handle. The arm brace and grips keep your wrist in the neutral position. You can purchase tools with extra-long handles, or to save money you can also extend the handles of your tools with a length of plastic pipe. If your wrists are weak, you can strap the long handles to your forearm and do your impersonation of Edward Scissorhands while you work.

Pruners can be particularly hard on the hands, especially if you have arthritis; make sure they are the right size for you and that they have good padded grips. Loppers or scissors may be easier to use. Tools with relatively large handles are usually easier to grip than ones with skinny handles. Similarly, cushiony, textured grips require less effort to hold, and reduce or eliminate blisters. When choosing new tools make sure they fit your hand. Your favorite old tools can be modified by adding bicycle handlebar grips or by wrapping the handles with waterproof tape.

Shovels, rakes, and hoes that are too long or too short can strain even the strongest backs. Look for tools that are comfortable to use and are

adjustable to suit the task. Tools with new designs labeled as ergonomically correct may work well for you, but if you are aware of the twisting or
awkward positions you put yourself in as you work, you can adjust your
methods to reduce the strain.

If you're headed to the garden for an extended weeding session, you
might be more comfortable if you use a kneeling pad or a low seat built in
on a rolling garden cart. It's also better if you vary your tasks. You might
do some weeding, get up to haul the weeds to your compost pile, water
your seedlings, stretch up to trim your hanging baskets, have a long drink
of iced tea (with crushed mint from your garden), and then come back
to weeding. That way your body won't be cramped into one position for
a long time.

Be realistic in your gardening goals and take frequent breaks during
heavy work. Gardening tasks usually can be interrupted for a few days or
weeks—they'll be waiting for you when you get back to them. Question
the way you've always done a certain task—maybe there's a better tool or
an easier method. Sustaining the gardener should be an important part of
your sustainable landscaping strategy.

Good Gardening Is Sustainable

When you use better gardening techniques and good design, you'll improve your results. While we'll never develop a no-care garden, an easier-
to-maintain garden requires less time and money. Sustainable gardeners
have more time to be creative.

Resources

Web Sites

The Florida Native Plant Society has chapters throughout the state. This organization is a good source of information on Florida's native plants: http://www.fnps.
org.

The Institute for Regional Conservation's zip code tool can help you find native plants for a South Florida locale: http://regionalconservation.org.

Use the Association of Florida Native Nurseries' Web site to locate a nursery
near you that sells native plants: http://www.afnn.org.

The Center for Plant Conservation provides ideas for increasing our native plants and promotes codes of conduct for the gardening public: http://www.centerforplantconservation.org.

The Florida Yards and Neighborhoods Web site lists ergonomic tools: http://cfyn.ifas.ufl.edu.

The United States EPA Web site has information relating to regulations and environmentally friendly practices: http://www.epa.gov.

Books

Kaufman, Sylvan Ramsey, and Wallace Kaufman. *Invasive Plants: A Guide to Identification and the Impacts and Control of Common North American Species.* Mechanicsburg, Pa.: Stackpole Books, 2007.

Compost and Mulch

In a natural environment, plants and animals litter the ground with their waste as they live and die. Floridians can reproduce this process and quicken the cycle by using composting bins or piles to recycle various plant materials. Composting can be quite efficient in Florida's warm climate.

Weeds are rampant in Florida, so mulching may be more important, and somewhat different, than in other parts of the country. Various materials and mulching strategies can be successfully used to enhance your landscape and reduce its maintenance.

What Is Healthy Soil?

Soil found in native habitats is a complex ecosystem of **bacteria**, fungi, nematodes, **earthworms**, ants, salamanders, toads, insect larvae, moles, and more—all living in a substrate of minerals and humus. In a rich woodland, that wonderful, earthy smell of good soil that all gardeners love is caused by **actinomycetes**, a type of soil bacteria. The minerals are a mixture of rocks, sand, silt, and/or clay. The humus or organic matter consists of fully or partially digested plant and animal parts. As humus is broken down into simple compounds, it provides a living for the decomposers and eventually yields nutrients for plants. And just think what a

Composting and Mulching Are Sustainable Strategies

Compost and mulch are important ingredients in the recipe for a healthy and more sustainable landscape; they save water, time, energy, and money, too.

Plants growing in good healthy soil require less attention from the gardener or landscape manager. Compost is the best amendment to improve either sandy or clay soils. Compost helps plants by providing nutrients, balancing acidity, and holding both moisture and air in the soil. Creating compost recycles organic materials that might have added to the volume of landfills.

Mulching in the garden protects the soil from drying out or heating up, so plants require less water. Mulch is also an important part of a gardener's battle plan against Florida's weeds. Using materials on hand, such as leaves, pine needles, or wood chips from tree trimming, is more sustainable than purchasing packaged mulch.

mess we'd have if we didn't have those soil inhabitants to clean up all that dead stuff.

One gram of soil (about ⅕ teaspoon) can contain as many as one hundred million bacteria, one million actinomycetes, and one hundred thousand fungi. (If all the fungi in that ⅕ teaspoon of soil were strung together, their filaments or **hyphae** would measure about 16 feet long.) This same gram of soil could also contain hundreds of nematodes living on the damp surfaces of the soil particles and maybe a few insect eggs or larvae and some earthworm cocoons. The exact proportions of each of these organisms will depend on soil conditions such as moisture, aeration, amount of humus, and what's growing above the soil. Chemical conditions such as **acidity** will change the balance of organism populations. For instance, fungi are more plentiful in acidic soils, while actinomycetes and other bacteria prefer more alkaline conditions.

The types and amounts of minerals, and humus, if it's present, determine the acidity of the soil. South of Miami, the minerals consist mostly of limestone, so the soil is quite alkaline. In much of peninsular Florida, the soil is mostly acidic and sandy. In parts of the panhandle, the red Georgia clay soil predominates. Before you begin any big project, test your soil. As your extension agent would say, "Don't guess; do the test." A complete soil test will assess the acidity or **pH** of your soil or soils, plus the major nutrients. You can buy soil testing kits in hardware stores, but regional extension offices also provide a for-fee soil testing service, along with information sheets and soil sample boxes or bags preaddressed for mailing to a testing laboratory.

Amending your soil with various conditioners, such as lime or sulfur, will alter its chemistry temporarily, but you can't really change the nature of your soil for the long run. Find plants that thrive in your particular soil and don't fight Mother Nature. If you're in an area that's not conducive to growing your favorite crop or flowers, raised beds or containers will allow you to better control soil chemistry.

Soil texture is determined by its relative portions of sand, silt, and clay particles. These proportions cannot be readily changed. You should direct your efforts instead toward improving soil structure. Soil structure is defined by the way that soil particles are assembled as aggregates. Your aim in improving soil structure is to achieve a loose, crumbly, or granular aggregation of particles.

Enriching the Soil

If the soil particles run through your fingers and don't stick together, your soils is sandy. At the other end of the spectrum, if the soil consists of hard or gooey lumps, your soil is clayey. Add compost or other humus-rich material to improve the structure and increase the richness of any soil, allowing it to hold more moisture and more air. Good rich soil is possible in most of our state, but it may take several years of adding organic materials to reach the point where your soil has good **tilth**. A handful of moist soil should contain mostly rounded particles of different sizes, with enough body to hold together under gentle pressure. The glue that holds soil together like this comes from all the activities of its inhabitants.

If the topsoil was scraped from your landscape during development or if it's very sandy or clayey, you may want to bring in large quantities of topsoil, composted manure, mushroom soil, or other material rich in organic material to work into your existing soil. If your landscape has good topsoil that was left in place during development or has been enriched over many years of good landscape management, then you'll have less initial work to do.

Of course, you'll need a plan before you start importing new soil so you'll know how much enrichment you'll need. If you are planning for a vegetable garden, then you'll need the richest soil possible. If you are creating a wilder habitat, you'll need much less enrichment—just enough to emulate the natural state of the environment for your region. The very best time to work on the soil is before you start planting, because you'll probably not have such good access to the root zone again.

Florida's warm climate raises the metabolism of its soil organisms, and they don't take a holiday in the winter. Since our soil's microbes are always working, they require more organic material for energy than they would in cooler regions. Keep this in mind as you work humus into soils—you'll need more here in Florida than you would in a temperate climate like North Carolina's. Fortunately, our compost production is also greater in Florida, because our long growing seasons produce more material to compost, and our compost piles or bins are more efficient. A highly managed compost system in Florida can turn out finished compost in two or three months instead of the six months to two years it takes in places with cold winters. Sustainable landscape management will produce enough compost to keep the soil enriched. It's a balance.

Composting

Composting is a form of recycling. Instead of throwing away kitchen scraps or stuffing the dead leaves and other yard trimmings into unsustainable plastic bags and leaving them for pickup, gardeners can be more sustainable when they deposit Mother Nature's offerings in a compost pile. A couple of months later, dark rich compost will be ready to enrich your soil.

It's most sustainable to process your yard waste onsite, but in many Florida counties you can obtain free compost or mulch made from curbside yard trash collections and county landscaping activities. Ask if the compost has been hot composted and if it's free of plastic from yard bags and other trash. The hot composting kills most of the weed seeds and disease-causing organisms. While you can pick it out as you use it, trash reduces the value of the compost. If you need a large amount of compost or mulch for big projects or if you haven't had time to build up materials for your own compost, a source like this is invaluable. Keep in mind that some of this material may have been treated with pesticides, so use it with caution in and around your edibles.

While there are many methods of setting up a compost system for homes, schools, and businesses, there are some general composting guidelines.

- Use equal amounts of green and brown materials in alternating layers when constructing a new pile.

  - Brown materials are mostly dry and are high in carbon. Examples include dead leaves, wood chips, pine needles, straw, and shredded paper.
  - Green materials are softer, have more moisture, and are higher in nitrogen. Examples include freshly pulled weeds, grass clippings, coffee grounds, kitchen scraps, manure, and waterweeds like hydrilla and water hyacinths.

- Do add gardening waste, but not diseased plants or noxious weeds with aggressive roots or tubers unless you dry them out somewhere else and know they are dead. Regular weeds and sod are fine, though. If weeds sprout from the pile, pull them out and put them on top of the pile to dry.
- Don't use materials that have been treated with herbicides—this could have a detrimental effect on the plants you're trying to nourish. Don't use materials that have been treated with fungicides or insecticides as they could kill the decomposers in your compost. It doesn't matter whether these pesticides are made from artificial or organic materials—they'll still do damage. The heat in an active

compost pile will break down some of the poisons, but whether or not they'll become benign is hard to predict.

- You may add manure from horses, cows, chickens, or other herbivores, but don't use pet or human feces, which can introduce harmful bacteria into the soil.
- Do add kitchen scraps, but not meat, oils, or dairy products. This keeps odors down and also discourages raccoons, opossums, crows, and other scavengers from raiding your pile.
- Don't add twigs larger around than your fingers unless you run them through a chipper. In general, the more finely chopped the initial materials are, the faster they'll decompose.
- The more often you turn the pile, the faster it will become fully composted. (Turning is rearranging the pile so the materials on top end up on the bottom and those on the outside are on the inside. Turning also discourages weeds and tree roots from invading your pile.)
- Keep compost moist, but not wet. Cover the whole pile with a layer of pine needles, straw, or other persistent mulch. In drier periods, create an indentation on the top of the pile, so the water is more easily absorbed. In the wet seasons, create a peak on the top and cover it with pine needles or some other material that sheds water. You might even use a tarp during really wet periods.
- If your compost smells like ammonia, it has too much green material. If the compost smells sour or more like rotten eggs, it indicates that **anaerobic** decomposers are working. To solve these odor problems, turn the pile to introduce air, add some dry brown material, and leave it uncovered until it becomes just slightly moist to the touch. A good compost pile should not stink.
- Compost piles need to have enough mass for the microbes' activity to raise the temperature. Rule of thumb is that an open pile needs to be at least three feet on all sides, but not greater than five feet in any direction to allow air into the pile. In the initial stages of composting the temperature will rise to 140 degrees Fahrenheit or more.

- Do not import earthworms for your compost unless it is entirely contained and the worms have no way of escaping into your soil. Use only earthworms you find in your landscape for the compost pile, and then not until it cools down some. In some parts of the country there are too many worms and they are devouring humus at such a great rate that forested areas have become stressed.

- You may use a bin or not. A closed bin will be neater and easier to turn. It's not a good idea to construct bins with pressure-treated wood, which often contains arsenic or other poisons. Untreated wood will last for a couple of years or more. Compost piles constructed directly on the ground will attract earthworms and other soil inhabitants.

- Make sure open compost piles are at least two feet from any building.

- Don't add lime to your compost pile even if your original materials are acidic. The decomposers will neutralize most of the acidity, and lime could kill many of the decomposers.

- Use caution when composting poison ivy, poisonwood, Brazilian pepper, or other plant materials with persistent toxicity. Urushiol, the oily toxin in poison ivy and related plants that causes a rash for many people, may last for a year or more after the plant is killed. If you decide to compost these poisonous-to-touch plants, protect yourself with long sleeves and gloves when handling the compost. Composting these toxic plants is probably the best way to get rid of them, though, because burning them is absolutely not an option.

- If you use compost before it's ready, its decomposers will absorb the nitrogen from surrounding soil as they continue to work the compost. Timing of gardening projects may require you to use compost early, so add an extra nitrogen source, such as composted manure, to supply the need. Otherwise plants in the area may suffer from the shortage of nitrogen in the soil. If you're using compost as a mulch, unfinished compost offers more weed control.

Create a Spot for Your Compost Piles

Open compost piles can look messy. Here are a few strategies for disguising or hiding your composting areas.

You can create a spot hidden from view with cinder blocks dry-stacked into two or three U-shaped stalls, with the working space facing away from view—maybe arranged diagonally in a back corner of your lot. Lay the blocks so that the pair of hollow spaces in each block faces in a horizontal direction to let air into the piles. You can then plant small trees, shrubs, or vines in front of the cinder blocks to integrate the area into your landscape. A space like this can also be used to store containers and other gardening items that don't need cover. While partial shade works well for compost in Florida's heat, remember that foot traffic might be frequent in this area, so plan to keep the working area ten feet or more from the base of trees. Otherwise the compacted soil might injure shallow-rooted trees. Because the cinderblocks can act as a firebreak, this system is recommended for firewise landscapes, as long as the compost stalls are set up at least 30 feet from any building.

If you don't have a good shady spot, create almost instant shade with vines. At the beginning of spring, with chicken wire or other fencing, construct a cylinder that is at least three feet tall and three feet in diameter. Place it in an out-of-the-way location in your landscape and then dump three or four shovels of manure (composted or bagged) in the bottom. Fill the cage with composting material, alternating greens, browns, and thin layers of soil until there is a mound above the top of the cage—like a scoop of ice cream on a cone. Make an indentation in this mound. Then plant three or more fast growing vines next to the bottom of the cage. If you want edibles, you could plant vegetables such as indeterminate (or vining) tomatoes, cucumbers, squash, or pole beans. Annual flowering vines such as morning glory, moonflower, or decorative peas would work well for a more exposed spot. Instead of vines, a circle of annual sunflowers planted around the cage would also hide it, and those rangy sunflowers appreciate having something tall to lean against. The compost inside the cage creates a lovely environment for the plants' vigorous growth. At the end of the season, after you harvest your vegetables or when your flowers

3 FEET +

3 FEET +

VINES
GROWING
UP SIDES
HIDE
COMPOST

TEMPORARY COMPOST BIN

A seasonal compost bin can be set up anywhere. Soften its appearance by surrounding it with vines or tall flowers.

have gone by, cut the vines down, and harvest your compost. The material will shrink significantly during the season.

Another way to disguise your compost pile is to recycle wooden shipping pallets by using them to build the sides, and maybe bottoms, of compost bins. You can wire, tie, or nail the pallets together to create three-sided bins. You may find that two vertical posts set into the ground at the back corner of the bin will stabilize the structure. Pallet bins allow for good aeration and make use of materials that might otherwise have been discarded. The untreated wood will last for a few years before rotting.

Buried compost has almost no visual profile at all. Dig a narrow trench into the edge of a garden bed or between planting areas. This hole should be deep enough so that after you deposit your kitchen scraps into it and cover them with six inches of soil, you're at or just above ground level. Keep track of where the holes are so you don't dig into the same space in one season. The next season, your scraps will have been assimilated into the soil. This is called "trench composting."

TRASH CAN COMPOSTER

Turn a standard trash can into a compact composter. Drill holes in the bottom, top, and lid; sink it into the soil; then fill with layers of brown and green composting materials.

You might also try containerizing your compost. Start with a 60-gallon plastic garbage can. Drill several half-inch holes in its bottom and several more on each side of bottom fifth of the can. Also drill several holes in the lid. Dig a shallow hole in the ground for the can, deep enough for the side holes to sit below the soil surface. Fill in around the can with soil. Add your layers of composting material and keep it covered with the lid.

Passive, Moderate, and Active Management of Composting

Passive Composting

Maintaining a passive compost pile requires the least amount of work, but it takes the longest to produce good compost. As you gather clippings, weeds, or other appropriate organic materials, toss them on the top of a pile until it gets too big for its spot or taller than five feet. Then start a new pile. When you think about it, throw a worm or two on top of the pile.

When a passive pile is working, it may stay approximately the same size even after adding materials to the top at a moderate rate. The centermost and bottom parts of the pile will shrink as they decompose.

In four or five months, check the middle of the first pile. If you can still see distinct shapes of the original matter, it's not done yet, but if the materials have become dark brown and crumbly, it's finished compost. To harvest the compost, disassemble the pile and shovel the finished compost into a container for use. Then replace the newer, undecomposed materials from the top and sides of the old pile into a new pile, and start again.

It's probably not a good idea to add kitchen scraps to a totally passive pile, because the process is slow and the kitchen waste may start to stink. In a case like this, you could have a passive pile for your yard waste and a different method, such as trench composting, for your kitchen waste.

Moderately Managed Compost

To hurry the composting process, you can better plan the ratio of components and build a whole pile in a day or two. Don't add newer materials to it while it's ripening. Instead, accumulate your new materials in a new passive pile that you can use in the next managed pile.

Here is one method for constructing a moderately managed pile. For either a freestanding pile or one in an open bin, arrange your materials by category—green or brown. The best tool to use for composting work is often a pitchfork or garden fork, although a shovel will be more suitable for woodchips, soil, and the like. Gather sticks up to one inch in diameter and lay them on the ground in a cross-hatch pattern over an area slightly larger than your desired pile size. As you cross-hatch the sticks, keep them about six inches apart. (This step will not be needed if you're using a wooden pallet as the bottom.) Create a four-inch-thick layer of brown materials followed by an equally thick green layer, and then spread a shovelful of garden soil evenly over the pile. The soil introduces microbes at different levels, so the pile will start to "work" sooner. Poke numerous holes through the top of the soil layer with your garden fork. This will help to settle the pile and ensure passageways for air, water, and critters between the layers. Water the soil layer with a gallon of water—nonchlorinated, if possible. (Rain barrel water is perfect.) Skip the water if your green materials are wet, as with water hyacinths, hydrilla, or rinsed seaweed just pulled from a body of water.

Lay five or six sticks, long enough to extend beyond the edges of the pile, on top of the soil layer. The sticks allow air to reach the middle of the pile. Repeat the layering process until the pile is three to five feet tall. Create an indentation in the top of the pile and pour a gallon or two of water into it. If you stop the construction halfway through the process, end with a thicker brown layer to hold in moisture. When you continue the pile at a later time, scrape away a little of that top layer before adding the next green layer. Finish by covering the pile with a layer of persistent mulching material, such as a mixture of pine needles and dead leaves or straw. This will keep the pile moist and retard weed growth on the outside.

The pile should heat up after one day if your ratio of green to brown materials is even and if there's enough moisture. Within two weeks, turn the pile to aerate it and keep the heat up. Pull the sticks out as you disassemble the pile and replace them every foot or so into the newly turned pile. You'll obliterate the layers when you turn it, but that's okay. The layers are mostly for creating the proper ratio of green and brown materials. This is when you'll be happy to have a second pile location, because it's easier to fork the pile into an empty bin or space than to mix a pile in place or move it twice. If the weather is dry, water it every week or so. If it's very rainy, you may need to cover it temporarily with a tarp. The pile should be damp, but not so wet that it starts to smell bad. Wiggle the sticks at each level every so often to let in some air. After that first turning, turn the pile when you can get to it. The more frequently you turn it, the faster it will ripen—perhaps as quickly as two months depending upon your initial materials but more likely three or more months.

Highly Managed Compost

You start a highly managed open pile the same way you do a moderately managed pile, but you'll need a chipper to chop your materials to a finer texture before you use them. Also for more productivity, invest in a compost thermometer to monitor the temperature at several levels of the pile. You'll want to keep the temperature between 110 and 150 degrees Fahrenheit. After each turning, the temperature will rise at first and then decline after a few days. When it does, turn the pile again. This keeps the microbial activity at the highest rate. After a month or so, when the temperature no longer increases after a turning, add a dozen or more garden worms. Worms will probably have found your pile already, but adding more at this stage will hasten the composting process. When the pile cools down, turn it every week or two to keep it mixed and aerated.

In general, highly managed, open piles are too much work to be considered a sustainable activity from the individual gardener's point of view, but if you need the compost for a specific project, creating compost fast can reduce the project's completion time. In contrast to an open pile, if you use a closed compost system in a barrel that turns on its axis, then the job of turning the compost is very easy. After you add your materials, turn the compost by rotating the bin. Frequent rotation keeps the compost well aerated so that the microbes can work full time. With this method, your compost should be ready in a month or two. Watch out for too much moisture, though. If this happens, as with an open system add some brown material. Enclosed composting systems tend to cost more (it's generally easier to buy a turning unit than to build one), and the amount of compost produced at one time is fairly small. But because the composting rate is so much higher and requires so little labor, a closed system may be worth the cost in the long run. Also, a closed bin may offer the only reasonable option for small lots or for courtyard and balcony gardening.

Vermiculture, or composting with special composting worms, should be done only in a closed system where the worms cannot escape into your soil. Some folks use this method for composting their kitchen scraps. Use shredded and dampened black-ink-only newspaper as brown material and kitchen scraps as green material, with maybe a little soil and composted manure thrown in to balance things out. To harvest the compost, lure the worms to new food and then clean up their leavings (usually called "castings"). This is a highly managed system, because you can't starve your worms or let them dry out. Remember, no worms from these systems should be released outside. To ensure this outcome, place the harvested castings in an airtight container for a week or two. This should give any worm eggs time to hatch. Search the container for leftover or newly hatched worms before you introduce the compost into outdoor soils.

Using Compost in the Landscape

At the end of the composting process, the compost should be dark brown and crumbly. Some people recommend sifting the compost through a hardware cloth screen with half-inch or one-inch mesh, in order to separate out materials that have not completely decayed. Screening will produce compost that is uniform in appearance, but its usefulness in your soil will not be significantly increased.

The nutrients contained in your compost depend upon the starting materials and the decomposers. If you've used nutrient-rich materials like manure or waterweeds (water hyacinths, hydrilla, or rinsed seaweed), your compost will usually contain high amounts of useable nitrogen (N), phosphorus (P), potassium (K), plus secondary and trace elements. If your starting materials were lean in nutrients (shredded paper, grass clippings), your compost might look rich, and it will be an important soil additive, but you may need to use more of it to get an equivalent number of microbes working in your soil. It's probably a good idea to send your compost for a complete soil test every so often, so you know what you're working with.

Keep in mind that compost is not used the same way as an artificial fertilizer; it's applied more generously and provides more than nutritive chemicals. After applying compost as a topdressing to the landscape, you'll notice that it won't take long for it to disappear. This doesn't mean that it's stopped working; it indicates that the compost microbes were absorbed into the soil, and the organic materials in the compost provided food for the soil's ecosystem.

As the microbes live and die, they break down the animal and plant parts and release the nutrients in a form that's useable by the plants. If the soil is dominated by fungi, as it is in most wooded areas, nitrogen will be released as ammonium (NH_4). When bacteria dominate the soil, most of the nitrogen is released as a nitrate (NO_3). This is the form that vegetables and other herbaceous plants prefer. You can alter your compost to favor bacteria by adding more green materials. More brown, carbon-rich materials will produce compost with more fungal decomposers. But mostly it doesn't matter much, because the compost will adjust to the environment in which it's placed. After repeated applications over several seasons, your soil will be in much better shape. It will start to resemble compost.

There are many beneficial ways to use compost in the landscape. Here are a few.

- Work it into vegetable beds. After initial clearing of weeds or plowing under of **green manure,** such as clover, apply three inches in the planting areas and work it into soil. You can also mix it with composted manure for more nutrients. This is especially important for heavy feeders such as tomatoes and squash.
- Use it to condition soil in and around perennials, shrubs, and trees. If the bed is covered with a layer of persistent mulch, scrape it away, and apply a ring of compost around each plant out to the **drip line** and not touching the stem or trunk of the plant. Then replace the mulch.
- Mix it with potting soil and use it as a topdressing for your container plants. It will keep the soil working and reduce the need for repotting. This is particularly important for long-term container plants. Soilless potting mixtures tend to deteriorate after a while; compost adds structure and microbes to the soil.
- Using a two-inch layer of compost as the medium for planting new grass, whether it's seeded or sodded, will greatly enhance the success of that turf. This practice works so well that the U.S. Environmental Protection Agency (EPA) now recommends it for erosion control on roadside projects.
- Use it mixed with sandy soil as a topdressing for turfgrass. Spread a ¼-inch layer evenly across the area. The microbes in the compost will filter into the soil to fertilize the grass and will help reduce the **thatch**.
- Use compost instead of unsustainable peat moss. Compost has more nutrients, is not inherently acidic, doesn't dry out as much, and adds beneficial microbes to the soil.

Compost Tea and Compost Extract

There are three liquids that can be produced from your compost pile.

1. Compost leachate is the liquid that leaches out of the bottom of the compost pile. While rich in soluble nutrients, in the early stage of composting it may also contain pathogens. Reduce the

leachate by using less water and adding more brown material to your pile.

2. Compost extract is made from completed compost suspended in a cloth bag in a container of water for a day or so. You'll need to experiment with volume and proportion based on the volume of your containers and bags. Don't soak the compost too long or the **aerobic** microbes (ones that work in an aerated environment) will be replaced by anaerobic ones that can cause the compost to stink. Compost extract can be used as a liquid fertilizer and to enhance soil microbes.

3. Compost tea is made from compost extract that has been fermented or brewed with the addition of sugars to culture the microbes. You need active aeration for this process to produce large populations of microorganisms. Compost tea has been widely touted as a foliar spray to reduce pathogens, but scientific studies have not verified its efficacy for disease control. It is not registered as a pesticide and cannot legally be recommended nor applied as one. Compost tea creates a culture of compost microbes. Because you don't know what microbes are actually in your compost, by providing this enriched environment, you could be multiplying *E. coli* or other pathogens. Stick with the extract and the "normal" levels of microbes.

Compost extract has many uses, but mostly it's used as a liquid fertilizer to water your seedlings, container gardens, or **epiphytes**—those air plants such as ferns, bromeliads, or orchids. Use compost extract to water in compost around trees and in your garden beds. This will enhance the nutrient delivery and provide good soil microbes.

There are several methods commonly used to brew compost extract. The simplest, lowest-tech way is to fill a loosely woven cloth bag (like burlap) with completed compost and set it in a bucket of rain-barrel water for a day or more. Off and on during that time, pick the bag up and dunk it like a tea bag to allow more water to run through the compost and to aerate it. (If you're using city water, let it sit for a day or two until the chlorine dissipates before using it. Don't use water from a system with a water softener.)

Your compost extract should be an almost black or dark brown liquid that smells sweet or earthy. Dilute the extract so that it has a lighter color, like tea, before using it. If it smells sour, don't use it on your plants. You can thoroughly aerate the sour tea to get rid of the anaerobic organisms, or you can throw it onto your working compost pile and start over. Once it has a good smell, use your extract liberally for a healthier soil and landscape. The extract makes your compost go farther and increases the ways that you can use it.

Mulching

Mulching adds sustainability to landscape management in many ways. Organic mulches, such as wood chips, sawdust, pine needles, straw, or bark nuggets will suppress weeds, help hold in moisture, prevent the soil surface from crusting, help prevent erosion on level grades or gentle slopes, and protect trees and other plants from mowing injuries. Because they are organic, mulches will eventually add compost to the soil. Mulching with organic materials in a garden area is called "sheet composting": it is slow to decompose because there is not enough mass to raise the temperature.

Mulching works to suppress weeds in two different ways. First, it creates a physical and a light barrier, so that weed seeds stay dormant. Weed barrier cloths, layered mulch (using newspaper), and gravel all create physical barriers. Second, organic mulch materials—unfinished compost, wood chips, sawdust, pine needles—also work chemically. As they decompose, their microbes absorb nitrogen from the surrounding soil to live. This temporary nitrogen depletion suppresses weed seed germination.

So many Floridians have embraced mulching that it has become the standard "look" for their garden spaces. But there's more to consider than throwing a new bunch of mulch onto every garden space and around the trunk of every tree each season

Best Mulching Practices

Do not allow any type of mulch to touch the plants' stems or trunks. It's not uncommon to see a foot or more of mulch leaning against tree trunks.

This practice, called "volcano mulching," is harmful to trees in several ways.

- Water is shed from the mulch away from the tree because of the steep angle.
- Rodents and other animals can burrow and nest in large amounts of mulch and chew the tree.
- Fungi and bacteria harbored in the mulch can rot out the base of the tree, making it prone to falling.
- Some trees and shrubs will create new roots within a thick mulch layer. The plants' roots should be in the soil for the best stability and the best drought resistance. In droughts, the mulch will dry out first, and trees with roots in the mulch can be strained.

Layered mulching may be used to keep down weeds in an established bed, or it may be used to start a new bed or other nonlawn area. First remove highly aggressive plants like torpedo grass, Mexican petunias, poison ivy, and catbriar from the area. Dig a trench along the edge of the area that you plan to mulch so that the plants under the layers aren't supported by those that are still in the open. Then tromp down the plants in your mulching area. Cover them with eight to ten overlapping layers of newspaper or one layer of corrugated cardboard. Wet the paper and top off with a thick layer (four or five inches) of mulch, such as leaves, pine needles, or shredded tree trimmings.

This is not the same as putting down a layer of weed barrier; the intent is different. We do want plants to grow here, just not turf or weeds. The paper layer provides a physical barrier for a month or two. After a few weeks, most of the covered plants will die and you may then plant shrubs or other understory perennials. Scrape back the mulch and cut right through what's left of the paper.

Types of Mulch

A wide variety of both organic and inorganic materials may be used for mulching. Sources of plant material for mulch are vast, and many will be on hand on your property or in your neighborhood. Each type of mulch has its pros and cons in relation to sustainability. Here are some considerations for the more commonly used mulches.

Shredded tree trimmings: This is a mix of shredded wood and green leaves—the tree parts that have been run through a chipper. As a mulch, it consists mostly of nicely chopped wood mixed with leaves and some thin branches that slide through the shredder. This mulch will last for a year or more as a garden or pathway mulch. It will eventually decay and become part of the soil.

Because nothing has been added to it, the look is quite natural, and if leaves fall on it, no removal is necessary—it all blends together. For beds that are in full view, you'll probably want to pull out or bury the larger sticks in the mulch to reduce its rustic look.

Using shredded tree trimmings is one of the most sustainable mulching solutions. First, you're using biowaste, often derived from old or hazardously located trees that need to come down; you're not wasting healthy trees raised or torn out for the mulch

Shredded tree trimmings from arborists working in your neighborhood are the most sustainable mulch. The tree trimmers save gas by dumping locally, you save gas and money by not paying someone to deliver mulch or picking it up yourself, and the landfills are not used. Commercial production of bagged mulch, no matter what type, uses energy in the packaging and delivery.

industry, like cypress. The production of bagged mulch, no matter what type, uses energy in the packaging and delivery. You're also helping to save gas. Commercial tree services save gas by dumping in the neighborhood where they're cutting, and you save gas by not having to pick up mulch at a lumberyard or recycling center or by paying someone to deliver in a dump truck. You're also recycling—instead of ending up in a landfill, the tree trimmings are nourishing your yard. Finally, you're saving money. Tree services—especially those that trim trees for the power companies—are often happy to dump a load of mulch for free or at nominal cost. Even if you have to order this mulch from a local tree service, it will be far less expensive than a comparable amount ordered from a lumberyard or service center.

Compost: Unfinished compost, in which you can still see the shapes of some of the original ingredients, provides a soil-enriching mulch. In compost at this stage, the microbes are still doing their decomposing work and will extract available nitrogen from the soil in order to live. This suppresses germination of weed seeds. Compost doesn't moderate the temperature or moisture of the soil below it, because it doesn't provide much of a physical barrier. Finished compost is probably best used in the landscape as a topdressing around plantings and on lawn areas.

Leaves and shredded leaves: These, of course, are Mother Nature's own mulch, and she's used it successfully for a really long time. As leaves fall from deciduous and evergreen trees, they mulch areas under the trees. It's best to let the leaves remain under the trees from which they fell—they supply just the right mix of nutrients. When leaves fall on lawn areas, rake them into the surrounding beds. If the leaves are large or leathery, you may wish to shred them before using them as mulch. If you don't have a shredder, you can use your lawnmower. Shredded leaves don't last as long as a mulch, but they may stay in place better than whole leaves.

Pine needles: Pine needles make such a long-lasting and good-looking mulch that they are harvested from tree farms and sold as pine straw. A waxy or resinous coating on the needles makes pines more drought resistant than many other trees. It also makes pine needle mulch shed water to some degree and resist decomposition longer than other materials. Pine needles make a durable path mulch, but if you use them in your gardens or around your trees, don't pile them too thickly or they will shed water. If you are harvesting pine needles from a pine forest, it's recommended that you clear them only every third year, so that the forest trees have enough of their own mulch.

Hay or straw: Hay consists of grasses that have been allowed to go to seed before they are mowed and gathered. Straw generally does not include the tops or seed heads, just the grass stalks, so it should have fewer weed seeds. Either of these makes a great, light-colored mulch. The long strands make it more pliable and easier to maneuver and plant around. The maneuverability of a mulch is an important consideration for a vegetable bed, where something is always being planted or harvested. The light color also reflects some of Florida's hot sun, so the soil heats up a little less than it does under a dark mulch.

Pine bark or other bark: Bark's purpose is to protect the tree from injury and to prevent water loss, so it contains waxy materials to repel water. For this reason, when you mulch with bark, use only a two- or three-inch layer. Bark mulches last longer than some other organic materials. Bark nuggets are easier to handle and stay in place better than the larger bark chunks. Bark is usually a by-product from lumber mills and is generally a sustainable product. Don't use bark for mulching rain gardens or bioswales—it tends to float away.

Shredded wood: A number of trees are used to produce mulch in Florida. Choosing mulch made from invasive species, such as eucalyptus and melaleuca, is sustainable, because using them is part of the ongoing effort to reduce their number in Florida's ecosystems. Cypress is probably Florida's most popular mulching material—dyed many colors. Do not use it. It used to be a by-product from lumber mills, but now whole cypress forests are being ripped out to accommodate our demand for this mulch. So while cypress is a good mulching product, its use is unsustainable because high demand has outstripped the supply. Cypress is also susceptible to fungal invasion—what you'll probably notice most are the smelly **stinkhorn fungi**.

Sawdust: A by-product from lumber mills, the small particles pack together and often cause anaerobic conditions when it's stored in a pile. You'll notice a sour smell when this happens. As a mulch, it reduces nitrogen from surrounding soils more than other mulches. This means that it's a good weed suppressant. Sawdust makes a great path mulch, but mix it with manure or compost for use around sensitive plants in order to increase nitrogen levels.

Gravel: Gravel is often recommended for low-maintenance succulent gardens and for firewise landscaping. Photographs of such landscapes look nice, but the reality is often quite different. When you think about the vigorous jungle-like weeds that grow here in Florida, gravel may not be much of a deterrent, and using herbicides on a regular basis makes your landscape less sustainable.

Keep in mind, too, that rocks, big and small, retain and reflect the heat long after the sun has set. A layer of rocks can turn a sunny spot into an oven. Gravel also does not improve the soil, and once you add it to the landscape, it's difficult to remove if you change your mind later on. Gravel can be thrown by power mowers or lofted by hurricane-force winds. On top of that, it's difficult to keep gravel clear of leaves and other debris without the use of leaf blowers, and we're all trying to reduce their use.

Gravel is not a natural feature in most of Florida, so for use in most landscapes it has to be trucked in. Coral limestone gravel is mined in the Keys, so in that part of the state it might earn a few sustainability points as a local product. If you decide to use it, despite all its negatives, use heavy weed-retarding cloth under three or four inches of clean, tightly packed or heavy gravel. Use some type of edging that will keep gravel from migrating into the surrounding soil. Don't use **crusher run gravel,** which contains a lot of small particles—it quickly turns into soil and loses its mulching properties.

Shredded rubber: Recycling tires is certainly an admirable goal, but using shredded rubber as a mulch may have problems. Some studies have shown that rubber leaches potentially harmful and persistent chemicals into the soil. Rubber mulch is highly flammable, and it does not add nutrients to or improve the structure of the soil beneath it.

Plastic sheeting: Used as a mulch, plastic is impenetrable by even the most vigorous of Florida's weeds. In many agricultural operations, plastic sheeting is stapled to the soil between vegetable rows. If you use it, you'll need to supply drip irrigation to your plants because the plastic doesn't allow water to penetrate. Any plastic heats the soil and in fact is recommended if you wish to "solarize" it to kill nematodes and other microbes. So yes, plastic suppresses weeds, but it disrupts the soil's ecosystem, is labor intensive to lay it in place, and plastic, a petroleum-based product, is not usually considered sustainable.

Maintaining Mulched Beds

There are several ways to set up and care for your mulched beds, and the method you use will depend on your goal for the area. For restoring most types of native habitat, the mulch that works best will be the one that looks most like what Mother Nature would use in that region. Shredded leaves and wood trimmings laid directly on the soil may be the right choice—simply let the leaf falls and deadwood stay on the ground. This mulch decomposes into the soil and needs reapplication only if your own trees and shrubs are too small to create enough of their own. Neatness does not count here.

If your mulched bed is in a conspicuous area around your home or building and its walks, then you'll probably be happier with a neater look. If just a few strategically placed specimens will fill the landscape space, you may wish to consider using a nonwoven weed barrier cloth or several layers of newspapers under the mulch for a more complete physical barrier that discourages aggressive weeds from sprouting from deep in the soil. If this area will be where you place your container gardens, then you may wish to lay a thicker layer of mulch so that it lasts longer.

In an area where there are many plantings including bulbs and perennials, don't use weed barrier cloth. Instead apply a two-inch layer of mulch on the soil so the plants and the gardener have easy access to the soil. The mulch will hamper weeds from below to some degree, but new weeds will continue to sow themselves on top of the mulch unless you've used sawdust. Wood chips, bark, or other wood mulch will also fade or age in the sun. A light raking of the top layer uproots the small weeds and turns the mulch to refresh its look. When you find that the mulch is less than an inch thick, add another inch of new mulch as you rake.

If your mulch becomes infested with stinkhorn fungi, rake the surface and harvest the egg-like sacks that are waiting to sprout. Dispose of the "eggs" in the trash, not in your compost pile. Spread the mulch out on a tarp, rinse it with tap water, and then let it bake in the sun before replacing it in your beds.

Composting and Mulching Are Easy Sustainable Activities

Of all the sustainable activities that you can pursue in your landscape, composting and mulching are two of the most important. Because they condition, build, and protect the soil, they provide the foundation for many other sustainable landscape management undertakings. Your plants will thank you.

Resources

Web Sites

The University of Florida's IFAS extension offers the *Living Green* Web site, with many composting and mulching resources. See http://livinggreen.ifas.ufl.edu.

The Compost Guide is a commercial operation and its Web site features information and supplies for composting: http://www.compostguide.com.

The United States EPA Web site has information on the many environmental benefits of composting, including erosion control: http://www.epa.gov.

Washington State extension agent Dr. Linda Chalker-Scott's Web site has articles on compost tea and more: http://www.informedgardener.com.

Books

Lowenfels, Jeff, and Wayne Lewis. *Teaming with Microbes*. Portland, Ore.: Timber Press, 2006.

Stewart, Amy. *The Earth Moved: On the Remarkable Achievements of Earthworms*. Chapel Hill, N.C.: Algonquin, 2005.

Smaller, More Sustainable Lawns

Americans have a long-running love affair with lawns, and Floridians certainly have their share of large, thick lawns that are forced to stay unnaturally green all year long. All too often, developers clear-cut all the woody plants from the land before construction and install lawns afterward, because it's easier and cheaper. The long-term maintenance costs, both monetary and environmental, are not the developers' concern. The EPA estimates that more than 30 percent of residential water is used on irrigation of lawns and that 50 percent of landscape irrigation, both residential and commercial, is wasted because of wind, over watering, and improperly designed irrigation systems. There are more waterwise and less expensive strategies for managing your landscape. Homeowners in Las Vegas have been paid to rip out their lawns. Maybe we can find some lessons there. Save water, money, time, and Florida's waterways with smaller, more naturally maintained lawn areas.

A More Sustainable Lawn Is Possible

There *are* sustainable ways to maintain an attractive, mowed grassy area for outside activities, whether you're a homeowner, business owner, or property manager. To make your lawn more sustainable, reduce its size and choose the lowest-care turf for your area: growing several types of

Lawns Are Not Sustainable!

Lawns in any form are not sustainable. Even a minimum-care lawn requires mowing during growing season. But, oh, those high intensity lawns are the epitome of unsustainability. It's hard to count all the detrimental effects of these high-wattage, "perfect" lawns.

The time and money required to maintain the **monoculture** of a single turfgrass species in a well-manicured lawn are extreme. Mother Nature will do what she can to diversify lawns with other plants, but people battle against her diversification with poisons that kill bugs, fungi, and weeds indiscriminately. Extreme fertilization is required after pesticide applications, because the sterile soil, without its microbes and bugs, serves little purpose except to hold up the plants: the turf is now on artificial life-support. After all the fertilization, the grass grows quickly, requires more water to keep up with the growth, and more mowing. Trimming the vigorous growth requires frequent, year-round use of power tools. The small two-stroke engines often found in leaf blowers, string trimmers, and other yard care equipment emit as much as 25 percent raw, unburned gasoline. Then there is the noise pollution. And at the end of the process, the grass clippings are bagged and put on the curb for collection or blown into storm drains and bodies of water, adding to the nutrient content of Florida's already overburdened aquatic ecosystems.

turfgrass together might be more sustainable than growing one type alone. If you have irrigation available, water less often but always deeply to encourage deep rooting. Halt the use of pesticides and reduce both amount of fertilizer and frequency of fertilization. Use only slow-release fertilizers or compost mixed with sandy soil. Mow at the highest setting for your grass and mow less often. During dormant periods, don't mow at all. Arrange gardens so that adjacent lawn areas are easy to mow.

Develop a tolerance for a mix of plants in the mowed areas on your property. A more naturally maintained lawn contains several types of grass or grass-like plants, such as wild garlic, blue-eyed grass, sedges, and rushes. It will also have various broad-leafed plants, usually referred to as weeds, like clover, sour grass, dollarweed, and many others. In the shift from an artificially supported monoculture to a regime without pesticides, dead spots will probably develop where cinch bugs, mole crickets, or other critters do their damage. Here in Florida, though, it won't be long before other plants take over and green that spot. If these patches really bother you and you can't wait for them to grown in on their own, scrape or rake away the dead grass, flush out the bugs with soapy water, and re-plant the bald spots with some sod or plugs taken from areas where you are removing lawn.

After you stop using all the poisons, you'll find that the soil will come alive again and repopulate with fungi, bacteria, worms, and beneficial insects. You'll also find that insect-eating birds will start dive-bombing the bugs in your lawn. If you're lucky, moles and armadillos will use their keen sense of smell to root out your grubs, cinch bugs, and mole crickets. Replacing the divots left by these four-legged insect feeders is a small price to pay for their faithful, beneficial services. If you work with Mother Nature to create and maintain these more sustainable and pleasant mowed areas for outdoor activities, you won't have to worry about pesticides harming you, your family, your pets, or the larger environment.

Here's another thought. Even though it may be a petroleum-based product, you might consider using artificial turf for high-traffic or problem areas that must remain "presentable." The quality has vastly improved since those ugly turf doormats first came out. The initial cost may be steep, but installing it isn't too much different than installing high quality sod, but you can simply lay it over poor soil. Over a year or two, the costs will even out. Just think: no water, no fertilizer, and no mowing or other maintenance expenses. Choose artificial turf made from recycled plastics for a more sustainable choice. Make sure the weeds cannot sprout through the turf by laying down a durable, nonwoven weed barrier under the turf. If it's good enough for football on high definition TV, it may be the most sustainable choice for tough, high-traffic situations including athletic fields.

Reduce the Size of Existing Lawns

Reduce the lawn: stop mowing places where the grass is not doing well on your lot. The first areas to target for delawning are those under and between trees, in low or wet areas, and in back corners. Instead of grass, spread a mulch of leaves or pine needles (or both) directly under trees. (Remember not to pile mulch against tree trunks.) This is good for the trees because it reduces their competition for water and nutrients that would be absorbed by the turfgrasses. When the trees drop their leaves (in Florida, there are always *some* leaves dropping no matter the season), leave them on top of the mulch. This will save you time, because there will be fewer leaves to deal with and it will make mowing easier. You might want to add native shrubs and shade-loving perennials to these mulched beds (Beauty berries, coonties, and ferns are good choices.) to add interest to your landscape and to provide better screening and wildlife habitat.

In low, wet areas, you can replace lawn with a rain garden or dig out a groundwater pond here to take advantage of your natural drainage. This way you won't be forcing turf to grow in places it wouldn't grow naturally or trying to mow in difficult areas. In sunnier locations, you can manage unmowed areas as natural or wildflower meadows or create butterfly gardens. Turfgrass on steep banks is difficult to mow, and there are many other landscaping treatments you can put into service that look good, provide habitat, and require less maintenance than turf.

Other targets for lawn removal are paths where people have worn through the turf in their normal comings and goings. Instead of trying to resurrect turf in these highly compacted areas, create defined pathways. Set stepping-stones or pavers in the turf so that people walk on these instead of the grass. The turf left between the pavers may recover and grow well without the traffic, but you'll still need to mow the area. To make less work for yourself, you can opt to lay mulch over weed barrier cloth along your yard's natural pathways, with or without the pavers, or you can plant tough groundcovers in between the pavers. The beauty of removing well-worn turf is that the foot traffic shows you where folks are walking already. Go with the flow.

Gated or controlled communities present a challenge, because they're often overseen by homeowners associations with specific and rigid rules about property maintenance. In such cases, you may have to be careful as you downsize your lawn that the result looks neat and cared for. Maybe you could work together with other sustainable gardeners in your community and organize a "no grass roots" group that works to promote landscapes appealing to butterflies and birds. Maybe your group could even get some of the restrictive lawn rules relaxed for the sake of Florida's environment.

Remove Lawns Adjacent to Waterways

Nothing says "Florida" like a broad green, palm-treed lawn that fronts a bulkheaded waterfront or sweeps downhill to the edge of a lake. But the location of managed lawns next to waterways can be particularly harmful, because fertilizer and pesticide runoff, plus grass clippings, all contribute to the pollution of the water. You can still plan a space for human activities near the water, but minimize the lawn area.

Even if you don't use pesticides on your grassy areas, it's highly recommended that you create a buffer zone between lawn areas and the water's edge. Recommendations vary as to how wide this buffer should be (and any buffer will help), but many of Florida's extension offices cite 30 to 50 feet as a safe bet. Here, you can grow shrubs or low-growing perennials that don't require any fertilization. If your property abuts a wetland, the same kind of buffer is recommended to help filter pollutants, to mitigate flooding, and to provide habitat for wetland wildlife species.

If the water body is salty or brackish, choose plants that can tolerate salinity—either salt spray or occasional high water intrusion into your beds. If flooding is a possibility, plan for it by planting deep-rooted species, especially those that tolerate inundation. In a high flood, even full-grown trees aren't safe, but you can plan for moderately high water with appropriate planting and grading.

Starting a New Lawn

Map out the smallest area possible for your lawn area and plan for mulched beds, hedgerows, and other nonlawn features. There are several turfgrasses commonly used in Florida—each has its pros and cons. If you are starting from scratch, choose the types that are best suited to your soil, irrigation capability, climate, salinity, and predicted traffic. Recently developed cultivars, such as varieties of seashore paspalum, require less fertilizer, less water, and have such a high salt tolerance that you can use table salt as an herbicide for weeds. So don't just accept what's available at a big box store; do your homework, and find the best choice for your long-term needs. You may even find a mix of native grass seeds. Over time, whatever grass or grasses you started with will become interspersed with other species, as you care for your lawn using natural and sustainable techniques. Even so, healthy turfgrass slows down the influx of other plants.

Before you seed, sod, or sprig your new lawn area (sprigging is planting evenly spaced plugs of turfgrass), invest the time and resources into preparing the soil. Plopping sod or seed on unprepared or poorly prepared soil may appear to be the faster, less expensive method, but it's a false economy in the long run. The very best time to work on the soil is *before* installing the grass. First test your existing soil to see which grasses will do best there. Then talk to your local extension agent for good, region- and condition-specific recommendations.

Good rich soil with plenty of humus will increase the durability of your turfgrass and its ability to withstand drought and other stresses. Whether your soil is sandy or clayey, add plenty of compost or topsoil (or both). The point of this exercise is to increase the volume of organic matter or humus, which increases water retention in sandy soils, provides more air spaces in clayey soils, and creates an inviting substrate for beneficial organisms in all kinds of soils. If the soil is rock hard, a powered tiller may be required to work your amendments into the soil, but most of the time the compost mixture can just be laid on top of the soil. Then rake the surface smooth before you seed or sod. If you're laying sod, use a roller on it after it's down to ensure good contact between roots and soil. Unless there's heavy precipitation, irrigate deeply every other day or so for several weeks until the sod is established. Irrigation rules allow exceptions for new lawns.

Connecticut's Department of Transportation performed controlled tests on using compost to establish grass to reduce erosion on roadsides. They found that whether they used a two-inch topdressing of compost or one-inch tilled into the soil, the composted sections performed far better than those that received their standard treatments. During the establishment phase, the composted sections held up very well during a six-inch rain event—this sounds like Florida weather.

Lawn Irrigation

Each of Florida's five water management districts determine their region's water supply and regulate its usage. You may be allowed to water only a certain number of times per week or only between certain hours and on specific days according to your address. Be sure to follow these regulations, and be comfortable knowing that for established lawns, less watering is almost always better. You want to train your lawn to withstand drought when irrigation might not be an option at all.

During the growing season, using automatic or manual irrigation, be sure to water deeply. For sandy soils, this means about a ¾-inch water total per week between rain and irrigation. Less water is needed for heavy clay soils. Let the grass go dormant during winter in central and northern sections of the state and don't irrigate at all. This will encourage deep roots: your turfgrass, along with the other plants growing in and around your lawn, need those good deep roots to withstand droughts and attacks from root-munching insects. Light and frequent waterings bring roots close to the surface making them more vulnerable to both root-eating bugs and drought. If this is the regimen your lawn is accustomed to, gradually shift toward less frequent and deeper waterings. This practice is also better for your trees and shrubs: even though your irrigation system should be designed to water lawn areas separately from other landscape features, it's good to have their watering cycles synchronized.

If there is no irrigation, choose a drought-resistant turf. Once it's established, the grass should be able to survive by going into dormancy whenever it doesn't receive the rain it needs or during the shorter days of winter. The one exception to allowing dormancy is if your property is in a fire-prone area. Here it's important to keep your lawn area mowed and relatively green near buildings. Dormant or tall grass can become fuel for a wildfire.

Mowing Strategies

Mow less often and set the blade on your mower to the highest recommended level for your grass. This allows the grass enough leaf area to photosynthesize and to shade the soil to reduce weeds. As new species work their way into your turf, set the blade higher. Don't mow at all when the grass is dormant. Some weeds may continue to grow while the grass is dormant, so take this opportunity to locate them and pull them out if it's important for your situation. You may even wish to transplant some of your attractive turf invaders, such as ladies tresses orchids, blue-eyed grass, and rushes to gardens or wild areas. You'll never notice them if you don't stop mowing, though.

Use a variety of patterns when mowing, so the soil compression along the mower's tracks is more evenly distributed and to cut across the grain. Keep your mower well tuned and keep its blade(s) sharpened. Dull blades tear rather than cut, and torn grass blades are more susceptible to fungal infections than clean cut ones. A mulching mower uses vacuum action to better chop up the blades of grass and other organic matter. These smaller pieces will sink through the turf and quickly rot to become part of the soil. Consider purchasing a propane-powered mower to save on fuel costs and reduce your pollution by nearly 80 percent.

If you can, reduce your lawn areas to the extent that using an electric or, better yet, a hand-pushed reel mower will be both practical and comfortable. Pushing a modern reel mower is almost as easy as pushing a standard rotary power mower, but it's quiet and it doesn't pollute. The only carbon emissions will be what you exhale! A reel mower provides a kinder cut—it works more like scissors—and cleanly cut grass recovers faster than shredded grass. Today's reel mowers work much better than ones you might remember from the '50s or '60s, and you can easily buy blade sharpening kits at hardware stores or online.

Mind Your Edges

Sustainability for lawns and other landscape areas is enhanced if they are designed for easy maintenance. Mowing the center of the lawn is straightforward, but edges can be harder to keep neat. Strive to eliminate the need

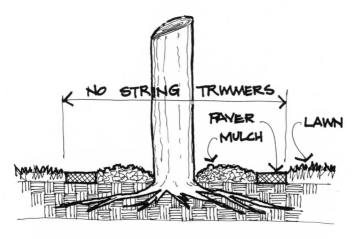

SUSTAINABLE LAWN EDGES

Flat pavers along the edges of lawn areas make mowing easier and save trees from lawnmower and string trimmer damage.

for string trimmers and edgers by incorporating better edge design. If you do need a string trimmer or edger, consider an electric or rechargeable model that is quieter and pollutes less than gas-powered models.

Avoid vertical dividers such as timbers or bricks set on edge around the edges of mulched beds. Set the timbers, bricks or other pavers flat and just slightly higher than the lawn—maybe an inch. Make sure the soil underneath is firm and the pavers don't rock when you stand on them. This way the lawnmower's wheels can ride smoothly along the pavers and cut that edge grass easily and without any additional machinery. This strategy might also be good for areas under or along fences.

Replace difficult-to-mow sharp corners with gentle curves that the lawnmower can easily negotiate. Broad, gentle undulations in the borders of the lawn provide interest in the overall landscape, but too many tight or angular turns may be difficult to mow and may make the garden area look too chaotic.

It's ironic that even though grass did not do well in an area, when you cut it back and install a mulched bed instead, the grass will try to repopulate the very same area it hated before. One way to handle grass runners that crawl into beds is to bend them back and weave them into the lawn area instead of cutting them. Cutting the runners will cause them to sprout new runners, but folding them back does not.

Plants in beds abutting the lawn may need to be trimmed back periodically so they don't hang over the pavers or interfere with the mowing process. If the plants are growing well and you don't want to prune them back any further, expand the bed and move the pavers out to make a new edge. If you keep this up, pretty soon the lawnmower won't have anything to do.

Raised beds are recommended in many parts of Florida where the soil is inhospitable for certain trees, flowers, or vegetables. They are also useful for marking the edges of outdoor rooms or other spaces. If the lawn abuts a raised bed, your best bet is to lay a solid row of bricks or pavers at the base of the bed's walls. Again, make sure they provide a solid footing for the lawnmower. If you have several raised beds in an area, it's probably best not to grow any grass between them at all. Instead, plant a high traffic groundcover or moss punctuated with stepping-stones. If folks tending the garden use wheelchairs or motorized scooters, the pavers should provide a smooth and wide enough surface to accommodate easy navigation around all sides.

Manage Your Lawn Service

Many folks use lawn services in Florida. Work with your lawn service so they practice more sustainable methods tending the lawn you decide to keep. Some services promote themselves as green; you should try to work with a green company, but it's probably a good idea to quiz them on why or how they're able to make that claim. Negotiate your service contract to be more sustainable, based on the following guidelines.

- Minimize the use of machinery. Leaf blowers are out. You can arrange your lawn's edges so string trimmers won't be necessary.
- Use the absolute minimum of fertilizer (slow-release only) and no pesticides.
- Excess grass clippings and leaves must not be swept into the streets, storm drains, or directly into a body of water. All these

extra materials turn into nutrients and place a strain on our waterways. Blowing debris into a neighbor's yard isn't very neighborly either. Leave most of the clippings in place and add excess to the compost pile.

- Don't mow during the dormant phases of the grass. It makes little sense to mow the lawn when there is nothing to mow. If your service contract is year round, have the crew work on other projects, like removing sod from around your trees or removing thatch from the lawn.

Thatch Reduction

Thatch is the buildup of dead and living plant material above the soil and under the growing turf. Thatch buildup is most prevalent in turfgrasses that spread by above ground runners, called "stolons," such as St. Augustine and centipede grass. Thatch makes the turf feel spongy, and when it's an inch or more thick, it repels water and anything else applied to the lawn. It also provides habitat for chinch bugs, sod caterpillars, and other damaging insects. Thatch elevates the growing part of the turf, and because lawnmower wheels sink into the thatchy spots, the turf here may get scalped or mowed too close for optimum health and growth.

Thatch is generally the result of turf growing faster than the soil microbes can compost the dead plant parts. This can be caused by a combination of too much fertilizer, frequent irrigation, and root damage from fungi, nematodes, mole crickets, or other pests. The causes and effects of too much thatch in your turf can work together to produce quite a problem.

To reduce thatch, cut back on both irrigation and fertilization. Once a year, during a dormant cycle, rake the lawn area vigorously with a flexible metal leaf rake to pull out much of the dead plant material. (This debris is a great addition to your compost pile because it's already partially rotted.) If you have a significant thatch problem and a large lawn, annual raking may not be a realistic option because it's hard work. One solution is to divide your big lawn into several smaller areas and rake one section each winter.

If raking simply isn't feasible, three methods can be used to fight thatch on a large scale.

1. Core aeration uses a coring machine to pull up plugs of soil and lay them on top of the turf. This procedure penetrates the thatch and provides access for water. It also puts soil in direct contact with the thatch so that the soil's microbes can decompose it.

2. Topdressing the turf with a light layer of compost, soil, or sand allows microbes to work on decomposing the thatch, but doesn't increase water absorption as quickly as coring. Repeated top-dressings over the years, however, will improve the soil's health and benefit the grass.

3. Vertical slicing, which uses a machine to slice grooves through the turf, is the most drastic treatment. The cleanup after this pro-cedure is staggering, because it pulls up the thatch and as much as half of the grass. The turf then has to be treated almost like a newly seeded lawn to allow for recovery.

Poking holes in the lawn with cleated shoes or other devices may in-crease water absorption, but it does nothing to reduce thatch. You may decide to use this method combined with regular compost topdressings, though. It's most sustainable to reduce thatch buildup and prevent other problems from expanding by sticking to good lawn management prac-tices.

Feeding Your Lawn

If you must fertilize, do it once a year late in the fall (after the hurricane season), and use an organic-type fertilizer with a slow-release formula. The plants don't really care whether a fertilizer is organic or contains manufactured chemicals, but you should. Organically produced fertilizer is made from plant and animal products and its manufacture is usually more sustainable.

Before you fertilize, test your soil. It makes no sense to spend time and money applying an ingredient that's not needed. Phosphorus is usu-ally not needed in Florida's soils; so don't add any. In the parts of Florida where the soil tends to be acidic, you may want to mix some lime with your fertilizer to reduce acidity, and that white trail makes it easy to see where you've been.

You don't want any of your lawn fertilizer to leach into Florida's lakes, rivers, or groundwater, so make it very light and plant your waterfront buffer with self-sufficient plants that need no added chemical nutrients. Using less fertilizer also means you won't have to mow as often, and it significantly reduces thatch buildup. The best fertilizing techniques build the health of the soil so the grass can become part of a living ecosystem. Using compost mixed with sandy soil is probably the most sustainable lawn fertilizing strategy.

Ideas for Large-Lawn Owners

Churches, schools, businesses, counties, and other large landowners may wish to replace the majority of their expansive, boring, and expensive-to-maintain lawns with community gardens. Create butterfly gardens, vegetable gardens, rain gardens, or wildflower meadows. Strategic plantings of trees and shrubs on the southern and western exposures of buildings can also reduce the need for air conditioning. Plantings around air compressors produce shade that can help them operate more efficiently.

Businesses looking for ways to be more energy efficient and contribute to the community could use more sustainable landscape practices around their buildings. Installing rain gardens to capture stormwater runoff before it goes into the retention ponds will improve the quality of our waterways. Your organization could work with youth groups to define and implement this project. As the students learn about nature and gain firsthand environmental experience, your business can gain attention as a green company working with and for the benefit of the community.

Just think what a church group could do with the money saved by not mowing a large portion of their land. And then think about what would happen if members created a community vegetable garden there. They could raise vegetables for their own families and share the excess harvest with those who are less fortunate. So many people live in condominiums or in houses on small lots that they might love to have this chance to show their children where food really comes from. It's all part of being good stewards of the earth.

Counties and the state are already working to replace mowable rights-of-way along roads with wildflower meadows, cabbage palms, sea grapes, ornamental grasses, and the like. More work needs to be done to make these areas more sustainable and to give the mowers less and less to do.

Local governments could set a good example for their citizens by replacing the lawns around their buildings with other alternatives that:

> cost less to maintain,
> improve the air and water quality, and
> add to the diversity of the landscape.

They could go even further, setting up workshops to educate their citizens and urging them to remove their lawns as well. Perhaps local governments could encourage gated communities within their borders to be better citizens by eliminating or, at least, relaxing the stiff requirements for flawless lawns. When new development companies apply for project approvals, local governments are in a strong position—before they sign off on a proposal—to encourage sustainable land use patterns, including cluster developments with greenways, bike paths, and much less lawn.

Replacing Lawns Has Many Benefits

When you reduce the amount of lawn on your property, you'll save time and money. You'll provide more interest in your landscape and create places attractive to butterflies and other wildlife. Mother Nature will thank you for reducing the fertilizer, herbicides, and pesticides that flow into her waterways. Using thick greenways of native trees and shrubs to replace lawn at the edges of properties usually increases both the area's shade and biomass, cooling the air. This will save on air-conditioning costs and make your immediate environment more pleasant.

Resources

Web Sites

The University of Florida's IFAS extension offers online information on mole crickets and links to other lawn pest resources: http://edis.ifas.ufl.edu.

For information and sources on environmentally friendly turf, visit http://www.environmentalturf.com.

The United States EPA has information on reducing water usage: http://www.epa.gov.

Connecticut's Department of Environmental Protection (DEP) documents its tests using compost with grass to reduce erosion along roadsides: http://www.ct.gov/.

Visit *LessLawn.com* for lots of ways to shrink your lawn and create environmentally friendly landscapes: http://www.lesslawn.com.

Cornell's Waste Management Institute documents the effects of compost on fields and compacted soils: http://cwmi.css.cornell.edu/turf.htm.

Books

MacCubbin, Tom. *The Perfect Florida Lawn*. Nashville: Cool Springs Press, 2004.

Trenholm, Laurie E., and J. Bryan Unruh, eds. T*he Florida Lawn Handbook*. Gainesville: University Press of Florida, 2005.

Habitats and Meadows

Much of Florida's native habitat with its abundant wildlife has been replaced with acre upon acre of housing developments, shopping centers, malls, tourist attractions, highways, and intensively farmed croplands. These artificial and managed environments have obliterated much of the original character of Florida's lands. Low-lying areas, including ponds and wetlands, have been filled in, rivers have been straightened, and ridges and bluffs have been scraped off to produce tabletop-flat lands.

The Audubon Society estimates that since 1967, populations of many common Florida birds have declined sharply. The numbers of some individual species have nose-dived as much as 80 percent. Habitat destruction is the primary cause. Some of Florida's threatened birds include the black skimmer, the American bittern, the northern bobwhite, the American kestrel, and the clapper rail.

Property owners and landscape managers can make a significant difference in helping to maintain Florida's wildlife—one property at a time. Taken together, all those single lots, corridors, and large blocks of newly diversified land can become greenways and provide important wildlife havens. Forward-thinking landowners, homeowners associations, and commercial and municipal land managers are becoming greener by changing the way things are done. Sprawl development is being replaced,

Creating Habitat Is Sustainable

Creating or restoring habitat is sustainable on several levels. Provide food, shelter, and water for wildlife and you'll be rewarded with a balanced population of **beneficials**—those birds, bats, predatory insects, and other creatures that prey on bugs, including those that damage landscapes and crops.

Meadows and wooded areas are not lawn—and that alone makes them more sustainable—plus they support many types of plants and animals. On a larger scale, a properly restored native habitat should be able to sustain itself with only very occasional maintenance, such as removing exotic invaders. This helps balance loss of habitat as more land is cleared across Florida.

albeit slowly, by greener "cluster development," where new buildings are grouped in close proximity to one another in order to preserve large green spaces for recreation and wildlife. Native and often waterwise plantings are being used in residential communities, along roadsides, in drainage ditches, and in other hard-to-maintain areas. Landscaping with native plants saves water and money, enhances the water quality, moderates the temperature and humidity, provides food and habitat for local wildlife, plus you'll feel better knowing that you are working with Mother Nature.

Backyard Habitat

Creating wilder areas in your landscape reduces the labor, energy, and water consumption needed for maintenance, especially when compared to lawns. Backyard habitat certification programs for individual homeowners, schools, and communities can provide a good framework and starting point. When you have a list of tasks to accomplish in order to have your property certified, you may be more likely to complete the project.

Backyard Habitat Certification

The National Wildlife Federation (NWF) (http://www.nwf.org) has been encouraging homeowners, schools, and communities to create habitat with their Backyard Habitat certification program since 1973. Here is the to-do list for certification.

1. Provide food
2. Provide water
3. Provide cover
4. Provide places to raise young
5. Use two sustainable gardening practices. In addition to the four habitat features your yard must provide, NWF requires that you practice at least two sustainable gardening practices, such as installing rain gardens, mulching and composting, reducing lawn areas, reducing erosion, reducing the use of chemicals, and more. Hmm . . . this sounds familiar.
6. List the plants on your property. Identifying and listing the plants on your property is part of NWF's certification process, because it enables you to know what you have—for instance, you need to know if any of your plants are invasive so you can start removing them.

Schools and Communities Can Work toward Certification

In addition to the requirements listed above, schools must include learning opportunities for all ages across the curriculum in order to be certified. A schoolyard habitat will also:

- provide areas for teaching and learning about nature;
- restore habitat for wildlife;
- decrease mowing maintenance costs;
- provide alternative classroom settings;
- create beautiful places on campus; and
- enhance biodiversity in the neighborhood.

NWF also offers a program that provides habitat certification to whole communities. When an entire neighborhood or town works together on such a project, the cumulative effect is huge.

Note: There is a participation fee for individiduals that includes a year's membership in NWF.

After receiving their initial certification, many people keep expanding and refining their habitat over the years, because the rewards of more birds, butterflies, and other wildlife can be intoxicating.

Don't Use Pesticides

Before you start any habitat project, stop using all pesticides. Allow your bugs and their predators to reach a balance. The predators' populations will vary depending upon the abundance of their prey. Using poisons requires more rather than less of your continuing attention. Letting Mother Nature alone to do the heavy lifting saves you money and time. Plus, chemical pollution from your property will be minimized. These two concepts are part of the integrated pest management (IPM) strategies discussed in chapter 9.

Food for Wildlife

Good habitat should have a wide variety of flower types, berries, seeds, and nuts. Adult butterflies, hummingbirds, and other pollinators are attracted to flowers for their nectar and pollen. Hummingbirds favor reddish tubular flowers, while butterflies prefer broader flower heads like asters, milkweeds, or goldenrods that serve as landing pads. In Florida, we can have flowers all year, even during the winter months. In northern regions of the state, the warm days bring out a few bees and butterflies—so your habitat should accommodate these winter beauties. In central and southern regions of the state it's easier to maintain year-round flowers and their pollinators.

Berries and seeds are important food for many songbirds, particularly when they are migrating. Some insect-eating birds shift to berries when the bug population is low. Work to create a selection of native berry-bearing shrubs and trees. In Florida, some plants hold their berries through the cooler months and are available in the spring, but the majority will provide food from late summer through late fall. To provide seeds large and small, don't deadhead all of your flowers—leave some of them in place and let them go to seed.

Provide caterpillar food plants where female butterflies and moths will lay their eggs. Group the food sources together so caterpillars can crawl to the next plant to satisfy their voracious appetites. After a plant has been stripped of vegetation, treat it with a topdressing of compost to help it grow back for the next generation of caterpillars. Florida's mild climate means that butterflies can go through several generations or "flights" in one season.

To plan for particular butterfly species, concentrate on the larval food plants, because they are the most crucial for the survival of the species. For instance, plant native passion vines to attract our official state butterfly, the zebra longwing. For monarch butterflies, plant groups of milkweed plants. You may find that scarlet milkweed is easier to obtain and grow in a garden area than a native milkweed species, such as the bright orange butterfly weed. To attract polka-dotted wasp moths, plant oleanders. This native insect used to feed on a native plant in the oleander family, but switched to the more plentiful imported oleanders. If you find that you're sharing your parsley with some caterpillars, smile because they will become beautiful black swallowtail butterflies. Butterfly gardeners hope for a moth-eaten landscape, because it means they've successfully attracted female moths and butterflies and soon will enjoy the beauty of the color-in-motion adults.

Food for wildlife is best supplied by plants and animals in a balanced ecosystem, but you may on occasion need to supplement naturally occurring food with feeders. Hummingbirds pollinate our flowers and eat insects, but for transitional times when no or few flowers are in bloom, you can support them by providing sugar water. Mix one part granulated table sugar with four parts of warm water. Don't dye the liquid red—use a feeder with red parts instead. It's important to keep the sugar water fresh and to clean the feeder regularly: every three to four days in warm weather and once a week or so during cooler months. This will keep the liquid from growing mold, which is harmful to hummingbirds. Food for seed feeders is quite popular, but make sure that you keep the area relatively clean. Seed should never be allowed to mold or rot. Once you start feeding, you should reliably maintain these food sources during the same time each year. You never know when a flock of migrating cedar waxwings will come and strip every berry from your trees and shrubs or when a group of gold finches will be looking for some seeds.

Water Features Attract Wildlife

Birdbaths are probably the simplest way to provide water, but you may find that here in Florida the water gets so hot in the sun that birds won't use it. You can, of course, install a birdbath in a shady spot. More birds will use a water source if there are nearby trees and shrubs with branches suitable for perching. Empty the water every three days to prevent mosquitoes from hatching. A birdbath with a solar-powered recirculating pump running a fountain will keep the water cooler and be easier to maintain. Moving water may also be more attractive to birds.

A larger water feature, such as a pond, provides habitat for more wildlife. If you build a pond, either an inground pond or a preformed water garden, make sure that there are shallow places where small birds can take baths, mud flats for the butterflies, and gentle slopes for easy access in and out for turtles and frogs. **Emergent plants**, which are rooted in the pond bottom or in submerged pots and emerge from the water's surface, provide hiding places for underwater animals and landing places for hovering insects and small birds. Replace the lawn at the edge of ponds with ferns, rushes, native irises, and other water-loving native plants to provide more cover and more interest in the landscape.

Create Sheltered Areas

Birds, butterflies, frogs, toads, and other wildlife need places to hide from predators and places to protect themselves from heat, wind and rain. Create areas where vegetation ranges all the way from the ground to high in the trees. Use shrubs and trees of varying heights, imitating the arrangement of plants in natural communities. Vines are particularly good for filling in spaces between low-growing plants (groundcovers, grasses, wildflowers) and taller shrubs and trees. This vertical layering simulates the natural **ecotones** or edges between different habitats (between meadow and forest or understory and **canopy**, for example) and provides shelter for many types of wildlife.

Snags—dead trees that have been left standing—provide food and nesting sites for many birds and other animals. Woodpeckers are primary cavity nesters and chisel out holes in deadwood for new nests each breeding season. Other animals, including birds, snakes, and small mammals,

WOODPECKERS
MAKE HOLES
WHICH CAN ALSO
BE USED BY OTHER
WILDLIFE

DEAD SNAGS
LEAVE SNAGS IN WOODED AREAS

Snags left in wooded areas make good habitat for birds.

such as bats, are secondary cavity nesters and use old woodpecker holes for raising young. If a snag might do damage by falling, chop off the top part to a safe, stable level: it can still provide good habitat. You can plant some vines at the bottom to make it more attractive to you and the wildlife. Brush piles provide good cover for birds and other small animals, so don't haul away or burn all your fallen limbs and twigs. Both snags and brush piles occur in naturally forested areas, but for firewise landscapes, snags and brush piles should be located at least 30 feet from buildings.

If you don't have any snags in your landscape, you can make up for a lack of nesting cavities by providing bat boxes and nesting boxes designed specifically for the birds you wish to attract. Insect-eating birds and bats are particularly important in your balanced ecosystem. Do some research and find the best design and hole size to welcome native birds. Plan and design your birdhouses so they can be opened for annual cleaning. Scrape out the nesting material and scrub with a highly diluted bleach solution to reduce infection and parasites. Let the box dry before reassembling.

Manage Pets

Cats and dogs harass and prey upon wildlife. Remove these subsidized predators, especially cats, from your landscape, particularly in the areas where you have attempted to restore habitat. It isn't logical or fair that you and your neighbors encourage birds, butterflies, and other wildlife to your properties only to have your pets scare them away or injure or kill them.

Remove Invasive Non-native Plants

It's important to know which plants are growing on your property so you can make informed decisions about how to handle them. Part of restoring or creating good habitat, then, involves removing the invasive exotics that have crowded out our native plants. The Florida Exotic Pest Plant Council (FLEPPC) publishes its list of invasive exotics (non-natives) in two categories. Considered the most noxious, Category I plants have already harmed Florida's native plant communities and habitats. Category II plants are regionally invasive and show signs of becoming more widely invasive. The FLEPPC lists are revised and updated on a regular basis. Millions of dollars have been spent to remove plant invaders from parks, preserves, and other public lands. You can help with this effort by not purchasing these plants and by removing invasives from your property.

As Florida's original habitats are reduced and replaced, many indigenous animals are left wanting. Native plants provide the preferred food and shelter for our native birds and animals, and native plants have adapted to Florida soil microbes. Before installing native plants, make sure you've created a situation where they will do well and that you know how to care for them. It's not sustainable to purchase native plants and then kill them with improper handling—most often over watering.

Your garden areas will work best as habitat if they extend into more naturalized areas. Integrating some naturalized habitat into your landscape is sustainable because these garden areas help support a balanced ecosystem of interdependent plants and animals.

Expand the Scale

By enlisting other people in your community to the cause of creating or restoring native habitats, you can have an even greater positive impact. Greenways, belts of undeveloped land, provide wildlife connections between habitat areas and increase territory size for larger species. When neighbors agree to create and link their backyard habitats, they create semiwild spaces that attract animals back to an area. As you add Florida's native trees, shrubs, perennials, and groundcovers to your landscape, you will find that they not only help wildlife but also reduce temperatures compared to surrounding regions with too much pavement and lawns.

Florida Backyard Landscapes for Wildlife

This important certification, sponsored by the University of Florida's wildlife extension, places more emphasis on wildlife than does the Florida Yards and Neighborhoods program described in chapter 1. These two Florida certifications go hand-in-hand. For more information and a printable application form, visit http://www.wec.ufl.edu.

Ten Tips for Landscaping for Wildlife

1. Limit the amount of lawn.
2. Increase vertical layering.
3. Provide snags and brush piles.
4. Provide water.
5. Plant native vegetation.
6. Provide birdhouses, bat houses, and bird feeders.
7. Remove invasive exotic plants.
8. Manage pets.
9. Reduce pesticide.
10. Expand the scale of habitat.

Meadow Management Strategies

Meadows, open areas filled with a wide variety of herbaceous plants, are important habitat for native birds, butterflies, bees, wasps, and more. Depending upon your situation, methods for creating and maintaining meadow areas will vary, but no matter which strategy you use, a meadow provides far more habitat value than a lawn.

When developing large meadow areas near homes, create paths wide enough for easy wheelbarrow or garden cart access. Install a bench or a couple of chairs and a table in the shade at the edge of a meadow to integrate the area into surrounding landscape. The edges of meadows are also great places to locate bird and bat houses. When you take the time to design your meadows, they'll look more like a natural and planned part of your landscape and less like a bunch of weeds that you forgot to mow.

Mow-Once-a-Year Meadow Maintenance

If the space where you want to start a meadow is lawn, stop mowing it every week. Give it a good boost by spreading a topdressing of compost mixed with sandy soil. You'll be surprised at the variety of plants that grow, especially if no weed killer has been applied for a while. Depending upon your location, in addition to various grasses, you'll find rushes, sedges, goldenrods, asters, clover, dog fennels, and many others. There's no shortage of volunteer plants in Florida.

At the end of winter, mow everything at the very highest setting on your mower. Before mowing, you may need to chop down some of the tallest plants by hand, but leave them in place. The mower will chop off newly sprouted pine trees and other small woody plants. Leave all the shredded materials in place as a mulch. Leaving the tops of last year's plants provides seeds for the birds and for the spring growing season. As the spring growth begins, the cycle will start again. You'll probably notice a wider variety of plants growing in your meadow during the second and following years. Be sure to remove invasive non-native plants that might volunteer in meadow areas—early removal is important, or you may find those invasives crowding out or crawling over everything else.

A good meadow will sort itself out into waves of plants according to sun exposure, average soil moisture, and other conditions. This variety of plants will bloom and provide seeds or berries at different times through-out the season. Sturdy perennials in your meadow areas will provide more predictability from year to year, but freely seeding annuals provide new arrangements every season. You could leave the mix of plants in your meadows as is, or you may decide to replace or add to the volunteers to add more diversity of form, flowering, and color.

When you pull out a large plant from a meadow, you can fill in the open gash of bare soil with a single replacement plant, or you can rake out an area of soil, apply some compost, and seed with one or two types of suitable wildflowers. Use a mix of wildflowers you create yourself, not one of the premixed combinations that you can buy. Florida is sometimes lumped in with Texas, so you might end up with too many prairie flowers and not enough Florida natives. Experiment with small quantities of vari-ous seeds until you find those that work well on your property. Mother Nature makes her own rules, so some plants that are supposed to do well in your region may not be successful.

If you are looking for more wildflowers faster, there are a few ways to add color to the meadow. You could just sow wildflower seeds over the meadow with no soil preparation in the fall, but the weeds and established grasses and other perennials will probably not allow many of those deli-cate seeds to survive. To give your seeds a better chance, find a few thin spots in the meadow and work some compost into the surface of the soil. You could add a thin layer of sterilized soil to the surface to deter some of the weeds until your seeds become established. After your soil prepara-tion, sow the seeds. In the fall don't water, just pat the seeds in, but in the spring, water the seeds to bring them out of dormancy.

At the end of the season, mow your meadow. Mowing chops down the woody plants and also helps broadcast seeds left on stalks of wildflow-ers and grasses. You'll need a heavy-duty power mower for this—a hand mower won't cut it.

An extreme meadow management method is to kill all the plants in the area with an herbicide before sowing new meadow flower seeds. This procedure is described in several of the highway or roadside meadow pro-grams. The use of herbicides might make this method at first appear to be unsustainable, but the fact that meadowed roadsides aren't mowed every few weeks makes them much more sustainable than manicured roadsides requiring regular mowing. Large-scale wildflower programs also have the option of spraying a slurry of seed, mulch, fertilizer, and binder to plant the wildflowers quickly from a truck. At the end of the year, the area is mowed. The roadside flowers provide long, narrow habitat and nectar sources, plus they increase our pleasure as we're driving or biking by. Maybe folks will stop throwing their trash along the roadsides if they look more like gardens. Wishful thinking.

No-Mow Meadow Maintenance

If your wildflower mix contains lots of perennials, which should come up reliably from year to year, annual mowing may not be needed. In most parts of Florida, a meadow area, if it's not mowed or burned, will change gradually over the years through succession. Depending on the region and the soil type, various trees and shrubs can germinate in meadows. If allowed to grow, these woody plants will transform the meadow into a wooded area.

If you want to maintain your meadow but don't want to mow it once a year, you can pull or dig up the trees and large shrubs every two or three years. If you have other spaces where these woody plants will work well, transplant them. This "no mow" regimen allows for a wilder meadow area, and it may offer better habitat for more wildlife than annually mowed meadows. Either method of meadow management, though, is easier and much better for the environment than maintaining a lawn.

Hedgerows

A mixture of shrubs and small trees planted to form dense thickets provides wonderful habitat and shelter, especially for birds and butterflies. Choose plants that produce flowers and berries or seeds at different times during the year. Also choose plants that should do well in the one or more environments on your property. Pay attention to predicted growth patterns (heights and spreads), foliage types and textures, flower shapes and color, and other features so that your plantings complement each other visually.

In naturalistic settings, you don't want to install woody plants in straight lines or in predictable checkerboard patterns. Such installations appear stiff and artificial. You can still arrange hedgerows in a more or less linear pattern, where the lines swell and recede in gentle arcs. You may want to create double or triple rows of plantings so that each plant has its own space, but the general effect is that of a thicket. Also, while the end result will be rather dense, space your plants slightly closer than the projected breadth of each specimen in the row. In other words, say, if the two species of medium-sized trees or shrubs you have chosen for your back row will grow to produce branches or canopies four feet wide, space the plants three and a half feet apart so that their limbs will interpenetrate.

A hedgerow can be quite effective as a visual, wind, and sound screen. See chapter 6 for more information on choosing woody plants.

Remember: a hedgerow is not the same thing as a hedge—those unsustainable monocultures planted in rows and trimmed every few weeks to unnatural, boxy shapes. While hedgerows serve a similar screening purpose in the landscape as hedges, they do so more sustainably by providing varied habitat and greater visual interest with much less ongoing maintenance.

Creating or Restoring Wooded Habitat

There are numerous strategies for creating or restoring wooded habitat. For most homeowners and businesses, small groupings of trees and shrubs will create pockets of woodland. This may be all that can be accomplished on small lots, but don't discount such groupings as unimportant. If everyone in a neighborhood landscaped this way, ambient temperatures would be lowered, and birds, frogs, lizards, and other wildlife would come.

To produce the best habitat on residential or commercial lots when planting woody plants, try to emulate groupings that would occur naturally in your region. Visit state forests or parklands in your region that have been allowed to grow naturally. Take note of which species occur together and their spacing.

If you've modified the lay of the land to promote the best drainage or if the topsoil has been scraped away during development, you may need to improve the soil before you start planting a lot of trees and shrubs. It might take a year or two to emulate normal succession for your region of the state. Get local advice from your extension agent on the best course of action for creating wooded areas on your property.

Here's one strategy that could work in many parts of the state. Sow native grasses and wildflower seeds—legumes are a great choice in poor soils, as they **fix their own nitrogen**—bacteria in their root nodules can extract nitrogen from the air and make it usable as fertilizer. If you're starting with lawn, let it go to meadow first, as described above; but either way, provide a topdressing of compost. If you're covering a large area, you'll want to take advantage of the free compost or mulch that's available from many of Florida's counties, often at waste management or wood reclamation facilities.

The microbes from the compost will migrate into the soil and start to rebuild the topsoil layer. Better topsoil will hold more water and provide more nutrients for your plants. After a year or two of letting the herbaceous plants grow, begin planting your native woody plants in this naturalized setting. Leave the grasses and other herbaceous plants in place between your planting sites, but remove them from the immediate vicinity of your woody plants, where you'll build a "saucer and mulch" system to better catch and absorb the water (as described in chapter 6.)

When selecting your woody plants, be sure to choose a variety of sizes and branching patterns for the best emulation of native habitat. Keep in mind how much care these plants will receive when you select the plants. Smaller trees and shrubs will require much less ongoing care than older, larger specimens. Larger trees will require regular watering for several months until they become established. So if you decide to get a head start on your habitat by planting sizeable trees, find a way to provide water on a regular schedule.

Waterside Habitats

Florida's abundant water-rich habitats include the Atlantic and Gulf beaches, riversides, clear, free-running springs, canals, large groundwater ponds, lakes, small lined ponds, wetlands, seasonally flooded low spots, and retention ponds. They all can provide important wildlife habitat. Depending upon the nature of the water body, your approach for habitat creation will vary. Bulkheads and other unnatural treatments have been installed in many areas to reduce erosion and preserve land, but they may have compromised much of our waterfront as habitat. Innovative treatments can invite wildlife back to these areas.

Before you embark on waterside landscaping projects, though, learn about state and local regulations governing modifications to waterfront areas. In many cases permits are required (see A Note on Waterfront Regulations on page 231). These regulations and restrictions protect Florida's most fragile ecosystems—aquatic and wetland.

Littoral zones are the transition areas between the water and the wetlands or the uplands. If they are designed well for habitat, they'll furnish cover and access in and out for turtles, frogs, wading birds, and other small animals. Mud flats attract butterflies and will support various invertebrates such as crawfish and mussels. A successful habitat supports a large variety of inhabitants, and as an ecosystem, is self-sustaining.

The process is twofold. First build the physical substrate that will withstand forces of erosion, provide the various depths for different types of plants, and protect the area from pesticides, siltation, and nutrient-rich runoff. Then install the plants most likely to succeed and ones that have the best wildlife habitat value. See chapter 13 for more on waterside gardening.

If you're building a small, inground pond, creating various depths of water and some surrounding moist garden areas will increase its usefulness as habitat. Place logs, rocks, and mounds of soil arranged at the edge of the pond and the wetlands to emulate a natural environment. Make sure that everything is secure and won't roll or rock if someone steps on them.

A small pond will probably require a water circulation system to keep it aerated and cool. If it's located in full sun, use a solar pump and add more depth to act as a reservoir and to moderate the temperature. Plan for minimal disturbance of the surrounding soil and rocks once you've completed the installation, so toads, frogs, and salamanders will have stable areas for hibernation, egg laying, and hiding.

Rain gardens and buffer areas around the shoreline of a natural body of water should be designed to absorb the first flow of rainwater and to allow only a small amount of well-filtered overflow into the waterway.

This reduces the erosion and siltation, plus it reduces the flow of nutrients into our aquatic ecosystems. The rain gardens and buffer zones also can be designed as transitional habitat to support wildlife that lives in both water and terrestrial environments during their different life stages.

If you are dealing with a bulkheaded waterfront, the rain gardens and buffer areas on the inside of the bulkhead, as described above, serve as a substitute for a wetland. Don't use weed barrier cloth in this area, because it compromises habitat—direct access to the soil allows toads to bury themselves and turtles to scoop out depressions for their eggs. Create some type of ramp or pathway that animals can use to access the water. You might also want to build or install basking logs that turtles and wading birds can use.

If the depth of the water is consistently a foot or more at the bottom of the bulkhead, you'll need either to build up the bottom with large stones or to lash the logs to the bulkhead so the lowest ones are at or just below the normal or average water level. (You can use both techniques at the same time, of course.) The logs should be arranged to provide a pathway to the top of the bulkhead. As an alternative, you could remove a small section of bulkhead to provide the access animals require. Be sure you have stabilized the exposed land on the inside of the bulkhead to prevent erosion and that you have planted a good barrier of emergent plants such as rushes, pickerelweed, or mangroves, on the water side.

If you have relatively shallow water, even if it experiences tidal or seasonal changes, consider installing a **living shoreline**—combinations of shoreline plants that may be planted on the natural bottom, natural sandbars, or man-made berms to protect the shoreline from erosion due to wave action. Living shoreline designs vary depending upon type of waterway. Barriers can be T-shaped, with the top of the T parallel to the shoreline, or C-shaped; but no matter what their structure, water is allowed to flow throughout. A living shoreline can become an important nursery for fish and a good substrate for shellfish. The scale can be large or small, but any living shoreline, no matter its size, will replace some of the wetlands habitat that Florida has lost to development over the last few decades.

Install plants that can tolerate wet feet—that is, plants adapted to different levels of submersion. Selecting a wide variety of plants with various structures is the key to success—plants need to be water tolerant, salt tolerant, or both, and they must be appropriate to your region and its specific climatic and environmental conditions. Plant to provide food and hiding places for terrestrial, amphibious, and aquatic wildlife. You may even decide to plant prickly barriers to keep out some of the more aggressive animals, such as geese, while allowing access for the smaller and more desirable wildlife, such as turtles, frogs, and toads.

It's best not to allow invasive non-native plants to take over your waterside habitat because they will compromise its habitat value as they crowd out native plants or solidify beachy areas required for nesting. A specific example of this in Florida is the Australian pine that has grown so thickly along the beaches that some species of turtles can't find good nesting sites. To start, you may have lots of weeds to deal with, and the best way to reduce their population is to hand pull them or use a sharp hoe. Because herbicides can be especially harmful to fish and aquatic invertebrates, herbicide use normally is not an option near the water. On the plus side, water weeds make excellent compost material.

Increasing Habitat Matters

Property owners, landscape managers, and communities can make a significant difference one yard and one property at a time. Taken together, new pockets of restored habitat will become greenbelts or greenways for a wide variety of birds and bats, frogs and toads, turtles, butterflies, moths, and other beneficial insects. It matters and great progress can be made one yard at a time.

Resources

Web Sites

The National Wildlife Federation has been spearheading backyard and school-yard habitat certification programs since 1973. See http://www.nwf.org.

The Wildlife Habitat Council helps large landowners manage their unused lands in an ecologically sensitive manner for the benefit of wildlife and the environment. It also has projects for backyard conservation: http://www.wildlifehc.org/.

The United States Department of Agriculture's Natural Resource Conservation Service Web site has information on backyard habitats and conservation: http://www.nrcs.usda.gov.

The Florida Fish and Wildlife Commission Web site lists and describes native plants by region: http://myfwc.com.

The Cornell Ornithology Lab's Web site provides detailed information on birds and their diets: http://www.birds.cornell.edu.

The University of Florida's wildlife extension (administered through IFAS and the Department of Wildlife Ecology and Conservation) offers several master naturalist courses (http://www.masternaturalist.ifas.ufl.edu/) and opportunities for backyard wildlife habitat certification: http://www.wec.ufl.edu.

Brooklyn Botanic Garden's Web site has information on changing schoolyards into wildlife sanctuaries: http://www.bbg.org.

The Audubon Society's Web site provides descriptions, plans, guidelines, and kids activities for creating and maintaining bird-friendly backyards: http://www.audubon.org and http://www.audubonofflorida.org.

The Florida Wildflowers Growers Cooperative has information about growing wildflowers in Florida: http://floridawildflowers.com.

The Florida Department of Environmental Protection (DEP) has information on permits for altering wetlands and advice on maintaining and creating living shorelines: (http://www.dep.state.fl.us).

The Florida Exotic Pest Plant Council maintains lists of plants that are invasive in Florida: http://www.fleppc.org.

NOAA's habitat Web site has detailed information on living shorelines and other wetlands and coastal restoration projects and resources: http://www.habitat.noaa.gov.

Books

Daniels, Jaret. *Your Florida Guide to Butterfly Gardening: A Guide for the Deep South*. Gainesville: University Press of Florida/IFAS, 2000.

Langeland, K. A., and K. Craddock Burks, eds. *Identification and Biology of Nonnative Plants in Florida's Natural Areas*. Gainesville: University of Florida, Institute of Food and Agricultural Sciences, 1998. (Available to download at http://www.fleppc.org.)

Miller, James H. *Nonnative Invasive Plants of Southern Forests: A Field Guide for Identification and Control*. Ashville, N.C.: USDA Forest Service, 2004. (Available without charge from Southern Research Station, P.O. Box 2680, Ashville, N.C. 28802.)

National Audubon Society. *National Audubon Society's Field Guide to Florida*. New York: Knopf, 1998.

Schaefer, Joseph M., and George Tanner. *Landscaping for Florida's Wildlife: Recreating Native Ecosystems in Your Yard*. Gainesville: University Press of Florida, 1998.

Walton, Dan, and Laurel Schiller. *Natural Florida Landscaping*. Sarasota, Fla.: Pineapple Press, 2007.

Trees and Shrubs

Trees and shrubs, the woody plants, provide the most obvious structural plants or the "bones" of the landscape. In Florida we have hundreds of wonderful trees and shrubs from which to choose. The most sustainable action is to preserve the appropriate existing woody plants on your property and, when selecting new trees and shrubs, do as your extension agent would advise, "Select the right plant for the right place." With proper selection and maintenance your woody plants will provide shade, privacy, and habitat for wildlife. They prevent erosion, cool their surroundings, and absorb carbon dioxide from the air. That trees and shrubs add beauty and stability to any landscape is a lovely bonus.

Evaluating Existing Trees and Shrubs in the Landscape

Evaluating existing woody plants in your landscape is an important initial step in prudent and sustainable landscape design. Preserving your existing trees, if they are in good health and growing in appropriate locations, is more sustainable than replacing them all with new saplings or, worse yet, lawn. Large trees that have been weakened by disease, old age, injured roots, or physical restrictions, such as sidewalks, foundations, or roads may need to be pruned or removed before they do harm. Periodic evalua-

Planting Woody Plants Is Sustainable

Woody plants cool the air more than smaller, herbaceous plants by moving a greater volume of water from the soil into the atmosphere through transpiration. Shaded areas beneath woody plants can be twenty degrees cooler than sunny spots. Properly placed trees and shrubs can reduce air conditioning costs, prevent erosion, and soak up excess stormwater. Depending on the severity and type of storm, groups of wind-resistant trees may reduce storm damage from winds by disrupting the air currents and protect your property by intercepting flying debris.

Trees and shrubs generally contain the most biomass or living matter per square foot in your landscape. This means that they will absorb the most carbon dioxide and produce the most oxygen during photosynthesis. The long growing season in Florida means that our trees form an effective carbon sink and may absorb and lock up greater amounts of carbon than trees in colder regions. This is good for the planet.

tions of this kind are part of preparing your landscape for hurricanes and other strong storms. Read more on stormwise landscaping in chapter 14.

Here are some of the conditions to look for (see below for a separate section on palms):

- Rot at the base of the tree, indicated by gaps in the trunk or by evidence of fungal invasion, such as mushrooms sprouting from the trunk, suggest the tree is diseased and weakened. It will be more likely to fall during a storm.
- Trees with split or divided trunks are usually weaker than those with single trunks. There are some exceptions, such as live oaks with their large horizontal branches and sea grapes with their branching, mounded shapes. These natives fare quite well in high winds.

- Dieback in the tree crown or other evidence of damage, disease, or pest invasion, such as piles of sawdust or weeping wounds also indicate a tree in a weakened, vulnerable state.

- Trunk damage from string trimmers and lawnmowers may signal a tree weakened by repeated abuse from machinery. Replace turf next to trees with a ring of mulch around each tree and between groupings of trees to prevent damage and reduce competition from turf and weeds for water and nutrients.

- Large trees growing in restricted spaces, such as close to buildings or next to driveways or other impervious surfaces tend to have unbalanced roots and may fall easily. Young or recently planted full-sized trees situated in this type of root-restricting site should probably be relocated to more appropriate spots before becoming too large to move.

- If several of a tree's major roots have been cut less than 20 feet from the trunk during a construction project or if heavy equipment has compacted the soil within 20 feet of the trunk, that tree is more likely to fall than an uninjured tree. Even if a tree doesn't die as a result of construction trauma, its vulnerability to storm damage and other forces can linger for ten years or more. Proper pruning to thin the crown can reduce the tree's wind resistance and help it withstand storms while it recovers.

- If surface soil is limited, trees growing there will have shallow root systems and may be more likely to uproot. Test for shallow soil by digging several holes just outside the drip line of a tree (where the branch ends drip after a rain), but don't cut into major roots as you dig. If you hit hardpan soil or solid rock within two feet of the surface, the tree's roots may not provide enough support to hold it up in a high wind. Be sure to mulch well and lighten the crowns of these trees to keep them healthy and well balanced.

- The bark of trees that were staked when planted may be damaged if the straps and supporting material were too stiff or not removed as soon as the tree was established. While most trees can heal, watch for signs of weakness at the strap marks.

- Trees planted in a **root-bound** condition may be strangled by their own roots years later. If you don't know the history of a tree, carefully remove the soil from the base of the tree and outward for a few feet to see if the surface roots are encircling the trunk. If you find this condition on a large tree, consult an arborist for advice. For younger trees, you can saw through the offending roots to prevent future damage. Cut one root at a time with at least a month between cuttings.

- If your property has remnants of a forest where, now, only a few solitary trees stand out in the open, those trees may be at risk for falling until they build up enough strength to stand alone. If you must clear out some forestland, it's better to leave groups of trees in the landscape. To reduce the vulnerability of isolated trees, plant smaller trees and shrubs near them to form a tree island, which will buffer the wind and provide a more natural microclimate.

If you notice any of these situations as you scout the trees on your property, you may need professional advice from a certified arborist, who can help you develop a sound management plan. Even if your trees show no external signs of decay, the pros can test for it. If decay is present, an arborist may recommend pruning to relieve stress on the trunk, but topping is never a good idea. Some of your more dangerous trees may need to be removed, but work to preserve as many woody plants in your landscape as you can.

Palms Are Different

What would the Florida landscape be without palm trees? Oh, those gracefully curved trunks and topknots of fronds—mainstays of any tropical setting. While many palms serve as trees in the landscape, they don't develop annual layers of wood like other trees, because they don't have a **cambium** layer under a coating of bark. Palms are **monocots** and are more like grasses, lilies, and bamboo. A cross-section of a palm shows a curly, random, fibrous grain rather than annual rings. This arrangement of woody tissue is usually quite flexible, making most palms especially wind tolerant and an excellent choice for stormwise landscaping.

PALM TREE BOOTS

Boots are the persistent frond stems (petioles) of palm trees.
They can support various plants and animals.

After a palm seed sprouts, the plant goes into an establishment phase
for several years, during which it looks and behaves like a shrubby palmetto. This phase is necessary for the development of the palm's growing tip and for the establishment of the tree trunk's diameter prior to its
vertical growth. Once the trunk is established, it usually doesn't increase
much in girth. Since they don't produce new wood each year on the outside of their trunks, palms have no mechanism for healing wounds. Any
gouges are entry points for fungi and insects, so take care not to injure
your palms.

Palm leaves, known as fronds, grow only from the terminal bud atop
the trunk. There is only one terminal bud per trunk, so if it is damaged,
that stem or the entire plant, for a single-stemmed palm, will be killed.
Depending upon the species, as the fronds die, they may leave behind a
persistent **petiole,** or leaf stem, known as a boot. Our native cabbage palm
often has **boots** armoring its trunk. Boots provide habitat for birds and
other creatures as well as growing ledges for ferns and epiphytes, such as

orchids and bromeliads. Boots may also host a strangler fig seedling that, if it matures, may eventually engulf and kill the palm.

Palm tree roots are different, too. Palms have hundreds of thin roots originating from the trunk. Sometimes the roots branch, but often they do not. A palm won't become pot-bound like a true tree, and when palms are transplanted, many species will develop all new roots from the trunk. This is why they are often staked for several months when first planted. Make sure that the staking does not damage the trunk and remove it as soon as the tree is stable. When you see truckloads of palms traveling down the highway, you'll notice that the trees have proportionally tiny root-balls for their size and that most of their fronds have been trimmed off. This trimming is done so that the roots won't have to support a full complement of fronds while they are trying to grow anew from the trunk. At no other time should a palm be treated this way.

When evaluating palms in the nursery or in your landscape, look for these conditions:

- Look for damage at the base of the trunk. Palms can't heal themselves like a normal woody plant. If string trimmers have nipped all around a palm's base, it will be prone to falling in a high wind. Prevent further damage by establishing a mulch bed around each tree.
- Palm trunks should have a uniform, slight taper. A narrow section of the trunk topped by a wider section, called "hour-glassing," is an indication of poor treatment during some part of its cultivation. This narrow area may fail during a high windstorm. Don't buy it, no matter how inexpensive. If it's on your property, consider removing it if it's in an area where it could do damage.
- Even though a palm may generate mostly new roots upon planting, examine the roots before purchase. They should be white and **turgid,** and they should have been kept in a moist environment since their digging—usually this means inside a burlap wrap.
- Do some research before you purchase palms to ensure that you select those that suit your climate and growing conditions, such as sun exposure and soil moisture. Choose the correct size for your

space. While palm roots are tolerant of close proximity to buildings, make sure you leave adequate space for the tree's growth. You surely don't want to ruin your roof or your palms by planting them so close that the fronds scrape against it. Also make sure that the palm you purchase won't make too much of a mess in your yard. Date palms, for instance, drop their seeds each year; if that's a problem for you, choose a different species or plan to remove the flowering stalks before their annual seed drop.

Arranging Your Woody Plants

Before you do any planting, develop a plan. Ideally you'd create a scale drawing of your lot and plan out different sections to suit your purposes for each area. You'll need to consider stormwater drainage and other water flows in your plans. Take care of the drainage and irrigation projects before you proceed with any permanent plantings.

Even if your plan is only a simple sketch in your garden log, you still should have ideas for the best use of each section. Consider the views from your windows and from outside areas where various activities are likely to occur. Your landscape plan could create wide-open vistas or enclosed garden rooms or courtyards defined by a combination of **hardscape** structures like walls, berms, large rocks, arbors, trellises, or pergolas. No permanent planting should take place unless it furthers your plan. This is more important for woody plants than other plantings because they're more permanent and a greater investment both in dollars and initial care.

As you plan for and create your permanent structures, keep in mind how they will affect your plants and how the plants may affect the structures. For instance, a wall or patio made of cement or limestone will sweeten the soil; so don't place acid-loving plants next to it. A good-sized tree or large shrub may have shallow, spreading roots that could lift patio stones or continuously send up sprouts in the middle of your outdoor space. Planting a tree near a garden pond or swimming pool might create wonderful shade, but it may also create a mess when it drops its leaves and flowers and fruit. Even evergreen trees drop their leaves some of the time—maybe all the time like southern magnolias. Think about the how the hardscape and the **softscape** elements interact as you create your plan.

Your plan should take into consideration both the underground and overhead utilities. You don't want to have the roots of your new trees wrapping themselves around your underground pipes or conduits. So call your utility companies and have them locate any underground wires, water and sewer pipes, or gas mains. In May 2007, the Common Ground Alliance launched a nationwide 811—"call before you dig" number. If you have an inground sprinkler system, you also need to locate the paths of its pipes and electrical wires. If you have a septic system, locate all the parts. Then look up. It's amazing how often folks plant full-sized trees directly under overhead power lines. You certainly don't want the power company's tree guys whacking off the tops of your trees. Be a wise planner and avoid all those utilities.

If your landscape has been wiped clean of woody plants during the building phase or if previously it was farmland, you'll have the freedom to begin your planting where it makes the most sense for your situation. If you have existing woody plants, your new plants should be sited to complement them. Here are some rules-of-thumb for the best results:

- No matter what purpose your trees and shrubs will serve, plant them with enough space to accommodate the adult plant—both the height and the width. Assume that each plant's root zone will be 30 percent larger than the crown when planting near buildings, sidewalks, or other inground obstacles. (Drought-tolerant plants usually have even larger root systems.) This doesn't mean that you can't plant anything else near a tree: roots may comfortably intermingle. Grouping compatible, shade-loving shrubs and perennials under trees is highly recommended to produce a pleasing green space and good habitat. The whole area around these trees and shrubs should then be mulched.
- When creating a grouping of more than three trees, work to make them look natural by combining more than one type of tree

and adding compatible understory shrubs. Use an odd number of trees, and for both aesthetics and wind tolerance; don't line them up like soldiers. Combine trees in ways they might occur in wild areas in your region. Avoid single trees plopped here and there in the landscape—groupings always look better, plus trees and shrubs grow better when assembled into their own microclimate.

- Don't pick out matching trees or shrubs for perfectly aligned borders or bookends for your landscape. Mother Nature will have her say, and her plants may grow at different rates even though, from your perspective, they are treated in the same way. Instead, plant a single tree with understory shrubs on one side of the landscape and three or five smaller trees or shrubs on the other side.

- For a small lot or a small space, where there is room for only three small trees, three different species might look too busy in a confined area. It's probably best to use the same tree species for this small grouping, but choose specimens that are different heights and that have different branching patterns. You might wish to use narrower trees like some of the magnolia cultivars, loblolly bay, or red cedar. Over the years you may want to prune the lower branches of these trees so that they feel open and airy. As understory plants, you might choose ornamental grasses, palmetto, beautyberry, or some other easy-care shrub.

- A group of deciduous trees planted 25 or 30 feet from the southerly and westerly sides of a building will provide shade in the summer months and allow sun in during the cooler months. This will reduce both your air conditioning and heating bills. In tropical areas where deciduous trees are not so common, go for good thick shade trees to provide the most cooling effect. Think about safety in windstorms, and use smaller, wind-resistant trees that will shade the sides of the building, but not necessarily overarch the roof. Don't forget to provide shade for your air conditioner compressor to maximize its effectiveness.

- **Wind groves** consist of wind-resistant trees in naturalized groupings 25 or 30 feet away from the windward side of buildings. By interrupting and dissipating winds, wind groves could possibly reduce storm damage to both the landscape and buildings. Shade trees, as discussed above, can also serve as a wind grove.

When planning for wind tolerance, create your tree grouping so that it has a mounded shape with some lower branching trees, like sea grape or dahoon holly, on the windward side. A wind grove's work extends beyond storm mitigation; it will shelter your property every day from prevailing winds and salt spray. Wind groves also play an important role in waterwise landscaping, because persistent winds cause greater transpiration rates in plants and increase their need for water.

- Woody plants can serve as screening for privacy, from street noise, or from other outside interference. Screening can also define your outside garden areas. Choose a combination of screening plants that don't require monthly trimmings. Go for a more natural and more sustainable hedgerow that needs only occasional trimming to maintain height and shade.

Depending upon your situation, you may want to build an earthen berm to help with a screening project. A berm has the advantage of immediate height and superior sound absorption. Create gentle slopes on the berm sides so the mulch doesn't slide off during hard rain events, and be sure to construct water-holding "saucers" in the berm for each of your plants. Arrange the trees and shrubs in waves up and over the berm and plant a good groundcover to help keep the soil in place. Keep in mind that the top of a berm will be drier and windier than the rest of your landscape. Even a small berm—just two or three feet high—and its plantings can make a big difference in the effectiveness of the screen.

Choosing New Trees and Shrubs

When choosing the ideal trees and shrubs for your landscape, plants native to your specific region are the best place to start. Native plants have a well-developed tolerance for Florida's soil, pests, and its wet and dry seasons. These plants also fulfill roles in the local ecosystem, and by planting them you will help restore some of the green space that has been lost to development.

Non-invasive, non-native woody plants and/or cultivars may provide alternate choices for particular situations. If you are considering a non-native for your landscape, make sure that it's not on the list of invasive plants for Florida. Non-natives are usually the less sustainable choice, but sometimes a non-native plant or a cultivar is a reasonable option for a highly modified landscape. Native plants are adapted to survive in the wilds of mostly unpeopled environments, not in today's concrete jungle.

Trees and shrubs planted on the edges of their normal ranges may survive, but they won't do as well as ones that are ideal for your climate and soil conditions. Choose plants that will thrive, not those that will just struggle along and need continuing attention. You'll also need to know about specific plant characteristics that may cause problems in your landscape. For example, you won't want to plant a sweet gum tree near a high-use outdoor area because of its many spiny gumballs and spreading surface roots that send up **suckers** more than 20 feet from the tree. And while bald cypress are fabulous native trees for wet areas, their knees—vertical root protrusions they often form—are hazardous for mowing and walking.

When purchasing new trees and shrubs, it's best if you can select your specimens from a reputable local nursery that can offer good advice along with its well-cared-for plants. When choosing trees, look for those with one main trunk or that can be pruned to a main trunk over a few years. A balanced crown will look better in the long run and require less corrective pruning. Look at the roots: they should be firm and white, and they should not be circling within the pot or rooted into the soil beneath the pot. In general, you'll want a tree or shrub with healthy roots even if it's on the small side. Healthy roots will adjust more quickly and show more growth sooner than stressed roots. Look for new growth or buds and good green color on the older leaves.

Once you have chosen the best specimens for your landscape, handle them with care. Do not handle woody plants by the trunk, but support the bottom of the root-ball or the pot as you move it to the nursery cart and then into your vehicle. If your vehicle is open, cover the foliage with a tarp to reduce loss of water during the transport to your property.

Planting Trees and Shrubs

In northern Florida, it is be preferable to plant deciduous trees and shrubs from mid- to late winter when they are dormant. In central and south Florida, plant at the beginning of the rainy season, late summer. When planting new trees, including palms, dig a hole that is two inches shallower than its root-ball or pot and at least twice as wide—wider is better. The base of the planted tree should be slightly higher in the ground than it was in its pot. Be sure that the center of the hole provides a solid footing so the tree won't sink once it's in place. Most trees have a slight flare where the roots start to spread; make sure that this flare it is above the soil line.

Before you remove the tree from its pot or wrap, set it in the hole to check for placement. Prop it up if necessary, and then stand back to view

Handling Pot-bound Plants

If you end up with a pot-bound tree or shrub, try to unwind the roots before you fill in the hole with soil. If they can be stretched out, but are too stiff to stay in place, you may need to brace them in place within the hole. Drive short, untreated wooden stakes into the hole to keep the roots from recoiling—these stakes will not usually extend above the ground level and will eventually rot away in the soil.

If the roots are too thick and woody to unwind, make three or four vertical slices into the side of the root-ball, cutting through the biggest roots. This harsh treatment stimulates the roots to branch out from the cuts, but the tree will require more irrigation over a longer period of time to survive. In the long run, the tree will develop a radiating root pattern, which will keep the tree from strangling itself and will provide a stronger structure against wind pressure.

Left: A pot-bound shrub

Below: When planting a tree or shrub that was pot bound, first rinse away spent soil from around the roots. Unwind the roots and spread them out. Plant your tree or shrub so it sits at the same level as in the pot—you might see a root flare. Use only soil from the hole to fill in—don't add any enrichments. Irrigate liberally.

it from all angles—look up as well. Also, go inside and view it from your windows to make sure that your planned location does not block a prized view. Remember to consider its mature size. Only after all this checking, remove it gently from its pot or wrap. As you place the root-ball into the hole, stretch out any roots that were growing against the edge of the pot or wrap to stimulate growth. Fill the hole with water as you gently shovel the soil back into the hole.

No amendments to the soil are recommended for trees or palms. It has been shown that compost and other soil-enhancing materials added to the planting hole can discourage the roots from spreading out as quickly into surrounding soil. The exception is in contained beds where plant roots can't spread too far from the planting site. Here, small shrubs or trees should be treated more like container plants.

After the hole has been filled in, press the soil gently in place and create a shallow saucer equal to the size of the root-ball or hole by creating a berm of soil two or three inches high around the circumference. Lay two to three inches of mulch over this whole saucer area, but not up against the trunk.

If the tree is wobbly and could be knocked over by a gust of wind, staking may be necessary until the roots grow into the surrounding soil. Make sure that no stakes enter the root-ball and that no wires or ropes abrade the trunk. You may wish to use wide flexible bands of rubber or cloth around the tree trunk instead. Except for palms, stake the tree in such a way that the trunk can bend slightly in the wind—this will enable the tree to build strength in its trunk. Remove the stabilizing stakes as soon as possible, so the tree is not damaged. Newly transplanted palms, as mentioned above, need to be held in place firmly while they grow a whole new root system.

Your new tree will need plenty of water to establish its roots in your landscape soil. The time it will take for your tree to establish itself in your landscape depends upon many variables—its size at planting, your hardiness zone, and the availability of regular irrigation. See page 103 for irrigation details.

Do not depend on an area-wide sprinkler system for watering newly planted woody plants. The amount of irrigation they require is over and above normal maintenance watering or what rainfall provides (at least

Irrigation Requirements after Planting Trees

Each time you irrigate, it's best to water with three gallons per inch trunk **caliper** (the diameter of the trunk at six inches above the root-ball of saplings). For example, use six gallons for a two-inch caliper tree. Apply slowly, so all water soaks into the root-ball.

If a tree is two to four caliper inches, the best practice is to water daily for one month and every other day for the next three months. After that, water weekly until the tree is established. If a tree is more than four caliper inches or if it's a palm, the best practice is to water daily for six weeks; every other day for the next five months; and weekly after that until the tree is established and new growth doesn't wilt during dry periods.

After the initial period, continue to supplement irrigation for your tree during drought conditions for at least a year— two or more years is better.

most of the time). On the other hand, if you've planted a tree on a site that is wet or damp all the time, extra irrigation may not be needed.

If you don't have time to give your newly planted trees the irrigation they need by hand watering, you may decide to install a temporary drip system or to use drip watering bags. (Some of these are horseshoe shaped and lie on the ground encircling the tree trunk, while others wrap around the trunk like a skirt and zip closed.) Drip bags deliver a slow drip of a measured, appropriate amount of water. (A 15-gallon bag takes about four to ten hours to empty.) The traditional advice that homeowners purchase the largest trees they can afford has, in recent years, lost much of its currency. If you have the time and inclination to provide large trees and shrubs with substantial, long-term watering, then maybe a live oak with a six-inch diameter trunk will be worth the extra effort, but one with a two-inch diameter trunk will adjust more quickly. It is often more sustainable to choose a smaller tree or shrub, especially if your situation doesn't allow for regular, long-term watering.

When your tree has been in the ground for at least three months or just before its next growth period, you can, if you wish, apply a topdressing of compost or a light application of a slow-release, organic fertilizer around the drip line. Do not topdress or fertilize during a drought period, though—your tree doesn't need the added stress of having to support vigorous new growth when water is scarce. As for palms, don't expect much in the way of frond growth while the root system is regenerating. When the fronds do start to grow, however, then some compost or organic, slow-release fertilizer would be useful. Apply the compost or fertilizer on the soil surface in a circle around or just outside the drip line for your shade trees and shrubs. For palms, spread the compost or fertilizer 18 to 24 inches from the trunk. There are several reasons for the light touch on fertilizer. If the plant absorbs a heavy load of nitrogen, it may grow too fast and produce a flush of growth that may be hard for it to sustain with normal watering. This weakens the wood, making it more susceptible to disease and pest invasions. Another reason for going light on the fertilizer is to help prevent any excess (that the plant doesn't absorb) ending up in our waterways and causing **algal** blooms or other problems. Compost is a safer alternative to fertilizer—even organics—and can be reapplied throughout the year as needed.

It's certainly more sustainable and less expensive not to have to replace new trees, so choose woody plants that are appropriate for your climate and environmental conditions and that have healthy trunk structures and roots. Make sure that you match the size of the trees you select with the level of ongoing care you'll be able to accomplish. The bigger the tree at planting, the greater the time commitment involved in getting it well established.

Transplanting Trees or Large Shrubs

If a tree or shrub has been growing in a location for more than a year or two, transplanting it will be more successful if you use the planting guidelines above as to best season and if you prune the surface roots at least two months in advance of moving it—earlier is better. Root pruning is most important for trees and large shrubs. Estimate the size of the root mass that you'll be able to handle; you will cut just outside the drip line or the saucer area that you created when you originally planted the tree or shrub. Use an extra-long bladed spade and make cuts straight down in a continuous circle around the plant. If you have time to draw the process out over six weeks, cut only one third of the way around the tree. Two weeks later cut the next third, and two weeks after that, finally cut the last third of the circle. Irrigate regularly inside the root-pruning circle between the time of the root pruning and the transplanting. This action will help the plant adjust to fewer roots and stimulate inner root growth. Two weeks before transplanting time, recut just outside your root-pruning circle so as not to cut through or damage the newly formed or forming root ends.

The day before you transplant your plant, irrigate inside the root-ball area. This will help keep the root-ball together while you work—maybe even in sandy soils. You'll need two or three tarps to keep the soil from burying other plants or obliterating the mulch as you dig your transplant out. Dig a wide, but shallow hole where you will be planting your tree and place the soil on a tarp. You'll finish digging the hole to depth when you know how deep the root-ball is.

Dig away soil from the outside of your root-pruned area and set it aside. For larger trees, you'll probably need to dig more soil away and go deeper to make sure that you've saved as many roots as you can. Then place a tarp on the ground just outside of the dug area. Dig under the tree on the opposite side from the tarp. You'll be prying the tree out of its hole up onto the tarp. Depending on its size, you may need blocks of lumber or more shovels or garden forks to put under the root-ball as you pry it up. Keep in mind that a shovel is not a crowbar and the handle could break if you apply too much pressure. Hopefully you won't encounter a massive taproot, but if you do, dig as much of it out as you can. The tree will tip toward the tarp as you work. Don't pull or pry by the trunk; handle only the root-ball.

Once the tree is on the tarp, drag the tarp to its new spot or, if it's light enough, lift the tarp with the tree into a wheelbarrow or garden cart. Keep the root-ball covered and moist while you work on the hole. Measure the depth of the root-ball using the handle of a shovel as a measuring tool. Finish digging the hole only as deep as the root-ball in the center—it could be a little deeper around the edges. After the hole is the right size, situate the tree on the high spot in the center of the hole and backfill and water as described earlier in this chapter.

Dividing Multistemmed Shrubs

The woody stems of shrubs are sometimes called "canes." While trees typically have one main trunk, shrubs may have many canes growing from the ground. In the event that you plan to leave part of a multicaned shrub in place, decide which portion that will be before you proceed. If the shrub is growing too close to a building or is crowding out a more desirable plant, plan to leave the portion that is farthest away from the area it is crowding. If you can arrange it, root prune the section to be removed several weeks before you dig, but don't root prune the portion that is to stay in place—the shrub will recover faster if more of its roots are left intact.

When you start the division process, you will probably find interconnecting underground woody stems or roots just below the surface that you'll need to cut before you can pull the portions of the shrub to be transplanted away from the part that will stay behind. Cut these stems with a sharp shovel or lopper. Then use a shovel or a garden fork to divide the root mass. Garden forks often work better for dividing because they allow for separation of individual roots, whereas a shovel will cut all the roots no matter where they are attached.

Keep as much of the soil with the sections to be transplanted as you can, and plant with care as described above for trees. Then fill in the gap next to the remaining shrub with local soil and plenty of water. While many of the original shrub's roots are still intact in the soil, this type of shovel pruning is a shock, so apply finished compost outside of the drip line, create a saucer around it like a new transplant, and renew the mulch around it. It's a good idea to treat this stay-behind shrub as if it were newly transplanted, too, and provide additional irrigation for a month or two. Wait to prune the stay-behind shrub into a better shape during the next growing season, but don't prune the transplanted shrub for two years—give it time to adjust. Gardeners need patience here.

Plan for Pruning Trees

Studies at the University of Florida have shown that for most species, a tree with a single trunk or leader is more wind resistant than a tree with multiple leaders. To provide a balanced crown, branches should sprout from all sides of, and be arranged six inches or more apart vertically along, the trunk. Exceptions include highly branched, shrubby or clumping trees that send up numerous shoots from the ground. For these, your best bet is to keep the healthiest, sturdiest shoots and to cut out the rest in order to avoid crossed trunks and overcrowding. Prune the excess trunks to the ground. Wax myrtle, sea grape, fringe tree, and crape myrtle are examples of trees with multiple trunks. They are useful in the landscape for screening and habitat.

As noted in the earlier discussion on evaluating trees for stormworthiness, many of the trees on your property may need pruning to reduce their chances of falling during a high windstorm. The thinning of a tree crown may take several years, because trimming more than 20 percent of a tree at one time can be too much of a shock for the tree to sustain. Your best and most sustainable management strategy is to develop a multiyear plan. Depending upon the type of tree, plan during the first year to remove or head back some of the **watersprouts** (thin vertical shoots growing from horizontal branches), multiple trunks or headers, crossing branches, branches with acute or narrow angles, and branches that could rub against buildings or walls. Again, don't cut all of these branches at one time, and be sure to work around the entire crown to keep it balanced. Over the next two or three years, continue to lighten and reshape the crown by cutting out these "problem" branches.

Most trees and shrubs develop a ring of growth tissue around the bases of their branches called "**branch collars**." Branch collars, which often look like swellings or wrinkles in the bark, grow around the scar when a branch is cut or lost. This way the cambium in the region is protected from invasion. When you make a pruning cut it's important to leave the branch collar in place so the tree will heal better.

When you have to remove a large branch, you need to reduce some of its weight so that the bark doesn't tear and peel away the branch collar. To reduce the branch weight, make three cuts. Make an initial cut on the un-

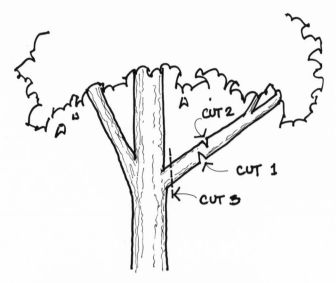

THREE CUTS FOR PRUNING LARGE BRANCHES

When pruning a large branch from a tree, it's best to remove the weight of the branch with cuts 1 and 2. Cut 3 removes the stub of the branch so it's almost, but not quite, flush with the trunk. Leave the branch collar intact to grow around the cut and seal it.

derside of the limb several inches away from the trunk. Then, not far from this first cut but on the top side, make a second cut down through most of the branch until it falls away. With the branch weight now reduced, make a third, more careful cut, just outside of the branch collar on the top side of the branch. After the cut is completed, the tree may weep, but no wound covering or dressing is recommended. Usually pruning should occur during the most dormant period for the tree. If you're pruning a flowering shrub or tree, it's often recommended that you prune it right after the flowering period, though.

If a new tree or sapling has two or more main trunks that branch off above the ground, choose the leader best situated to be the main trunk and prune the others back by a third. During the next growing season, your chosen main trunk will continue to grow, while the severely pruned header or headers will not grow as much. The next year you can cut the other leaders back to another crotch and wait another year or more to prune them back to the main trunk. Over several years, trim back small branches growing too low to the ground or too close to each other on the trunk. If too many branches sprout from one side of the tree, head some of them back—by thirds, as described for the secondary trunks. Continue this process, never cutting out more than 20 percent of the crown in a year, until the tree is in the recommended shape for its species. If a mature tree has a double trunk, it's probably too late to head back to one or two leaders. In this case, to save the tree, an arborist may recommend some type of cabling to strengthen the tree against its weak branching pattern.

In areas where lower branches could interfere with human or vehicular traffic, encourage the higher branches and prune back the lower branches. Don't completely cut off the lower branches on newly planted saplings, because they need as many leaves as possible to grow vigorously. Instead, prune lower branches back a little each year until the tree has gained enough height to survive well without them. This is called "**limbing up**," and it is a good strategy for creating a firewise landscape.

If a tree is leaning, even if it is mature, you'll probably need to balance the crown so the weight is more evenly distributed. If you need to reduce the size of the crown, not just thin it, you should prune some of the tallest or widest branches back to a crotch or a lateral branch facing in the direction you wish the branch to take: this is called "heading back" or drop-crotch pruning. The next year you'll continue the process and remove the rest of the watersprouts or tallest branches. This is not the same as topping, which is never recommended.

After several years, the crowns of your trees will be well shaped, balanced, and airy. From a distance they shouldn't look like they have been pruned. After this initial period of lightening the crown, you may need to retrim every four to five years to keep it in good shape. The frequency of trimming depends upon the species and previous maintenance practices. For large trees, you'd be wise to work with a certified arborist.

Palm trees don't have crowns and do not need drastic pruning. Never top a palm because it grows only from the top and removing its only growth node will kill it. Each year remove only the dead fronds, old flower stalks, and fruits, especially coconuts. These could become missiles in a

Pruning Fruit Trees

Fruit trees, such as pear and apple, tend to produce multiple watersprouts. If the trees aren't pruned on a regular basis, fruit production will be limited to only the ends of the branches or only the very topmost portion of the trees. Even a mature or well-established older fruit tree in the landscape may be pruned to a better shape so adequate light and air can penetrate throughout the crown. It will take several years to complete the process, and ongoing maintenance will be required after that. This will increase fruit set and improve fruit shape. Compared to a mature tree, it's easier to train a sapling because a sapling is still pliable and there are fewer branches and watersprouts to deal with. The watersprouts can be pruned back to the original branches. Depending upon the growth habit, you can brace the sapling's branches apart so the angle of growth is wide enough to create strong structure.

The extra effort to maintain fruit trees is worthwhile, because growing your own fruit is a sustainable activity. Most citrus trees, however, do not need much pruning when growing in a residential landscape.

high wind, and they put a stress on the trunk. Other annual pruning for palms in southern regions of the state might include removing strangler figs that may have sprouted on the palms, unless you'd rather have a fig than a palm. Don't prune back any green fronds, even if they droop. Because palms have so few leaves, they need them all to maintain vigor.

Pruning Shrubs

Pruning shrubs requires a different strategy. Quite often shrubs are pruned to keep them appropriately sized for their location. The typical shearing of shrubs into lollipop and gumdrop shapes is never sustainable, because the new growth that pokes out from the smooth artificial shapes has to be regularly trimmed. Choosing shrubs that will mature to the correct size is the best way to reduce pruning duties. Even then, shrubs may need occasional trimming, but instead of shearing them into artificial shapes, use drop-crotch pruning to head back individual branches.

For established, taller multicaned shrubs in the landscape or for shrubby trees with multiple trunks, trim the canes or trunks to different heights. This way you'll avoid ugly **hat-racking** hatchet jobs where all the trunks are sawed off at the same height.

Shrubs and some trees spread via new shoots sprouting from shallow roots. If new shoots begin to make the shrub too large for its location, pruning some of these shoots with your shovel is a fairly simple way to handle the situation. You may be able to transplant the new sprout to another location.

Woody Plants Warrant Extra Care—They Are the "Bones" of the Landscape

Trees and shrubs are the most permanent and prominent landscape plants. Their proper care is a long-term investment. Time spent planning for and choosing the most appropriate trees and shrubs for your landscape, and handling them carefully, will mean greater survival rates, fewer problems, and less work in the long run. Plus growing more trees and shrubs, with all their biomass, is good for the planet.

Resources

Web Sites

Use the International Society of Arboriculture's Web site to search for a certified arborist near you: http://www.isa-arbor.com.

The Web site for the Association of Florida Native Nurseries provides general information on native plants and has a locator for member nurseries near you: http://www.afnn.org.

University of Florida horticulture professor Ed Gilman maintains the Landscape Plants Web site, with detailed information on tree establishment, irrigation, pruning, and other care of woody plants: http://hort.ifas.ufl.edu/woody.

Books

Gilman, Edward F. *Illustrated Guide to Pruning.* 2nd ed. Albany, N.Y.: Delmar, 2002.

Gilman, Edward F., and Robert J. Black. *Your Florida Guide to Shrubs.* Gainesville: University Press of Florida, 1999.

Haehle, Robert G. *Native Florida Plants: Low Maintenance Landscaping and Gardening.* Rev. ed. Lanham, Md.: Taylor Trade, 2004.

Nelson, Gil, and David Chiappini. *Florida's Best Native Landscape Plants.* Gainesville: University Press of Florida, 2003.

Osorio, Rufina. *A Gardener's Guide to Florida's Native Plants.* Gainesville: University Press of Florida, 2001.

7

Container Gardening

Gardening in containers provides Florida gardeners with myriad plant and positioning choices. Containers provide a way to have plants in tight spots, in areas with troublesome soil, or even on pavement. You can feature your showiest plants in an entryway, on a porch, or on a balcony. When the flowering stops, move the containers to a more out-of-the-way location to make room for the next set of showy plants. When your garden beds serve only as a neutral background for your containers, they are easier to maintain. Hanging from porches, swinging from tree branches, gracing front stoops or courtyards, container gardens add charm and beauty to Florida's landscapes.

Containers for Planting

Gardeners may have set ideas about what a standard garden container is and how it should look—a pot, an urn, a window box. But there are many more possibilities. Appropriately sustainable containers are often recycled or repurposed objects, such as baskets past their prime, pieces of furniture, or interesting buckets. Some are more practical than others, but your container gardening projects can be seen as a recycling mission. (Be sure not to reuse containers that previously held petroleum products or poisons.) You can have fun choosing and artfully arranging your unique

Container Gardening Is Sustainable

Even though container gardens may require more frequent watering than in-the-ground gardens, they are sustainable for several reasons:

- Containers allow people to have gardens on impervious surfaces, such as driveways, parking lots, poolsides, and sturdy rooftops. Container gardens absorb rainfall and reduce the heat retention of these surfaces in proportion to the area covered.
- Container gardens provide folks who live in apartments, condos, RVs, or other places with no permanent access to the ground an opportunity to grow vegetables, herbs, and flowers. The more greenery we have, the better it is for our air quality.
- In areas where the soil is not suitable for growing certain crops, people can create soil mixtures for containers or raised bed systems that are tailor-made for specific plants.
- Small water features can be constructed in containers, such as half wine barrels, with or without pumps to circulate the water. Birds, frogs, and beneficial insects like butterflies and dragonflies are attracted to, and may require, water to complete their life cycles.

container gardens, but if you're short on time or more conservative, there are plenty of standard containers of various sizes and colors for sale in your local garden shop.

Containers need to be matched to the plants they are going to hold. Each container must be large enough to provide good stability for the plants as they grow and to hold enough soil to supply sufficient moisture and nutrients. Whether you purchase a standard flowerpot or decide to use an old porcelain sink, the plants should be the right size, shape, and texture to compliment the container. Drainage is necessary, so poke or drill holes in found containers or place a pot with drainage on a brick inside a closed container.

Container Types

Standard flowerpots and planters with built-in drainage come in a wide variety of sizes and shapes and materials. Mix and match colors and shapes for the best visual results in your container garden—there are so many to choose from. Here are some the pros and cons of various container types.

Clay or **Terra cotta**: The most traditional pot material, compared with which, as some people think, all other materials pale. Clay is heavy, which offers good stability for tall plantings, but it's also breakable and hard to move when full. Because clay is porous and retains heat, plants growing in them will require more irrigation. Clay containers come in many styles and sizes and age well.

Cast concrete: Less breakable than clay. Because cast concrete is lime based and will sweeten the soil, it's not a good choice for acid-loving plants. Otherwise it has many of the same advantages and problems as clay.

Glazed clay or ceramic: Offers the heft of clay and cement, but isn't as porous. Comes in many beautiful colors and patterns. Breakable.

Resin/fiberglass/plastic: Impervious, inexpensive, and lightweight. Comes in sizes and shapes reminiscent of clay. Does not retain heat or lose water like clay. Usually will last a long time, but may crack or split, and the colors may fade in the sun. Faded containers can later be used as liner pots or used to store soil or other ingredients in your work area.

Lumber (wood or fake wood): A good insulator that blends in with naturalized landscapes, lumber is popular for window boxes and patio planters. Untreated wood will rot over several years, but it will last much longer if you use liner pots so that the wood isn't in direct contact with the soil. Some wood, such as red cedar, will resist rot. Redwood and cypress also resist rot, but they've been so widely harvested that now there are serious questions about their sustainability. Don't use treated wood for edible plants. Fake wood—made from compressed wood and recycled plastics—is more durable. You can purchase manufactured containers or boxes or you can construct your own. Lumber is often used as the sides for raised beds, which can also be considered containers in a way.

Metal: Conducts heat, exposing roots to rapid temperature fluctuations. Some metals rust quickly in contact with soil. Use a liner pot for better results, especially if the container will be exposed to full sun. If planting edibles, make sure that the soil doesn't contact the metal—some metals can leach into damp soil.

Nonwoven cloth: Makes an excellent liner pot because plants won't become root bound and the soil is aerated. When roots reach the side of the pot, they sense the air and stop growing in that direction. Controlling root growth this way is called "air pruning." If you use this cloth as a liner in a nondraining container, set it on an inexpensive plastic catch tray with drainage holes and set that tray on some stones in the bottom of the container. If cloth pots sit directly on the ground, drainage trays may not be necessary.

Hanging or mounted planters: Can be solid and made from plastic, wood, or other material. They are sometimes fashioned from wire baskets lined with sphagnum moss or coconut fiber mats. While these are a popular choice for theme parks, porches, and street décor, they tend to dry out quickly. The beauty and ambiance they add, though, may be worth the extra care.

While all the pot choices have their pros and cons, you can usually compensate for the disadvantages. Before you can come up with a plan for which types of plants to use, you'll need to know the main purpose of the container and the exposure of its projected location to sun and wind.

Selecting Plants

So many available plants are adaptable to growing in pots, that it can be difficult to find a starting point. Choose plants that fit in with the resources available for ongoing care. If your realistic plan shows that the containers will receive water and other care only once a week, you'll need to choose succulents or other low-care, drought-tolerant species and plant them in large pots with good reserves of soil. If you're able to arrange for daily care or can install an automatic irrigation system, your choice of plant materials is vast.

If you'll be growing plants from seeds, start them six to eight weeks before you'd like to fill the container, or take the easy route and go to your local nursery to select seedlings for your container. Choose specimens with firm white roots just touching the sides of the starter pots for the best chance of success.

Some people approach container gardening like the Japanese art of flower arranging, governed by a three-level placement principle. (The tall plants represent the sky, the medium level plants represent mankind, and the lower level plants represent the earth.) In a container this translates into including a tall or spiky plant, a bushy plant of medium height, and a vining or trailing plant that will hang gracefully over the sides. Work with odd numbers of plants, and maybe add a nice rock or art object to enhance the arrangement. You can accomplish such three-level arrangements in one large, stand-alone container or by using several containers of different styles and a variety of plants.

When combining different types of plants in a container, do your homework to make sure they are compatible. They should require the same soil type and irrigation level and, if possible, choose plants so that their roots will occupy different levels within the pot. For instance, you could plant some bulbs below the roots of a shallow-rooted plant. If a plant is an aggressive spreader, a container is probably the best place to grow it, but it won't be easy to include other species—they'll be crowded out in no time. In such cases, multiple pots, each with a monoculture, can be arranged in a visually pleasing manner and will be easier to maintain.

If the container garden will be a more or less permanent fixture, say, for your front step, a kitchen garden, or for poolside screening, it is most sustainable to choose plants that thrive in containers and in the exposure where the container will be located. The soil mixture for permanent planters is normally a little heavy and should include compost or garden soil—microbes promote healthy root growth. Select a good heavy container that will stay upright in a thunderstorm, but have a way to move it in preparation for a hurricane. A liner pot inside the main container is easier to move before a big storm, because you can separate it from the heavy pot.

A one-season-only, short-term container planting can be treated more like a bouquet. Go ahead and place the plants too close together for maximum effect. This is not a sustainable planter, but if it's fun and dresses up the rest of your landscape, then break the rules. Plants will become stressed in this environment, so plan to water them heavily. Annuals are perfect for one-season containers—they are programmed to produce a big show in order to generate their seeds. If you use perennials, plan to transplant them into a better location at the end of the season.

Preparing Containers for Planting

Your pot choices and soil mix will depend upon the plants you choose and their exposure to sun and wind in the container's planned location. Whether it's a long-term container garden or a one-season pot, you need to plan for watering and care. Develop a realistic strategy that fits your time and resources and proceed accordingly.

Here in Florida it gets hot, especially on our front doorsteps where many potted plants live. Heat is retained in sidewalks, concrete steps, and even more in clay and cement planters. It's a wonder that any plant, unless it's a prickly pear cactus or yucca, can survive this environment. To help reduce heat stress in containerized plants and to meet their resultant need for more water, insulate plants and soil by putting them first in a liner pot. This way, there is a layer of air between the outside and inside pots to separate the soil from the heat. You can even stuff Spanish moss or packing peanuts in the space between the pots to increase the insulation.

This interior pot doesn't have to be pretty, but it should be lightweight enough that you can remove it, along with its plants and soil, without too much trouble. Fabric pots make the best liners: plants growing in confined spaces are less stressed when the soil is evenly aerated and when roots receive the benefit of air pruning.

If the exterior pot has drainage holes and if it's the right height, just set the liner pot on the bottom. If your exterior pot does not have drainage or if you need to raise the height of the liner pot for the best presentation

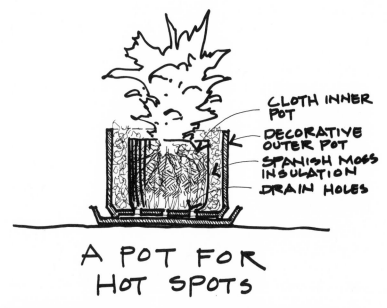

CLOTH INNER POT

DECORATIVE OUTER POT

SPANISH MOSS INSULATION

DRAIN HOLES

A POT FOR HOT SPOTS

Container gardens will stay much cooler with a liner pot inside the larger decorative container. Fill the air space with Spanish moss to add more insulation.

of the plants, then place enough gravel, packing peanuts, bricks, or other inert material in the bottom to raise the liner pot to the correct level. Then place the liner pot on top.

Whether you are using a new pot or reusing an old one, rinse or scrub out the pot to remove salts, disease-carrying organisms, or chemicals used in manufacturing. For a porous pot, such as clay, cement, or wood, thoroughly wet down the interior of the container. If it is a fabric pot, soak it in a bucket of rain barrel water.

Despite what we've been told all these years, covering the bottom of the planting container with inches of gravel is not recommended. University studies have shown that a layer of gravel or potshards actually impedes drainage, because water does not travel well from the fine substrate of the potting mix to the coarse gravel mixture. Plants are under enough stress in containers already; so don't add to it by reducing the depth of the soil in the pot with a gravel layer. Prevent soil from washing out of drainage holes by placing over them a piece of screen or nonwoven weed barrier cloth or even a few dried leaves. If you cut weed barrier cloth large enough to extend up the sides of the planting pot, you can sometimes discourage ants from using your containers as nests. Another alternative to keep soil from leaking out of the pot is a reusable fibrous mat of recycled plastic that sits in the bottom of the pot.

The soil mix for containers will vary depending upon whether you're planting a one-season pot or a long-term container garden. The usual advice is to use a soilless potting mix—for its lightness and because it contains no weeds or other organisms. The main disadvantage of this type of potting mix is that it is nutrient poor, so the plants are totally dependent on you to provide fertilizer. The light mix also dries out quickly. There are potting mixes that have chemical fertilizers and water retention granules built in to attempt to address these shortcomings, but studies have been unable to verify that the water retention balls make any difference at all.

A more sustainable solution is to use your own good compost made from many types of plant materials. It's full of beneficial microbes that promote good root health and has complete nutrients. Mix it with vermiculite and/or coconut coir to add absorbency. Vermiculite lightens the soil. Coconut coir adds more organic material or humus; use it instead of peat moss.

The ratio of these three items will depend upon the container and what you'll be planting in it. For a permanent container, create a heavier mix with more compost: that way, the plants will thrive for several years before they need to be repotted. For hanging baskets or temporary containers, keep it the soil light by adding more vermiculite to the mix.

On planting day, it's a good idea to prewater the plants in their nursery pots so they'll be easier to remove and so more soil will remain clumped around the roots. Water them first and let them drain while you work on the rest of the preparations.

Combine the soil mix and water it so that it's damp to the touch, but not soggy. Place the leaves, screen or weed barrier cloth in the bottom of the pot to cover the drainage holes. Fill the container or liner pot with soil mix up to the bottom of the root-ball of your largest plant. In order to minimize the rearranging and handling of your plants after they've been removed from their pots, arrange them in the container while they are still in their nursery pots. When you are satisfied with their locations, carefully remove each plant from its pot and fill around its root-ball with your soil mix.

Once a container is planted, water it all to rinse the soil from the leaves, to settle the soil between the plants, and to eliminate any big air spaces. Press down the wet soil gently, adding more as needed to smooth out the surface—don't pack the soil too tightly, because the roots need small air spaces in the soil. Depending on the type of planter or container, you may want to add a fine-textured mulch, such as coconut coir on the top. For even better protection from weeds and water loss, cut a piece of weed barrier cloth in the same shape and size as the top of your container, cut openings or slices into it that you can slide down over your plants, and then cover it with at least an inch of fine mulch.

To create a hanging or mounted pot in a wire basket with a coconut fiber mat or sphagnum moss liner, proceed as above in handling your plants and create a fairly heavy soil mixture—the aeration is so extreme in this type of planter that your plants will appreciate the extra moisture retention. You could install all your plants at the top of the planter and then wait for those to grow into a graceful, trailing arrangement. For quicker results, insert some plants in the sides as well. Place just a little soil in the bottom of the planter, split the coconut mat or sphagnum liner in three or five places. Slip the side plants, roots first, into those side splits. Fill in the rest of the soil up to the bottom of your top plants' root-balls and proceed as described above. This will not be a long-term planter but it will fill in quickly and will provide quite a show for a season.

Strawberry planters, with their pocket-like side openings, enable you to grow several different plants in one container. Insert the root mass of each plant into one of the openings from the outside of the pot. A big problem with this type of planter is that water doesn't always reach the plants in the lowest openings. By installing a watering tube before you plant the container, you can bypass the annoyance of trying to water directly into the tiny bottom pockets and of having to remove shriveled plants. Before you add soil to the pot, cut a piece of PVC or bamboo "pipe" slightly longer than the height of the planter. Drill holes every few inches in the sides of the pipe and seal the end. Place the pipe, sealed end down, into the middle of the planter so that the open end protrudes just above soil level. Then fill around it with soil. Put a screen over the pipe opening and hold it in

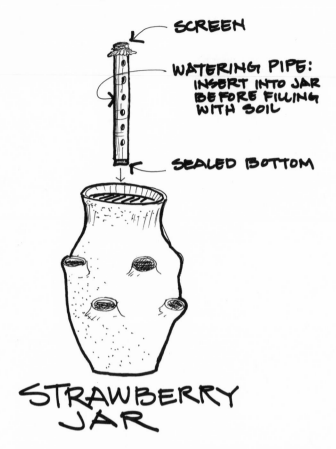

SCREEN

WATERING PIPE:
INSERT INTO JAR
BEFORE FILLING
WITH SOIL

SEALED BOTTOM

STRAWBERRY JAR

Use a watering pipe with a sealed bottom and a screened top for strawberry jars and other tall, multi-opening containers. This allows more water to reach the lower plants easily.

place with a cord or a rubber band. When you water the container, pour water through the screen so the water fills up the tube and makes it to the bottom. The water will seep through the drill holes and water your upper, middle, and lower plants evenly. There may be other containers that require even watering down to the bottom where a watering tube like this would also work.

No matter what type of container you've planted, you may want to set it in an out-of-the-way spot for a day or two while the plants adjust to their new orientation and where you can keep an eye on them. Some of the stems or branches may have been broken during the planting and will need to be trimmed. If one of the plants wilts while the others remain perky, it needs to be replaced. Plants will arrange themselves so that as many leaves as possible can absorb light for photosynthesis—when they do this, your planter is ready to set or hang in its permanent position.

Container Garden Care

Coming up with a watering routine is the biggest challenge in container garden care. Watch for wilting, and check the soil before and after you water to make sure that the water is soaking into the soil and not running straight through a gap somewhere: this can happen if the soil dries out, and a deep soaking will be needed to fix it. The faster a plant grows, the more water it needs. You may need to water most plants daily during hot or windy spells, but during the cooler months or rainy season, their need for water will be much reduced. One of the principal criteria for sustainability is consideration of all available resources—not just water and fertilizer, for instance, but your time and energy, as well. While hand watering is the most frequently used watering method for container plantings, it can become a chore if you have lots of pots. An automatic drip system will remove some of this maintenance time, but you'll still need to keep an eye on how your container plants are doing.

While the soil mix includes compost with its microbes and nutrients, your plants will deplete the soil in an enclosed environment, so add some compost to the soil's surface, or if you think it's needed, fertilize occasionally with organic fertilizer, such as a fish emulsion or compost extract. Don't stimulate new growth with fertilizer if the plants are entering a dormant period or a period with limited watering, though.

Trimming and pruning plants can increase their blooming, keep the arrangement well balanced, and reduce the amount of water and nutrient uptake. For a one-season pot, trimming will consist largely of deadheading and pinching back stragglers—this will cause new growth and will lengthen a plant's "season." In a permanent container, when you prune woody plants, be careful of their overall shape, because they are on prominent display. Herbaceous plants usually need to be trimmed back in the manner of one-season container plants—to stimulate new growth and to keep them from getting too leggy.

During the dry season, flush your permanent pots with an extra deep watering every six weeks or so. This rinses out the salts that build up from fertilizers, soil residue, and maybe salt spray. It's good if you can coordinate with Mother Nature by flushing your pots just before or just after a good hard rain. Right before a rain, set up your plants in an open area without their saucers, water them thoroughly with rain barrel water, and then check the soil for depth of moisture. Sometimes even what seems to be a thorough watering doesn't wet all the soil. Water again after a few minutes and then let the rain soak the soil again.

After two or three years growing in a container, most plants will appreciate new soil and maybe a larger pot. The day before repotting, water deeply. If you used a cloth liner pot, the plants won't be root bound, but they're likely to fill the whole space, so it might be easiest to cut the pot away. If you used a hard pot, the roots will probably be growing against the inner wall of the container. Carefully knock the plants from the pot. Don't manhandle the plants by the stems or trunks; support them by their root-balls.

Judge your container's ecosystem as if you were purchasing new plants. If the roots are white and turgid, your plants are still in good health. If your container soil is healthy, it should smell sweet or earthy, not sour. If the soil is sour, you've probably been over watering, which creates an anaerobic condition. If the roots are circling inside the pot or if they are tan or mushy, then you've waited too long to repot and there may be a soil-born disease in your container. It's not a good idea to repot mushy-rooted plants; they are not likely to survive. To attempt to save them, cut away all the mushy roots, thoroughly rinse the remaining roots, and use all new soil in the new or well-scrubbed pot.

Before you replant your healthy plants, knock away most of the loose soil from the roots and spread them out. If you plan to reuse the same pot, scrub it inside and out. Also unless you are going to move your plants to a larger pot, take a clue from the bonsai gardeners and trim back the roots (maybe one fifth of the volume) before replanting. If you trim the roots, don't prune the top for two or three months—the plant will need all the leaves it has to recover from transplant shock. Record the dates of planting and repotting in your garden log, so you'll have a better idea of when to repot next time.

Container Water Gardens

A container water garden is an excellent addition to your butterfly garden, enhances wildlife habitat creation, and can be one of your integrated pest management strategies. Having a water feature in a container allows you to bring water closer to your outdoor living spaces for greater enjoyment.

Your choices for water garden containers include, but aren't limited to, half barrels, metal or plastic tubs, bathtubs, and preformed pools. It's probably best that the container be more than a foot deep and more than two feet wide. You'll want enough water volume to support the plants and animals and to keep it from heating up too fast. The container should be watertight, of course, but if a barrel leaks you can seal the leaks with plumber's putty or line it with heavy-gauge plastic.

There are several considerations involved in locating a water barrel. Many water plants require full sun, but here in Florida, where the sun is so intense, you would be wise to locate your water garden where it gets some afternoon shade from a building, pergola, or fence. Avoid areas under tree branches, because leaves and sticks will increase maintenance labor and can clog your filter and pump equipment. To keep the water aerated and to enhance its appearance and usefulness for wildlife, you'll probably want to add a pump and filter system, so locate the water feature near an exterior electrical outlet. If you decide to use a solar pump (a more sustainable choice), make sure there is good sun exposure for the solar panel. It's also good to locate your water feature near a water supply—a rain barrel is perfect. If you use city water, you'll need to let it sit for two days so the chlorine can dissipate. Don't use water from a water softener system.

Once the location is decided, elevate the container an inch or two above the surface of the ground with some bricks or timbers. This keeps the water cooler, reduces rot (if it's a wooden barrel), and makes finding a leak easier. Fill the container half full with rain barrel water and let it sit while you install the pump and filter system. For container gardens, an aquarium pump offers a low cost, easy-to-use system. You may decide to include a fountain device to produce the trickling sounds birds are drawn to and to assist in aeration. There are many choices. Whichever pump or fountain you use, don't run it all the time because too much water will

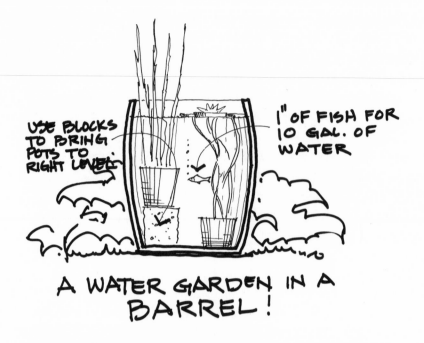

USE BLOCKS TO BRING POTS TO RIGHT LEVEL

1" OF FISH FOR 10 GAL. OF WATER

A WATER GARDEN IN A BARREL!

Containerized water gardens bring water features into small garden spaces or patios. A water garden is easy to care for once it reaches a balance, and it's important for habitat. (A 50-gallon container could have one five-inch fish or five one-inch fishes.)

evaporate. Run it when you are there to enjoy it or at certain times each day. A timer might be helpful.

Next, choose your plants. Each plant will stay in its own pot, so use dark green or black pots—they will be less obvious below the water surface. You can use plastic pots, nonwoven cloth pots, or special wire mesh pots. Fill your pots with a mixture of garden soil and compost. Don't use perlite, vermiculite, or fertilizer crystals, because they often float out of the pot. You can also use special potting mix specifically formulated for underwater use. After you set the plants in the pots, cover the top of the soil with clean gravel or sand to keep the soil from floating into the water. For even more security, you can use circles of weed barrier cloth covered by gravel or coarse sand. Use bricks or upside-down pots under pots to bring the plants to their proper levels beneath the water's surface.

Don't overplant—only a third of the water surface should be covered. Vary plant material to create contrasting textures and habits—couple spiky iris with floating water lilies, for example. Submerged plants, also called "oxygenators," absorb excess nutrients, slow algae growth, and replenish the oxygen supply. Don't use water hyacinths, hydrilla, or other invasive waterweeds.

A water garden is a miniature ecosystem: the plants, water, and fish must interact together to survive, but there will be a period of adjustment. When you first start, your water garden may develop an algal bloom that turns the water green. If this happens, use just enough chlorinated water from the tap to replace the evaporated water. This helps to control algae until the garden is balanced, usually two months or so. Don't use any extra bleach, it's too corrosive and could ruin your pump.

After stocking the tub with plants, wait a month or two while the plants adjust to the environment before adding fish and snails. Since the tub is outside, frogs, snails, dragonflies, and other creatures will probably make themselves at home during this waiting time, anyway. So will the mosquitoes, so initially you might want to use a special mosquito donut containing Bt-i, a specialized strain of **Bt** (*Bacillus thuringiensis*). These donuts are usually available at stores that carry organic gardening supplies. Don't poison mosquitoes with general insecticides. Wait for a balance in your container and then add fish that will feed on them. After that, Bt donuts won't be necessary or desirable.

Many nurseries sell pond supplies and can recommend the fish and snails that will work well in your region of the state. Snails eat algae and **detritus**. Fish eat foliage, algae, mosquito larvae, and other insects. A good rule of thumb is to use one inch of fish length for every ten gallons of water. For example, a 50-gallon container could have five one-inch fishes or one lonely five-inch fish.

The ongoing maintenance of a containerized water garden will include thinning excess plant materials, especially the floating plants. You'll also need to clean out the filter and follow the recommended conditioning of your pump. While this sounds like a lot of work, you may find that your water-filled container requires less work than those filled with soil.

Gardening in Small Spaces

If you've downsized your living arrangements, you may be discouraged about your gardening prospects; but there are many ways to arrange attractive garden spaces in tight quarters. Even if you have only a balcony or small courtyard, you can fit container gardens into your lifestyle.

Containers will give you flexibility in a courtyard, but they are a necessity for a balcony garden. If you're working on a balcony, you might want to reduce the weight of your garden by using packing peanuts in the bottoms of the larger pots. Make sure your pots and their soil are heavier than the plants inside them. You don't want your containers to be top heavy and blow over every time there's a thunderstorm or a gust of wind.

Lattice can provide a substrate for a wall garden, but make sure that it's mounted several inches away from the wall to reduce the chance for mold to grow behind the plants. In Florida we are fortunate to have a good variety of air plants or epiphytes (orchids and bromeliads, for example) that thrive here. You can strap them to the lattice in an attractive manner, and for the most part they will absorb their nutrients and water from the air. If your lattice is under a roof, you'll probably need to supply your plants extra water by misting them. You can also use one-sided hanging baskets on your lattice, but these will need more regular attention than epiphytes.

An out-of-sight potting area where you can store your potting soil components, your gardening tools, and maintain your compost piles is probably not possible when you're gardening in a confined area. You might have room for one of the small, closed composting barrels, though, where you can deposit your kitchen scraps and plant trimmings to produce some nice homemade compost. Even in a space as tight as a balcony, you can take care of seating and storage at the same time by using one or more storage benches. Stackable storage cubes are another good option for small spaces. By stacking your tool bin on top of a closed soil bin, for instance, you can create a small work area where no one will notice your gardening paraphernalia.

Container Gardens Add Flexibility to Sustainable Landscapes

Container gardens can set the tone for your landscape—they can be formal or informal. Container gardens can define outdoor areas, absorb rainfall on otherwise impervious surfaces, allow gardening in small areas, and provide changeable accents each season. Use your imagination and you may find that containers can solve some of your biggest gardening challenges. You may never go back to 100 percent in-the-ground gardens again.

Resources

Web Sites

Smart Pots is a source for fabric pots: http://www.smartpots.com.

Planet Natural is a source for coconut coir and other supplies: http://www.planetnatural.com.

Dr. Linda Chalker-Scott's Web site has more information about gravel in pots, moisture pellets, and other gardening myths: http://www.informedgardener.com.

Books

Chalker-Scott, Linda. *The Informed Gardener*. Seattle: University of Washington Press, 2008.

Greer, Jennifer. *Container Gardening (Southern Living Gardening Guide)*. Birmingham, Ala.: Oxmoor House, 1999.

The Edible Garden

The edible garden can take many forms. Replacing acres of nonsustainable lawn with community vegetable gardens is a great way to make better use of our public and private landscapes. A grouping of fruit trees can make almost any lot productive. Even a small cottage garden, planted with a few herbs and vegetables, does wonders for how you feel about your land. Some tomatoes in pots on your patio or deck can offer a wonderful addition to your salads for many months. We are fortunate to live in Florida, because we can plan our edible gardens for year-round production.

When we buy produce in a grocery store, we usually have no idea where those fruits and vegetables come from, how far they've traveled, or what pesticides may have been applied to them. Local farmers markets provide a better alternative to grocery store produce, but many people grow their own edibles because they want more control over what they eat. It just makes sense that fruits and vegetables are better for you if they are fresh from your own garden: you know that no poisonous residues will end up on your table. While organic gardening is not synonymous with sustainable gardening, both gardening schemes minimize the use of poisons.

The path you choose to take in your edible gardening is subject to your own agenda, schedule, and the microclimates of your landscape. Mother Nature may have her own ideas for your garden, so you'll have to find out what grows well on your property and which crops work best for your family.

Edible Gardening in Florida

Because of our warm climate, with little or no freezing weather, we must give special consideration to our edible gardens in Florida. Even where there are frosts, the soil doesn't freeze into the root zone, so pests can linger in the garden over the winter just waiting for the next crop to attack. Some crops don't do well during our long hot summers and, oh, those explosive weed populations!

Before you start, determine the purpose of your garden, making sure to decide who will do the initial and ongoing maintenance. The definition of sustainability has to include human resources, too. Unlike natural or native landscapes, a productive edible garden requires ongoing care to be successful. There's no point in letting your crops and good intentions die on the vine. It's probably smart to start small and expand with each season as you learn what works for you and what doesn't.

Eating from Your Garden Is Sustainable

Finding locally grown produce to put on your table has been promoted as a way to live a greener lifestyle. Growing your own food is even better.

Eating from the garden saves money and makes better use of your land. When you control how produce is handled from seed (or seedling) to the table, then you know it's good for you. Because grocery store produce frequently ships from great distances, food freshness and quality are reduced, the burning of fossil fuels is involved, and the shipping costs are passed on to you.

Determine the initial space on your property that is available and appropriate for edibles. Stay out from under large trees in your landscape for the following reasons.

- Most tree roots are aggressive and will outcompete your crops for water and nutrients.
- Trees may be damaged if you disturb their root systems with filling or digging.
- Most vegetables, herbs, and fruit do best with six hours of sun or more, and that's unlikely to exist inside a drip line. Monitor the sun in various parts of your landscape during each season of the year. The shadows will be longer in winter, but then again, the cooler weather crops may not need quite as much sun as the warm weather edibles. Most trees in your landscape will grow, so consider their adult sizes (including their root systems) as you locate your garden plots.

Keep an open mind—don't limit your plot search to the backyard or some hidden-away area. Many crops are attractive enough to appear in the front yard or in a container garden. For a small landscape, think

TOMATO TEEPEE

Vegetables do not have to be hidden away in backyards. Many crops make beautiful edging and may be incorporated into front yard cottage gardens or used as temporary playhouses for the kids. Have fun!

about planting pole beans along a fence among passion vines in your butterfly habitat. In cooler months, leaf lettuce is decorative enough for the front garden, or it can provide a frilly fringe for a container garden. Plant squash as a rambunctious groundcover for its coarse texture and clear yellow blossoms. Grow tomatoes and squash on a passive compost pile. Create a shaded summer shelter for the kids with indeterminate (vining) tomatoes and pole beans growing over a tall cone of poles set up like a tee pee. Use your imagination as you scan your property for places to grow edibles.

Preparing the Soil

After you figure out where you're going to put your different vegetables and herbs, work on the soil. In much of Florida, the sandy soil will need a good amount of compost or other organic amendments to help it retain water and nutrients. In the northern panhandle and other areas where there is more clay with poor drainage, these same organic amendments will lighten the soil structure and help your plants maintain healthy roots. In the Keys, you'll probably need raised beds for most of your crops, because the limestone substrate is not conducive to growing most edibles. In fact, raised beds can be a good choice in any part of the state.

Identify a good source of compost. While a sustainable gardener will have a personal compost pile, it may not yield enough material needed to start a good-sized vegetable plot. Especially in rural Florida, but in other parts of the state as well, you can find nearby horse farms, dairy farms, and cattle ranches where for a small fee (and sometimes for free), both fresh and composted manure are available for pickup or delivery. If your garden is near a mushroom farm, mushroom compost makes a great amendment for garden soils, although it may be a little alkaline. Many counties in Florida offer free compost made from collected yard waste as part of their waste management programs. While this material doesn't offer as much nutrient content as manure or mushroom compost, it will certainly improve the water retention and tilth of your soil. Building up your soil may take several years, but don't hesitate to plant your first edible crop just because your soil isn't perfect yet. The sweat equity invested in preparing your plot will pay you back even in the first year.

Here's one way to prepare the soil for a moderately sized vegetable bed in an area with poor soil—maybe ten feet long by four feet wide. The first year, about two months before it's time to plant, mark out planting areas no more than four feet wide with pathways between them—remember to plan for wheelbarrow or garden cart access. Going one shovel blade deep, dig out all of the soil—grass, weeds, and all—from the planting areas in your plot (but not the pathways) and set it aside. Line the bottoms of these planting troughs with a three-inch layer of crushed or shredded dead leaves and compost. Dig this material into the bottom soil using a garden fork. This procedure, sometimes called "double digging," improves drainage and moisture retention.

Add three-inch layers each of composted manure or mushroom soil, the original soil, and finally compost; then repeat the process. The plots will soon be several inches higher than the original soil. Stab a garden fork into the mixture every six inches or so to settle the soil and to make sure there are air passages between the layers. Cover the planting areas with leaves, straw, or other persistent mulch, and water deeply. Let this sit for two months and add more water if there's little or no rain. This is basically an inground composting project on a large scale. When it's time to plant your crops, turn the soil in your planting plots with your garden fork. The soil should have settled some, and you should have attracted earthworms over those two months. Don't walk on the areas to be planted.

The next year, the double digging won't be necessary, but add more compost and composted manure after you harvest each crop to keep the soil in good shape. Skip the composted manure in areas where you plant beans, peas, or other legumes. The bacteria in their root nodules fix nitrogen from the air, so the extra nutrients from manure aren't needed and could actually reduce flowering and fruit production. Also skip the manure in your herb garden. Complete soil treatments won't be easy to accomplish once you start planting: that's because for best production, you'll be interplanting crops, so there will always be something growing. Your composting opportunities will be limited to harvest time and to the areas between hills and rows. As discussed in chapter 3, between rows is the ideal location for trench composting.

Raised Beds

Raised beds work well for edible gardens in any part of the state, but they are particularly important where drainage is poor or where the soil is unsuited for growing crops. You can even set up raised beds on impervious surfaces such as decks, patios, driveways, parking lots, or flat rooftops (if they are sturdy enough). Six-inch-deep tray gardens for shallow-rooted crops can also be constructed on carts, saw horses, or tables for waist-high gardening.

For raised beds, depending upon their height, the digging out of so much soil may not be necessary, but follow the soil-building procedures described above nevertheless. If you don't have enough soil or if your soil is troublesome (too alkaline or too clayey), substitute purchased topsoil or potting soil for the original soil layers. Add enough layers so that the soil is within three inches or so of the top of the bed's walls.

In comparison with inground garden plots, after the initial work of constructing your raised beds' frames or walls, you'll have easier access for gardening chores, better control of the soil mixture, good drainage, fewer problems with in-the-ground critters, like grubs and cutworms, and maybe fewer weeds. Raised bed systems reduce the area you have to care for in proportion to your crops. A big advantage of a raised bed system is that the plants grow better in the loose, uncompacted soil—you don't walk in a raised bed. In other words, you'll harvest more with less work.

Traditional, in-the-ground gardens were once set up with rows sized wide enough to fit between the rumps of two mules with a plow between them. Farm tractors and their tillers are similarly sized, but using a raised bed system allows you to escape this long-standing tradition and forego the need for heavy tilling equipment. You may decide not to have long rows in your beds at all, but to plant your crops in groups instead. Wide spaces between garden rows increase your maintenance and use more resources, because you are tending (watering and weeding) not only the growing areas but also the unplanted areas.

Because raised beds are similar to containers, it might seem logical that they would require more irrigation than an inground bed, but this may not be the case. If you manage the soil mix well and use mulch, you're only watering the crops and not the large spaces between them. Also, there are no roots from nearby trees or shrubs to compete with your plants for water. Tray tables with only six inches of soil will probably require more frequent watering than either a raised bed or an inground garden, though; there's not enough volume to retain water or to buffer heat.

Set up your raised beds in the sunniest location in your landscape, where they won't sit within the drip line of any trees. Organize and size your beds so that you will have good access to all the planting areas without having to step into them—about four feet wide or so. The working areas between raised beds, as between inground beds, should be wide enough to accommodate wheelbarrows or garden carts. If your raised beds are built on top of lawn areas, get rid of the grass between the beds, too. It will be too hard to mow, and it probably won't grow well with all the trampling it will receive. Strip off the sod and use it as a lower layer in your raised beds or to fill in bare spots in your lawn, then line your path with a thick layer of woodchips or other mulch on top of heavy-duty weed barrier cloth. You might also want to use stepping-stones or pavers for a more solid footing, especially if people tending the garden will be in wheelchairs.

Measure out the area of your beds and figure out a plan for irrigation and drainage. Raised beds should be more or less level for the best distribution of water. The preferred irrigation for raised beds is a drip or microspray system where water is directed only to the root zones and avoids wetting the foliage. There are several good reasons for this: first, you'll use less water; second, dry foliage means reduced risk of fungi and mold on your crops; and third, fewer weeds will grow in the walkways when they don't receive extra irrigation.

You could set up a manual irrigation system: once or twice a week you fill a bucket, tub, or other container mounted on a stand or wagon that is higher than the bed and then connect it to a drip system or perforated hose. An automated irrigation system is hooked up to a water source with reliable pressure and a timer of some sort.

The drainage from the bottom of the beds, especially in a poor drainage area, could be directed into a rain garden area for better absorption. You could design an open **swale** leading to the rain garden, but a **French drain** or culvert will be called for if the drainage area crosses work areas and paths. Culverts are also useful for protecting your irrigation system's hoses or pipes. Tripping over or walking on your equipment isn't good for you or the equipment.

If possible, run the long sides of the beds in an east-west orientation, and plant the taller crops on the north side. This way, all the plants in the beds have good exposure to the sunlight. Start with one or two beds to see how they work in your own real-life setting and adjust future beds to further accommodate your situation. Experience is a great teacher. Start small like this, maybe even growing some of your crops in pots for a season or two, until you know better what to expect.

The height of the raised beds above the surrounding land can range from only six inches to two feet or more. If the bed is six to ten inches high, you'll probably need to work the soil as described above for a regular, inground garden plot, especially if there are deep-rooted or persistent

Accessibility for Raised Beds

For gardeners who use wheelchairs, scooters, or walkers, raised beds should be elevated 24 to 27 inches off the ground and be no more than three feet wide. Leave ample maneuvering room between beds—five feet is a good distance. The pathways around and between beds need to be solid enough for good traction. Mulched or gravel pathways are not recommended for this situation—use pavers or bricks.

It's probably a good idea to install some kind of seating at the edges of the beds so that folks using walkers can sit comfortably while they tend the garden. If the sides are made from lumber (either wood or fake wood), you can use 2×6s laid flat on top of the walls. If you're using cinderblocks, bricks, or some other stone-like material, make sure the tops are flat and that they won't catch or snag fabric when people sit on the walls. For more comfort, it might be best to install wooden seating along the tops of block walls.

Waist-high gardens-in-a-tray are great for accessibility, especially if they are set up on rolling carts. The gardens can be rolled into sunny areas for most of the day and then moved to shaded areas where people can comfortably tend them—maybe in the cooler mornings or evenings.

weeds, such as torpedo grass, wild blackberries, or catbriar, growing in that area. The ideal height of the bed and depth of the workable soil will depend upon the underlying surface, whether you'll need easy access, and the crops you will be planting. Leaf lettuce, radishes, and many herbs require soil depths of only six inches, but tomatoes, squash, and larger or perennial crops do best with more depth. Potatoes and other root crops may need even more soil. Choose crops that have the best likelihood of succeeding in your beds and those that will be the most popular with your family.

Keep in mind that the higher you make the walls, the more soil or other materials will be needed for fill and the more pressure there will be on the walls. Beds with higher walls will need sturdier construction and more drainage holes at the bottom along the sides. You may wish to lighten the load of higher walls by filling the bottoms of the beds with a lightweight and inert material such as chopped Styrofoam packing materials that would otherwise go to a landfill. Don't overfill with these materials, though; you want to ensure that your crops have enough soil in which to grow well. A greater mass of soil also does a better job of holding moisture and maintaining even temperatures.

Materials and Design Choices

A common material for the sides of raised beds is lumber: it's readily available, comes in a variety of sizes, is easy to work with, and looks good in the landscape. Don't use pressure-treated lumber, which may contain poisons, or creosoted railroad ties where you grow your edibles. Plan on replacing the lumber every few years if you use standard pine lumber. The old lumber sides can then be used for a few more years in your compost area before they finally rot completely and become compost themselves. A more durable wood, such as red cedar, will last longer. Cypress and redwood are also durable woods, but because demand for them is so high there is strong concern that these trees aren't being harvested in a sustainable manner.

Fake wood lumber, made from recycled plastic products or a combination of recycled plastic and sawdust, may cost a little more initially, but overall has the look of wood (sort of) and comes in the same sizes and

WOOD FRAME BED

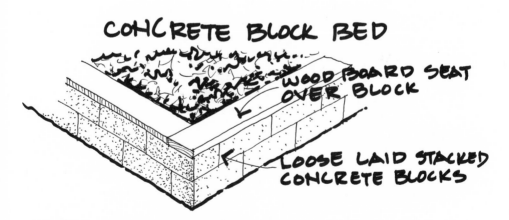

ATTACH BOARDS
TO STAKE

SET STAKE
IN GROUND AT
CORNERS OF BED

Raised beds may be built with lumber (either wood or fake wood). Drive corner
stakes into the ground to secure the corners.

CONCRETE BLOCK BED

WOOD BOARD SEAT
OVER BLOCK

LOOSE LAID STACKED
CONCRETE BLOCKS

Raised beds may be constructed with concrete blocks or bricks. Top off the blocks
with boards to make a more pleasant seating area while you tend the garden.

shapes. It is probably the most sustainable choice because it's made from recycled materials, won't warp, and will last for many years.

Using either wood or fake wood, you will enhance the stability of your frames if you use 2×2s or some kind of square post for the inside corners. The greatest stability can be had by sinking the posts into the ground before attaching framing to them, but you can also build your frames to sit right on top of the ground or other surface. Screw the side boards to the posts, overlapping them at the corners. (You could also use nails, but screws hold better and can be reused as you periodically replace the lumber or reconfigure the beds.) Metal corner brackets or hinges will take up less room in your bed and last longer than wooden posts. Make sure that any metal parts you use are galvanized. Some are designed specifically for constructing boxes out of lumber.

You can also use cement blocks or bricks to construct your raised beds. For low-walled beds, the blocks can be stacked loosely, but you may find that you need metal or wooden stakes to hold the blocks in place once you

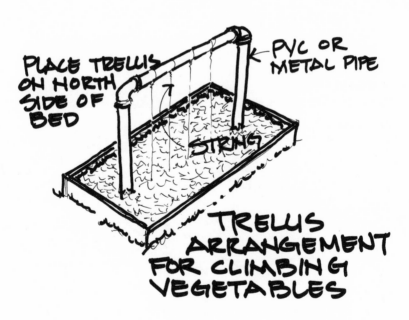

Construct a trellis with pipe and string on the north side of a vegetable bed for vines. Make sure it's sturdy and tall enough for your vining crops.

start working in the beds. Bricks and blocks offer good flexibility, because you can easily reconfigure the sizes and shapes of your beds as your needs change. If you are designing a higher-walled bed (more than 20 inches), the blocks may need to be mortared in place. Keep in mind that if you use cement and mortar, the soil near the walls will be more alkaline; so plant your acid-craving crops, such as tomatoes, away from the walls. If you use mortared or more permanent walls, plan for your irrigation and drainage before you start installing the walls.

For tall or vining crops, such as tomatoes, squash, cucumbers, or pole beans, plan for a sturdy support system before you plant. In a raised bed, cages might take up too much room, so plan for a flat trellis system on the northern side of the bed. This way, the wall of vines won't shade the other crops. You can purchase a trellis or construct it from lattice or pipe and string. Either way, build it five to six feet tall, make sure it is sturdy enough to support the weight of your crops, and place it to give them plenty of room to grow.

If there are pocket gophers, voles, or other burrowing animals that would like to dine on your vegetables, line the bottom of your bed with hardware cloth. Half-inch gauge is a good size to use. If rabbits or other above-ground critters acquire a taste for your greens, place removable fencing around the perimeter of each bed. To keep out squirrels, raccoons, and birds, cover the top of the garden with more hardware cloth or with fine netting.

There are many garden supply stores, both local and online, where you can find complete raised-bed systems or kits, including precut lumber (real wood or fake) that snaps together to form frames for beds of various sizes and shapes. Using a kit will certainly make the job of creating raised beds easier.

Tray Gardens

Tray gardens can be placed on almost any kind of stand, such as saw horses, an old table, or a rolling cart. Because they accommodate shallow-rooted crops, such as lettuce and spinach, your trays only need to be about six inches deep. Construct the tray sides with 2×6 or 2×8 lumber (wood or fake wood) with good corner bracing. Three feet by three feet is probably the largest tray you want to construct if you are going to be hand carrying it on a regular basis, but otherwise it can be sized to fit on top of whatever support system you decide to use. To reduce weight, create the tray bottom with half-inch-gauge hardware cloth secured to the inside or the sides with heavy staples or nails. Run two or three 2×4s parallel across the bottom and screw them into the side boards. Space the bottom boards to fit onto your cart, saw horses, or other support structure. Line the bottom and sides with heavy-duty weed barrier cloth to contain the soil and to allow water to drain.

The soil mixture for your tray gardens needs to be lighter and more absorbent than other soils. Your mix could include two parts compost, one part vermiculite, and one part coconut coir. When you handle the vermiculite, wet it down as soon as practical to reduce its fine dust. You may decide to wet the soil mixture before you place it in the tray to make sure that the moisture is evenly distributed—both vermiculite and coconut coir are highly absorbent and take in a surprising amount of water.

Just-In-Time Gardening

Designing the layout of your vegetables and crop rotation in a raised bed is the fun part. Square-foot gardening, as promoted by Mel Bartholomew starting in the early 1980s, provides sustainable ideas like planting only what you're going to use and planting only a few seeds at a time instead of sowing them thickly and thinning later. Think about how unsustainable we've all been when we've planted a whole package of seeds resulting in too many sprouts growing too close together. If you didn't get around to thinning the rows, chances were good that none of the crop was satisfactory because of too much competition for resources. If you did thin, you may have thrown away more than three quarters of your seedlings.

With the square-foot method, allocate the appropriate spacing (usually indicated on the back of the seed package) within the one-foot square for each type of plant and plant only one or two seeds in each planting hole. If they both sprout, cut one off. This way, the distance recommended for plants within the row is the distance from the center of one plant to the center of the next. For example, the recommended spacing for lettuce is four inches. Create a pattern of planting holes within the foot-square space where every hole is separated from every other hole by four inches, and sow two or three seeds in each hole. The close spacing tends to create a nearly solid leaf canopy, which decreases water loss and keeps weed problems down. You'll be amazed by how much more you can grow in a confined space where there are no wide spaces between rows. Seal the leftover seeds in a plastic box in the refrigerator for use next season—the germination rate will drop somewhat, so sow a few more seeds per hole the next time.

The next planning item is the timing of your planting. If you sow all of your lettuce, bean, or radish seeds at one time, guess what? They'll all mature within a short time period and maybe produce more than you can consume. Plant only the amount that you will use at one time. Then, depending upon the crop and room in your garden, several weeks later plant more seeds for an ongoing harvest. Of course, you'll need to pay attention to the proper planting times here in Florida. Even though we can grow vegetables all year long, cool weather crops will not do well in our summer heat, so don't plant winter crops, such as cabbage and collards, at the start of the hottest time of year. Restart your rotation again at the end of summer for fall and winter harvests. Starting seeds in pots is an important aspect of intensive gardening for many small-seeded crops that take well to transplanting. To get the most from the garden plot, a new crop should be ready to take the place of the crop being removed. You can be several weeks closer to harvest by having six-inch transplants ready to go into their allotted areas.

If you plan to use perennials in your beds, set them off to one side or put them in their own location, so they are not disturbed by all the jostling of tending the annual crops. Herb gardens often include easy-to-care-for perennials, but you should know how aggressive they are. For instance, if you plant monarda or other mints, they can cover the whole bed in short order if you let them. To keep them in check, plant them in a plastic or clay pot and sink the whole pot right into the garden with the rim protruding just above the soil level. That way, you add and enjoy their presence in the garden but keep them under control. Every year or two, you'll need to pull the pot from the ground, thin out the herb, and resink the pot into the garden.

Planting a good variety of crops and rotating them to different spots in your plot will prevent the soil from becoming depleted of certain nutrients and may reduce the buildup of diseases or pests specific to a particular crop. This is not an idle experiment, so plant mostly crops that you know you'll use, but go ahead and plant a few new crops to expand your horizons. If you and your family don't care for a particular vegetable, turn it under as a green manure or toss the whole crop into the compost. Hey, maybe you could even sell it to a roadside or fresh produce market—someone else may have a hankering for it.

Intercropping

In the simplest terms, intercropping is the practice of growing two or more crops in the same space at the same time. Because it groups plants with similar nutrient and water needs, intercropping makes efficient use of resources and increases yield, which is why it is considered a sustainable gardening practice. There are several types of intercropping, which use a combination of timing and spatial or physical arrangements to work well. Square-foot gardens encourage interplanting foot by foot. Here are some other examples:

- Sow seeds of a fast-growing crop with those of a slow-growing crop, so that the fast grower is harvested before the slow grower starts to mature. For example, plant some radishes between your bell peppers—you'll harvest the radishes and recompost the area long before the heat of summer when your peppers start to get serious about adding bushiness.
- Plant a cool weather crop close to a summer crop a few weeks before its harvest time. The cool season crop will get a good start in the shade of the previous crop until it is harvested and pulled up. Be careful in the cleanup of the summer crop so you don't damage your new fall crop.
- Use the physical characteristics of one plant to complement another. When you plant corn, pole beans, and squash together on the same hill, the beans crawl up the corn stalk and the squash's large leaves shade the ground to discourage the weeds. Native

Americans called these crops the "Three Sisters," because they represent a complete vegetable diet. If you decide to try this, place a large amount of compost in the hill to supply nutrients for all three of the crops, because despite what you may read in the literature, the beans fix nitrogen only for themselves, not for the benefit the other crops. Plant the beans and squash after the corn is knee high, because they'll grow quickly.

Companion Planting

Growing a variety of crops next to each other and in rotation discourages pest attacks and it maintains a better balance in the soil. (Growing one crop repeatedly in an area can deplete the soil of certain nutrients.) Much has been written in organic gardening literature about which specific plants work well together, but extension agents, university studies, and other professionals have been unable to verify most of the anecdotal benefits of "companion planting."

There are some combinations to watch out for, like the **allelopathic** chemicals exuded by crop plants such as broccoli and sunflowers or trees such as walnut, Australian pine, eucalyptus, and others. As you may have noticed under your own bird feeder, hulls of sunflower seeds inhibit germination of many types of seeds. So use spent sunflower parts as a mulch where you want to suppress weeds, but don't use them as a mulch around cultivated plants. You *can* put them in your compost pile, because the decomposers will digest the allelopathic chemicals and they will be highly diluted. If you plant broccoli in your vegetable garden, don't plant another cabbage crop in that same spot for two seasons. (Cabbage crops include broccoli, cabbage, kale, cauliflower, Brussels sprouts, collards, and kohlrabi. They are also known as cole crops and are all derived from one species, *Brassica oleracea*.)

It's also beneficial to plant flowers among or in the vicinity of your fruiting crops to attract pollinators. Marigolds planted next to your tomatoes, for example, make a tough, good-looking border that will attract pollinators. Don't count on them to prevent nematodes from attacking your tomatoes' roots, though. While marigolds ward off nematodes in

Fruit versus Vegetable

What distinguishes a vegetable from a fruit? If we eat the leaves, stems, roots or tubers, flowers or buds of a particular crop as we do, for instance, when we eat lettuce, carrots, potatoes, or broccoli, then horticulturally what we're eating is a vegetable. On the other hand, we're enjoying a fruit when we consume the part of the plant that is the swollen ovary of a flower that contains seeds, such as a tomato, an apple, a squash, or an orange.

Traditionally, the terms "fruit" and "vegetable" have had less to do with edible plant parts than with how particular crops are used and how grocery stores display them. In 1893, the U.S. Supreme Court unanimously declared the tomato to be a vegetable in a tariff dispute—tariffs were payable for vegetables but not fruits. Then again, the European Union declared the carrot a fruit in its 1979 Jam Directive, which set standards for how much "fruit" must be contained in jams.

Diet plans and nutrition diagrams tend to lump fruits and vegetables into one category. The USDA tells us that we need five servings a day. With a productive garden, that advice is much easier to follow.

their own roots, this resistance is not apparently transferred to nearby crops. Choose tomato cultivars bred to resist nematodes for the best success.

Legume crops such as beans or peas can provide their own fertilizer via **symbiotic** nitrogen-fixing bacteria in their root nodules, but this process does nothing for the fertility of the surrounding soil while they are growing. Legumes are an excellent choice for a green manure, though, because as you turn them under, that newly fixed nitrogen is added to the available nutrients in the soil. Be aware of legumes in your crop sequencing: as you won't have applied any extra composted manure to their space in the garden, be sure to add some for the next nonlegume crop in your rotation.

In summary, take advice on companion planting with a grain of salt and do your own research to see what works for your garden. It's a good

Put the right plant in the right place—take advantage of microclimates. These native prickly pears thrive in a dry, hot, full-sun corner. Lava rock adds to the heat. (Chapter 2)

Composting and mulching enrich and protect the soil. These are two of the most sustainable activities in your garden. When mulching around stepping stones you may wish to use weed barrier cloth to reduce the weed populations. The larger pieces in this mulch load were used in the bottom layer and then covered by more finely chopped wood. (Chapter 3)

This bird-friendly yard provides meadows, nectar-rich flowers (supplemented by sugar water), and habitat for nesting and hiding. (Chapter 5)

Reduce the size of your lawn by installing mulched beds around groups of trees and creating meadow areas in out-of-the-way spaces. Make the lawn easy to mow with wide sweeping curves and edges designed to reduce the need for string trimmers and edgers. Also, reduce the use of fertilizer, herbicides, and pesticides. (Chapter 4)

When creating habitat for butterflies, use flowering nectar plants for the adults and food plants for the larvae. Milkweed serves both purposes for monarch butterflies. Healthy butterfly habitat also includes water sources (including mud flats, so important for butterflies) and a variety of vegetation for shelter from predators and weather. Most important, stop using general pesticides. (Chapter 5)

Attractive meadows are possible anywhere in Florida. The field of yellow rain lilies makes a statement in Key West, while a mixture of black-eyed Susans and mist flowers thrive along a roadside in northern Florida. Meadows provide excellent habitat for a wide variety of birds, butterflies, and other wildlife. Meadow maintenance can be as simple as mowing once a year or just removing woody plants every other year or so. (Chapter 5)

When possible, choose native trees and shrubs for your landscape. This delicate wild azalea produces quite a show in the spring. (Chapter 6)

Palms don't have annual rings and can't heal themselves like other trees do. Their woody structure is generally more flexible than other trees, so they're especially recommended for stormwise landscaping. (Chapters 6 and 14)

Even in a small space, like this St. Augustine balcony, you can have a fabulous garden using containers. (Chapter 7)

A graceful container dresses up the area next to a pond. Both plants in this arrangement thrive in a moist, shaded environment. (Chapter 7)

Above: Growing fruits and vegetables is sustainable because no energy is used in transporting the produce. Controlling your edibles from seed (or seedling) to the table provides peace of mind because you know that no poisons were used. And really fresh vegetables taste better and have more vitamins. In Florida you can grow your own vegetables year round. (Chapter 8)

Left: Cherry tomatoes do well when the soil has been enriched with compost and composted horse manure. In Florida, we can plant two crops of tomatoes each year.

Above: A green lynx spider captures a beetle on this sunflower head. Integrated pest management allows bugs and their predators to reach a balance. (Chapter 9)

Left: Creating habitat for bug predators is an important step in your Integrated pest management. (Chapters 5 and 9)

This hornworm is covered with braconid wasp larvae. These larvae will consume their host and are some of Mother Nature's many biological tools to keep bugs in balance. (Chapter 9)

Water running down the street and irrigation running when it's not needed indicate that a "set it and forget it" automatic irrigation system is wasting too much precious water. Follow all irrigation regulations, and pay attention to the rainfall and the natural cycle of your turf. (Chapter 10)

Harvesting pine needles from the street keeps the storm drains clear of clogging debris that overloads waterways with organic matter. Plus pine needles make an excellent mulch. (Chapters 10 and 3)

This open rain barrel system consists of three barrels joined by overflow hoses between them, with the third overflow hose directed into a watering can. Excess water flows away from the building into a low wooded area. (Chapter 11)

The water collection feature of the first rain barrel (shown above) consists of a screen-covered plastic basket with a lip that sits loosely in a hole in the top of the barrel. The diverted downspout pipe empties all its water into the basket, where the screen catches roof debris and keeps out the mosquitoes.

Top: A downspout rain garden with a blooming rain lily and two types of fern just after its installation. A drywell is filled with gravel under the fake river rocks for better absorption of rainwater. The excess will flow into the grass. *Above:* A year or so later, the blue-eyed grass obscures the stones, a different rain lily blooms, and the ferns have spread. Rain garden plants help absorb water. (Chapter 12)

Top: A hard-to-maintain parking lot green space in Central Florida. It's so over-mowed that the bark on the trees' surface roots is skinned right off—weakening the trees. *Above:* A different parking lot swale—planted with a variety of rain garden plants—absorbs more stormwater and provides good habitat for birds and butterflies. This attractive space, also in Central Florida, requires less maintenance and reduces the volume of water entering the local stormwater drainage system. (Chapter 12)

Red mangroves, plants with their own stilts, create a tangled structure that adds to the stability of Florida's shorelines and creates habitat for fish and other wildlife. (Chapter 13)

A living shoreline has been created using biodegradable bags (or socks) filled with chopped corn stalks. They have been staked in place along a canal shoreline that was previously eroding. Tough native grass, planted just behind the bags, has spread into the water to create better habitat. Photo courtesy of Sanibel BioSolutions. (Chapter 13)

In Pensacola Bay, a living shoreline was created with the installation of a breakwa-ter and shoreline grasses planted on a shallow island. The shoreline is protected, but the water and wildlife flow freely. Photo reproduced by permission of Florida Department of Environmental Protection. (Chapter 13)

Trees in waterlogged soil are more vulnerable to hurricane-force winds, but expert pruning can lighten the crown. Stormwise and firewise landscaping may signifi-cantly reduce damage and save time and money. Preparing for disaster should be part of your sustainable gardening strategy. (Chapter 14)

practice to keep notes about your crops in your garden log. Your notes don't have to be fancy, but by developing your own record of planting dates and what crops worked well together, you'll save yourself time and energy in the future. Let Mother Nature be your teacher.

So Many Fruits and Nuts in Florida

From native blackberries that crawl on the ground to pecans or coconuts growing high atop trees, Florida's wide range of fruits and nuts provides you with a fantastic variety of choices for your edible landscape. One of the big attractions of fruit and nut trees is their longevity—new crops do not have to be planted each year.

In northern and central Florida, we have the opportunity to grow some traditional deciduous fruit trees such as apple, pear, and peach. In central and southern Florida, a wide variety of tropical and subtropical fruits do well, including our famous citrus crops. Some of these tree crops require little care and produce well year after year.

On the other hand, some fruit trees need applications of dormant oil or other means to keep their pests at bay. If you are considering a crop that is commercially produced in Florida, you could cause damage to nearby operations if you allow your trees to become infested. The citrus industry has been so concerned about outbreaks of citrus canker and other serious diseases that, in some years, the sale of new citrus trees to homeowners and casual farmers was halted, and in some cases citrus trees were removed from residential lots. It's certainly not sustainable to damage commercial crops by hosting pests with your informal gardening practices.

So pay attention and consult your local extension agent before you plant long-lived fruit and nut crops. Agents can provide you with up-to-date horticultural and regulatory advice, as well as with data sheets that list the best cultivars for your region and detail cultivation practices, including pruning strategies and whether or not your trees need to be cross-pollinated with another variety.

Some of Florida's smaller fruit crops make great additions to a sustainable landscape, including our native grapes, blueberries, pawpaw, passion fruit, persimmon, and blackberries. Your edible landscape can also be enhanced by the many non-native tropical and subtropical fruits available to Florida gardeners, such as banana, fig, pineapple, avocado, dragon fruit, and mango. Be sure to check that the cultivar is appropriate for Florida and that it is not invasive. Just because a plant is for sale here in our state does not necessarily mean that it's the best choice. It's much more sustainable to choose a native blueberry, or one that was specifically bred for our heat, than one that grows well in New Jersey. Jersey blueberries are delicious, but those plants don't grow well here. Choose southern high bush or rabbit-eye blueberries instead; they do well as far south as St. Petersburg and Vero Beach.

Heritage Seed Stocks

The fruits and vegetables that we see in the store have been bred for marketability. Grocery store tomatoes are usually round, red, and often tasteless, but they look good on the shelf, ship well, and are available year round. When you grow your own fruits and vegetables, there's no reason to limit your crops to the most familiar cultivars. Experiment with various sizes and colors and go for the ones with the most taste.

Various organizations have kept the old-fashioned fruits and vegetable stocks going, and you can find supplies of these seeds and plants on the Internet and also from local nurseries that cater to the organic gardening market. Keep in mind that these crops might vary in quality, but save space in your garden for some of these longtime favorites that your mother and grandmother might have grown.

Nonhybrid seeds will breed more or less true with open pollination, and you will be able to save seeds from the plants that grew best in your gardens. Harvesting your own seeds saves you money next year. Since you'll save only seeds from plants that performed well in your garden, over a few seasons you may produce better crops because, in effect, you will be doing your own breeding.

Diversity in our edibles keeps the gene pool rich and may keep some of the pests at bay. You may even decide to donate some of your seeds to one of the heritage seeds initiatives.

Pests in Your Edibles

Healthy, well-composted, and mulched vegetables should not need much attention when it comes to pests. Bugs seem to do more damage to weaker plants. For instance, even if a tomato worm goes undetected for a few days, the loss of those leaves won't make much difference to the plant's vigor. When you do find it, pick it off and kill it—unless larvae of a parasitic wasp are attached to it. Those rice-sized pellets sticking out of the worm's back is not a punk hairdo but larvae of a parasitic wasp that preys on the tomato worm and other hornworms. Leave the worms with the larvae alone; you want those wasps to survive and reproduce so they can kill more worms.

If you end up with squash borers hollowing out your squash stems, slice the stem open lengthwise—don't cut across the stem, because you'll interrupt the flow of water and nutrients. Pull out the worms and squash them—it's only fitting isn't it? Learn to distinguish the pests from the garden helpers. Keep in mind that the striped caterpillars on your parsley may be those of our lovely black swallowtail butterfly. If you treat your whole bed to keep out *all* caterpillars by using Bt (the bacteria designed to nonselectively kill caterpillars) or **diatomaceous earth** (made from pulverized diatom fossils that rip open caterpillars' bellies) you'll be defeating your butterfly garden efforts and your integrated pest management (IPM) program. Plant more parsley in more places, and learn to share it with the caterpillars that you've worked so hard to attract. This same sharing principal goes for the zebra longwing and Gulf fritillary larvae on your passion vines and the various kinds of sulphur larvae on your legumes.

Quite often pests are crop specific, so the interplanting and rotating of crops will make it more difficult for one pest to wipe out your entire garden. Mother Nature abhors a monoculture, so plan for diversity of crops, including different cultivars of the same crop to increase your chances of a successful harvest. You may find that a certain crop is damaged despite all your efforts. If your Swiss chard always ends up looking like Swiss cheese with hardly any leaf left to eat, try a different cultivar or find some other greens to plant.

Some problems in a vegetable plot that look like a pest problem may actually be due to uneven watering or a shortage of one nutrient or another. Blossom-end rot, a metabolic disorder in tomatoes and zucchinis, is due either to calcium deficiency or uneven watering. If you find this, work some crushed eggshells into the soil near the plants and even out the irrigation. Some varieties of tomatoes are more prone to this disorder than others—often the older ones or the heirlooms. The fruits are still fine for eating, although you may have to trim off the affected portion of the fruit. Don't reject a good-tasting tomato just because it has minor blossom-end rot or other minor deformities.

Some cultivars have been bred to resist damage from pests and diseases or to set fruits at high temperatures. Do your homework, keep notes, and purchase only the types that have been proven for your part of Florida. Your agricultural extension agent has lots of up-to-date information on recommended crops and cultivars.

A Family Garden

To reiterate advice from earlier in this chapter, gardeners new to raising vegetables will do best to start small and grow from there. If the purpose of your edible garden is to augment your family's groceries and maybe to convince more members of your family that vegetables are delicious to eat, then start with a plan to grow a few of the vegetables everyone likes that are also suited to your climate and soil. The next year, add a few new types for more variety. Make your edible garden a family project and keep it at a manageable level. A sustainable gardening system means that you plan for enough resources, including workers, to comfortably care for your plot. Include crops like beans and squash, with their large seeds and quick germination, so younger children won't lose interest in the project.

When you finish harvesting your summer crops, have a plan in place for the next set of crops: be ready to plant the lettuce, radishes, or other cool-weather vegetables. You may find after a season or two that your family's edible garden has increased enough in size and yield to significantly augment and alter your family's menu. You might even have enough to freeze or can for those off-season uses.

Four-by-four-foot raised beds are perfect for a family vegetable garden, because they present a set of easy-to-accomplish tasks instead of a huge span of chores. Weeding and hand watering one square can be accomplished in a few minutes. You may decide to assign each family member responsibility for one bed. For young children, build the raised bed only three feet wide, so that they will be able to reach all the way to the middle to plant, weed, and cultivate their crops.

Community Gardens

Community gardens are wonderful projects that enable people who have no land for cultivation to grow their own vegetables and flowers. There is underused or vacant land in almost every Florida town or city that could be set aside for this purpose and partitioned into plots of sufficient size to grow produce for any number of families. In northern states, plots are typically allocated one growing season at a time. Here in Florida, where crops grow all year long, other timetables can be devised for garden plot assignment. That way, vacant lots—even in Florida's largest cities—can be turned into productive landscapes at little expense and with only some basic initial planning and effort. Instead of grassroots movements, we could set up "no-grass" movements to lead the way. Grants might be available to help start community plots, and extension offices and other agencies could provide good local information. Once started, a community garden should be able to sustain itself through the efforts of the participants.

Initially, large garden areas in urban and suburban environments may require use of large tillers or plows to turn over hard-packed soil, but once the project is underway, the individuals in charge of the separate plots can keep up the soil quality without deep plowing. Regular workshops, presentations, competitions, and other educational efforts can be organized to bring community members together and keep them informed about and interested in their project. A sense of community goes a long way to ensure the success of the entire effort.

Compost piles can be maintained in each community garden for recycling wastes from both the individual plots and from the neighborhood. A yearly or seasonal delivery of composted manure or mushroom compost can increase the success rate of the individual plots.

If the garden area was originally part of a lawn, it may already have irrigation in place. If not, a plan will have to be developed for getting water to the plot. Gathering rainwater from the roofs of nearby buildings and then directing it to a cistern is one sustainable way to supply a water source. If local regulations allow it and if the quality of the water is good enough, a pump could be installed in a large retention pond to recirculate that water into the garden area. The water in retention ponds already contains nutrients from stormwater runoff, so gardens irrigated from this source might not need any additional fertilizer.

Community gardens can be set up and run by any number of organizations, including schools, homeowner associations, churches, youth groups, fraternal groups, and local governments. Anywhere there is cleared land that may be costing money to maintain is a good place for a community garden project. Vegetable gardens help teach kids that food doesn't always come from stores or fast-food places. Members of churches or other charitable organizations can grow food for their own needs and then distribute a portion of their harvests to the less fortunate. What better way to be good stewards of Mother Earth?

Become a Locavore: Plant an Edible Garden

Eating from local resources reduces the fuel required for transportation, and this saves money and energy. Eating from your backyard or local garden plot makes you the ultimate locavore. You'll also have peace of mind knowing exactly the kind of treatment your produce received as you put it on your table.

Resources

Web Sites

The University of Florida's IFAS extension offers Fruitscapes, a Web site on landscaping with fruit trees: http://fruitscapes.ifas.ufl.edu.

The IFAS extension's Solutions for Your Life site is loaded with information and resources for all types of crops: http://solutionsforyourlife.ufl.edu/agriculture/.

The Sustainable Table, a nonprofit organization, educates people on sustainable food supplies and eating habits: http://www.sustainabletable.org.

Visit the nonprofit Seed Saver's Exchange for information, book suggestions, and heirloom seed varieties: http://www.seedsavers.org.

Books

Bartholomew, Mel. *Square Foot Gardening*. Emmaus, Pa.: Rodale, 1981. (The associated Web site has updated information: http://www.squarefootgardening. com.)

Kingsolver, Barbara, Camille Kingsolver, and Steven L. Hopp. *Animal, Vegetable, Miracle*. New York: HarperCollins, 2007.

Marinelli, Janet, ed. *Kitchen Gardens*. Brooklyn, N.Y.: Brooklyn Botanic Garden, 1998.

Pollan, Michael. *In Defense of Food*. New York: Penguin, 2008.

Smith, Edward. *The Vegetable Garden Bible*. Pownal, Vt.: Storey, 2000.

Stephens, James M. *Vegetable Gardening in Florida*. Gainesville: University Press of Florida, 1999.

Integrated Pest Management (IPM)

Pests in the landscape come in a wide variety of sizes and shapes. A pest is any living thing you don't want in your landscape. In addition to the bugs, like mosquitoes, squash borers, aphids, white flies, fire ants, and spider mites, you can also include weeds, slugs, snails, and larger animals, such as geese, rabbits, voles, pocket gophers, wild hogs, raccoons, deer, and squirrels that help themselves to your vegetables and landscape plantings. Even the neighbor's cat that uses your garden for its litter box and kills or harasses your songbirds, bug-eating lizards, and other wildlife is a pest.

The biggest part of your IPM strategy is to encourage beneficial organisms and to discourage pests by making physical modifications to your landscape and by exercising vigilance. When problems do arise, the next step in an IPM program is to determine whether or not a pest is causing enough damage to warrant control. You also take time to consider which of the possible controls is most effective and appropriate in your situation. If a particular plant or crop is always under siege from a pest insect or fungus, sometimes the best solution is to get rid of it. Here in Florida there are so many choices for replacements.

IPM Is Sustainable Pest Management

Integrated Pest Management is one of the more sustainable actions landscape managers can take. When you don't use poisons, your landscape becomes an ecosystem working in balance between predator and prey species. Using good garden management practices and physical barriers can prevent many of the problems with pests.

Sometimes removal of vulnerable plants may be the best way to combat a persistent pest. Rarely, and only as a last resort, use the smallest amount of the most specific and most degradable pesticides. The goal is to mitigate pests while doing the least amount of damage to the surrounding environment.

Insects and Other Bugs

In a balanced ecosystem, predators will be in the minority. In other words, in a natural environment, there are many more prey organisms to ensure a continuing food supply for the predators. As Florida gardeners know well, there is no shortage of prey in our state, including aphids, white flies, mosquitoes, cabbageworms, leaf miners, mealy bugs, mole crickets, spider mites, and others pests we'd like to get rid of.

Let's consider what happens when you attempt to poison or zap those pesky bugs. A general insecticide (or bug zapper) will kill the majority of the insects in an area, but more than 90 percent of those insects are beneficial or benign. Some of those beneficial insects would have pollinated your flowers. Without them, you won't harvest any squash from your vegetable plot. Your butterfly garden will be missing the invited guests because you've killed the caterpillars. Some of the beneficials that would have eaten your pest insects are now dead. Other predators such as bats, frogs, and birds will go elsewhere to feed, and your land will become a poisoned vacuum.

As your landscape recovers from the poisoning, insects will begin to multiply again, but since you've killed off the beneficial insects and the birds have flown away, the harmful insects, possibly including new pests that were previously controlled, will recover in even greater numbers than before. You spray again, and the process repeats itself; and each time the most damaging insects will recover in ever-increasing numbers. Bugs can become resistant to insecticides, driving people to switch to even stronger poisons. If you've ever read the hazard statements on a pesticide label, you know that these poisons aren't just toxic to bugs—they can harm other wildlife, especially birds and fish and the animals that eat them; they can harm your pets; and, over time, they can harm you and your children. It's time to break the cycle of chemical escalation and manage your landscape as a complete ecosystem by using IPM, Integrated Pest Management.

Relying on insect predators and other eco-friendly strategies to control your pests is not a matter of sitting back and doing nothing. As with any other effective gardening method, it requires awareness, education, experimentation, effort, and patience.

Encourage the Beneficials

The beneficials include birds, bats, frogs, toads, lizards, predatory insects, and parasitoid insects. Encouraging them is an important part of your IPM program. You want to enlist Mother Nature's aid in keeping your pests under control, because she has a large arsenal of bioweapons and knows how to use them. There are a number of excellent advantages to this method of control.

- The predators do most of the work. You can spend your garden time doing other things.
- It helps prevent the development of pesticide resistance in target bugs.
- You are not contributing to environmental pollution.
- Insect predators will wax and wane in pace with pest populations.
- Your landscape will have a more balanced ecosystem. A poisoned landscape requires total life-support from you.

Predators of Bugs

Predators hunt and eat bugs or feed bugs to their young. Most are generalists and will devour any insect within their range. A bat will consume thousands of flying insects every night. Purple martins or tree swallows take over during the day, depending on the time of year. Bluebirds and blue jays will dive-bomb your yard to snag critters there, and wrens will pick through your container gardens looking for bugs to eat. Frogs, toads, and lizards are all excellent insect predators. Spiders do more for your garden than just decorate it with lovely dew-catching webs; they are efficient bug catchers. Armadillos and moles can smell grubs and other underground insects. While they might make a mess as they dig their prey from the soil, you should cheer them on. Smile as you replace their divots: you have great helpers in your landscape, and they don't eat your plants.

Predatory insects eat other insects. As an underwater larva (naiad), the dragonfly has a voracious appetite for mosquito larvae; as an adult, it continues to eat mosquitoes and other flying insects. Ladybug larvae eat aphids and other sucking insects. Lacewing larvae are also avid predators of aphids, but will also consume mites, scale insects, and small caterpillars. Hoverfly larvae feed on greenflies, but they also eat spider mites and small caterpillars. Praying mantises, those highly efficient predators, are fascinating to watch as they prowl around your garden and grab insects large and small with their wickedly barbed forearms. Yellow jackets are carnivorous wasps that feed on a variety of bugs, including mole crickets. In a balanced ecosystem, the prey vastly outnumber these predatory insects.

Parasitoid Insects

Parasitoid insects kill their hosts, but they are not considered predators. Most parasitoids are tiny wasps, such as the braconids. The adult female lays her eggs in or on the host. When the eggs hatch, the larvae consume the host gradually, allowing it to stay alive until the parasitoid larvae pupate and are able to survive on their own. Parasitoids tend to be host specific. The best-known types are the wasps that infest tomato hornworms, leaving behind rice-sized larvae protruding from the worm's back. Some are native, but many have been imported to target specific pests: phorid

Hand pick tomato hornworms from your tomato plants instead of using poisons, but leave the ones dotted with the rice-shaped wasp larvae. You want to encourage the wasps—one of Mother Nature's many bug controls.

flies pupate in red imported fire ants, and tiny wasps target various weevils, worms, white flies, and scale.

Attracting and Keeping Insect Killers

Just as would for other wildlife, you need to build or enhance habitat for your insect predators. Provide water, food, shelter, and places to raise young. You'll want to encourage a large insect population to keep the predators supplied with plenty of food. This may seem counterproductive since you're trying to get rid of problem insects, but letting the populations reach a balance is definitely the most sustainable option. The predator populations expand and contract in reaction to the pest populations.

As adults, parasitoid wasps, lacewings, and many other beneficial insects require nectar sources. It's a good idea to keep a variety of flowers with different colors and structures blooming year round in your meadows and gardens. That way, you provide nectar and pollen for both the beneficial and benign insects, including your butterflies. To provide good habitat, use native hedgerows to develop different layers in your landscape so that leaves extend from ground level to a high shrubbery level. Here are some of the specific plant types you can use to attract your voracious beneficials.

- Low-growing creepers provide cover for ground beetles.
- Small flowers arranged in a flat flower head are good for the adult phase of those tiny parasitoid wasps. Plants from the carrot

family (Apiaceae) work well. These are plants that you'd have in your herb garden anyway, like parsley, fennel, coriander, and dill.

- Flowers in the daisy family (Asteraceae), such as asters, daisies, and goldenrod, plus those in the mint family (Lamiaceae), such as monarda, catnip, salvia, scarlet sage, and various mints, attract hummingbirds, predatory wasps, hover flies, and robber flies. When you look at this list, most of the flowers that attract beneficial insects are also attractive to humans.

In addition to maintaining a large insect population, attract and keep carnivorous birds and bats on your property by supplying appropriately designed bird and bat houses and other shelter, such as snags and brush piles. Hummingbirds eat insects when they are raising young, so keep them coming to your property with hummingbird feeders. Install a purple martin apartment house in the open near a water source. Maintain some of your property as open meadow for the bluebirds.

Leave some out-of-the-way places uncultivated (with no weed barrier), so there's space for critters to make their nests in the ground. Create permanent toad shelters in and around your gardens—they'll return the favor by dining on your slugs and bugs. A toad shelter can be as simple as a piece of a clay pot or a flat rock with a small crevice under it.

To provide habitat for toads, frogs, and dragonflies, you need a pond so they can complete their life cycles. It doesn't have to be large, but it should

Build toad houses with broken potshards around your gardens to welcome these voracious predators—they'll dine on a wide variety of pests, including bugs and slugs.

include a good variety of plant materials, fish, snails, and both shallow and deep water. If your pond has a beach, or mud flats, the butterflies will also enjoy it. Ponds combined with rain gardens provide a wonderful focal point for almost any landscape.

Best Practices in the Garden

While you want to provide good habitat on your property for insects and their predators, there are some important garden practices that will reduce problems with known pests.

> **Mosquitoes**: While we all know not to leave water standing for more than three days, it can still collect in out-of-the-way places if we're not careful. Scout every nook and cranny in your landscape for items that could hold water. Start at your potting bench or work areas and work your way around the property. The catch saucers for your container gardens should be deep enough to hold water for half a day or so after you water, but the soil in the container should soak it up after that. During rainy periods, you can turn the catch dishes upside down under the pots so the excess water can flow away. Birdbaths and other small water features with no circulation pump and no flora and fauna need to be emptied every third day. To be most effective, make mosquito prevention a neighborhood-wide program.

> **Fire ants**: The red imported fire ant, an apparently accidental introduction from Brazil in the 1930s, is definitely a pest in the Florida landscape. It has also displaced native ants. Worker ants aggressively defend their nest and will bite and sting intruders: they bite with their pincer mouthparts and then inject venom with their stingers. Most Florida gardeners have firsthand (and first-ankle) knowledge of fire ants.

> Researchers from the University of Florida and elsewhere have been experimenting with parasitoid phorid flies from Brazil that pupate only in the red imported fire ants. Their release in agricultural areas has reduced fire ant populations in key parts of the state, but you'll still need to deal with your own populations. The

most sustainable method for treating anthills on your property is to slowly pour at least two gallons of boiling water on them. To eradicate the colony, the hot water has to reach the queen (or queens) that are usually deep in the hill. The hot water may cook nearby plants, though, so use it with care.

A gallon or more of cold water and other disruptions, like raking, will cause a colony to move. Repeatedly disrupt each mound until the colony relocates to an area where you can tolerate its presence. Unfortunately we will never get rid of fire ants altogether, but you can keep them out of the way with water treatments. If you feel that you need stronger methods, use a bait ant killer in moderate amounts and only around the most troublesome hills.

Sucking, boring, mining, and browsing bugs: When you depend upon predators to control pests, there will always be a certain number of them around. You can reduce their impact with the establishment of the proper growing environment and ongoing maintenance. Remember, too, that to keep your predators around, you need to have prey available for them to eat.

Follow your extension agent's advice—"Put the right plants in the right places." Your landscape will have a head start in bug resistance when your plants have everything they need to be vigorous: composted, mulched soil that provides the correct balance of nutrients and irrigation that is correctly adjusted. More is not always better. Providing too much soluble nitrogen in the soil and too much water will cause your plants to respond with fast growth, but those growth spurts can attract sucking insects—the softer cell walls of the new growth make it easier for them to feed.

Bugs and other pests often look for a specific type of plant to infest. Growing a variety of plants together can make it more difficult for species-specific pests to find their food source. A monoculture, by contrast, makes it easy. In the vegetable garden, intermix crops and rotate them. In other parts of the landscape, do the same. Use a variety of plants in your borders, hedgerows, beds, and other landscape features. Besides being more interesting than monoculture, plant diversity makes for better habitat, may confound pests for a while, and ultimately is more sustainable for both the gardener and the garden. Diversity also means that if one plant species is hit with a fatal attack, your landscape plantings won't be totally wiped out.

For those bugs that do come, make it difficult for them to survive. Each week, look for them under the leaves and stems or branches of your most desirable plants. Remove bugs by handpicking or knocking them off, and put them in a container of soapy water. You can also hose pests off of plants with water—be sure to spray both sides of the leaves. Remove badly infested plants or plant parts, and remove old, sick, or dying plants because they're more susceptible attack. Don't use them for composting. Instead, throw them away with the trash to reduce the chance of pests moving between plants.

Controls are more effective when infestations are caught early. Once extensive damage occurs, it is often too late to save the plants. Using traps to monitor pests provides another form of inspection. Sticky traps, pheromone traps, pitfall traps, and light traps are each used for different kinds of pests. Beer traps (tuna cans holding an inch of beer and sunk in the soil to their rims) are good for catching slugs. Whiteflies and aphids, attracted to bright yellow sticky cards, are trapped on their adhesive surfaces. Keep in mind, though, that some of your beneficials may also be trapped.

If your gardens have been plagued by a particular bug, experiment with timing your plantings. Perhaps you can plant your seedlings earlier or later. (Florida's warm climate provides a good deal of latitude in planting times.) Or, for a year or two, plant something in that space less vulnerable to the target pest. You might even install translucent row covers that allow plants to absorb the light they need while keeping flying insects out. By blocking access, you keep pest insects away from their usual food supply when they need it. Remove the covers periodically to allow for pollination and when the target bugs become less of a threat. Plants are most vulnerable when they're small. Once your plants mature, pests may not be able to do them as much damage.

If cabbageworms or other caterpillars are inflicting more damage than you can tolerate, supplement your handpicking program by spreading diatomaceous earth around each plant. Made from the pulverized fossil remains of ancient hard-shelled algae called "diatoms," the sharp, glassy particles of this powder cut open the undersides of caterpillars and worms as they crawl across it. Diatomaceous earth will work on all caterpillars, though, so use it only where the target pest is causing trouble. You'll want those swallowtail butterfly larvae to eat some of your parsley, so that you'll have visitors to enjoy in your butterfly garden.

Not By Bugs Alone

Bugs are only one of many potential causes of unhealthy plants. Fungi, bacteria, and viral diseases, nematodes, water stress, and nutritional imbalance can also be damaging. Many times, plants weakened by one problem are good targets for another. Just because you see aphids sucking on a stem doesn't mean that they are the only problem. Correctly identifying the foe can be tricky, but it's worth the effort so you can remedy the problem correctly and efficiently. As with insect pests, defensive gardening is essential.

Inspect the plant's entire environment for clues to the problem. Too much or too little moisture, wind, salt spray, humidity, and light may cause stress that results in susceptibility to damage from pests and diseases. In your garden log, record weather conditions, planting dates, and the type of attention you've given your plants. Such information may provide clues to growth patterns and problems from year to year.

You probably won't be aware of fungal invasion of your plants until it's too late. Fungi are everywhere, of course, and like bugs, most are beneficial. They play a significant role in your compost pile, for example, and some help plant roots absorb water from the soil. Some of the most commonly encountered fungal infections include powdery mildew, damping off of seedlings, downy mildew, rusts, leaf spots, root rots, and wilt.

Fungal infections are spread by spores. Though too small to be seen individually, masses of spores on leaf surfaces often look like furry or powdery growths. If conditions are favorable, once the spore lands on the plant, it will germinate there and penetrate the tissue to grow inside. Fungus becomes much more difficult to control once inside the leaf or root tissue, so prevention and early control are the best ways of halting infection. A healthy plant has defenses of its own against fungal attack: when fungus spores contact the tissue of a vigorous plant, they don't germinate because of the plant's innate resistance.

Your best defense against persistent fungus problems in the landscape, especially the vegetable garden, is to maintain the following practices:

- purchase cultivars resistant to specific fungi;
- water only in the morning, so leaves dry out during the day, or irrigate only the soil;
- clean up infected plants (and the debris around them) and dispose of these material in the trash, not the compost pile;
- in the vegetable garden, use a long crop rotation cycle (two years or more) so as not to supply the fungi in the soil with the perfect host each year.

Taken together, these defenses constitute good and sustainable plant hygiene that will save you time, energy, and money.

Nematodes are tiny worms that live in the water film that surrounds soil granules. They abound in soils, and while most are beneficial or benign, some are harmful to your plants. Root knot nematodes invade the roots of susceptible peppers and other crops in your edible garden and hamper their growth. The best defense against them is to purchase nematode-resistant crop varieties and to provide such a good growing environment that your plants can survive with fewer functioning roots.

Fungal infections are usually signaled by visual cues of one kind or another—spots, discolorations, sunken lesions, fuzzy coatings, and so on. Bacterial and viral infections on the other hand don't typically give obvious warning signs. Instead, what you'll see are the results of such diseases, which tend to be immediate and widespread. For example, if bacterial or viral disease is involved, one slightly yellowing tomato plant on Tuesday can be followed on Wednesday by a whole row of dead tomato plants. Unfortunately, there is little you can do about such diseases once a plant is hit.

Once again, prevention is your best defense. Bacteria usually enter plants through a wound, so be careful not to create entry points for disease. Make clean cuts when pruning: torn bark is an invitation to disease. So are puncture holes and other kinds of mechanical injury: never nail anything to a tree; don't tie anything around trees or shrubs that could cut into them, like wires or metal banding. Avoid nicking or cutting plants when you stake or otherwise tend them. Be careful to avoid tree trunks and roots when you mow or use landscape maintenance equipment. Even when working on apparently healthy plants, sterilize your pruning tools with an alcohol rub after use to reduce your chances of spreading bacteria. If a group of plants succumbs to disease (a sudden and widespread die-off is often evidence of bacterial or viral infection), remove the dead plants as soon as possible and dispose of them in the trash, not the compost.

Soil solarization may offer some relief from severe infestations of soil-borne pests, such as root-knot nematodes, and it may kill some weed seeds as well. In the hottest months, when parts of your vegetable plot may be fallow, cover sections of your garden with a heavy-duty, clear plastic sheet for four weeks or more. Because Florida's summer months are usually our rainy months, you may need to leave the plastic in place longer for the solarization to work completely. Before laying down the plastic, remove all plant material, loosen the top layer of soil, and water thoroughly—the water in the soil helps cook it. If you have a drip irrigation system installed, remove it so it doesn't melt in the heat.

Keep in mind that solarization will kill everything in the top two to three inches of soil, including all of the beneficials you've worked so hard to cultivate. Those top few inches will be disturbed again when you plant your first seedlings, so harmful organisms may continue to be a problem even after solarization. Plastic is a poorly degradable, oil-based material, so using it in this way is only sustainable because it might reduce the use of chemical poisons. Also, if you do decide to solarize your soil, do what you can to preserve the plastic so that you can reuse it.

Larger Pests

Depending upon your location, you could host a menagerie of landscape browsers. The most sustainable deterrents for woodland animals are physical barriers. Burrowing animals can be stopped from eating your root vegetables with a hardware cloth mesh affixed to the bottoms of raised beds. In the flower garden, if bulb-eating critters aerate your landscape, enclose each bulb or group of bulbs in a hardware cloth basket to impede the nibblers but not the plant (make sure the holes in the cloth are large enough for the plant to grow through).

Discourage deer by laying poultry netting (chicken wire) over the mowed areas near your beds and tack it down with garden staples. Their split hooves get stuck in the wire and they back off. You can walk on it and mow over it without a problem. Each season lift it up, rake the vegetation, and then replace it. This is easier, less expensive, and more sustainable than an installing and maintaining an eight-foot-high or electric fence around your property.

A Note on Wild Hogs

The wild hog population in Florida is second largest in the country. (Texas is first.) Wild hogs aren't native to Florida, and their rooting habits can damage the woodland understory and destroy native wildlife habitat. According to the Florida Fish and Wildlife Conservation Commission (FWC) (http://myfwc.com), if a wild hog is on your property, it is yours. (And hogs are definitely edible!) On the other hand, while there are no restrictions on hog hunting on private property, there are restrictions on discharging firearms in residential neighborhoods. Plus, firearms and crossbows should be handled only by skilled hunters. It is not sustainable to risk one's own or someone else's safety or to cause an animal undue suffering in order to get rid of even as big a nuisance as a feral hog.

The University of Florida's IFAS extension cites many nonlethal methods of nuisance wildlife control, including prevention, exclusion, habitat modification, and various forms of trapping. Where feral hogs are concerned, however, nonlethal methods are seldom effective. Both FWC and the Internet Center for Wildlife Damage Management (an affiliate of USDA and the University of Nebraska's Cooperative Extension Division) recommend trapping and shooting as one of the better methods of feral hog control available to both large and small property owners. Hogs' nocturnal habits will complicate the trapping process, however, and if you do trap one, you may not legally release it onto public land.

In the end, you might want to save yourself a headache by contacting a licensed nuisance trapper in your area. These trappers have the proper tools, know the laws, and are experienced. Extension offices and regional FWC offices usually have names and numbers of trappers that you can call for help.

If birds are eating your blueberries, grapes, or other fruit, use a fine netting to keep them away, but make sure the holes are small enough that birds can't get caught in the net. You can always reuse the material you cover your crop rows with at different times of the season. Scarecrows and contraptions that move and clang in the breeze are traditional deterrents, and they may work for a while, but birds will figure out in time that these devices mean no harm. After all, scarecrows have no brains, but despite the disparaging term "bird-brained," birds do. Happily, newer and higher-tech scarecrows *do* have brains—in the form of a motion sensor attached to a water squirter. Because these devices squirt anything that moves, they can effectively deter birds and other animal pilferers. (They'll learn to avoid getting squirted.) Be sure to turn off the motion detector before you go out to pick berries!

Rabbits, squirrels, raccoons, opossums, voles, pocket gophers, and wild hogs can all be a problem in your vegetable garden. Your best protection is a fence that is partially buried (about one foot) in the ground. Raised beds, if they're high enough, can deter large animals, like hogs, or animals that don't climb vertically, like rabbits and armadillos. As for squirrels and raccoons, no fence or raised bed will stop them. But wire cages that cover the tops of your plants might work most of the time. Sink the bottom edges of the cage below the soil surface to discourage tunneling. Otherwise, plant enough to share.

A secondary line of defense is to avoid attracting scavengers to your yard. Don't let old seeds build up under birdfeeders. Keep pet food stations indoors. When you add kitchen scraps to your compost pile, bury them deeply. If you see or hear scavengers, scare them away. It's all part of making your landscape inhospitable to pests.

Weeds Are Pests, Too

A weed is a plant that's growing in an inappropriate place. Florida's invasive non-native plants are not welcome anywhere in the state; other than that, what is and what is not a weed is a personal judgment call. Weeds are pests because they use moisture and nutrients in the soil and crowd out more desirable plants. Weeds are also pests because efforts to eradicate them can poison the soil (and possibly kill desirable plants), empty your wallet, and strain your back.

In most of Florida's habitats, weeds—lots of them—will sprout within a few days after the soil is disturbed. Our warm climate provides excellent conditions to maintain huge seed banks that can remain viable for many years in the soil. Keep this in mind as you work in your landscape. Disturb the soil as little as possible, but when you do, prepare for the onslaught. For example, when you establish your vegetable plot and double dig your beds, many weeds will sprout from that loosened soil. Pull them out when they are small and get mulch down between your plantings. If you are sowing seeds directly in the ground, use a sterilized topdressing, such as vermiculite, to allow your seeds to sprout without immediate competition from all those weeds. As the desired seeds sprout, mulch around them and remove any weeds that do grow while they are still small and definitely before they bloom.

As with other pests, your goal is to make your landscape inhospitable to weeds in a sustainable manner, without compromising the habitat of desirable plants. Mulching is the most recommended landscape treatment to prevent weeds. In Florida, though, mulching requires management to be effective. Over time, weed seeds will land on the top of your mulch, sprout, and, in most cases, continue to grow. Weeds with tubers, such as catbriar, with deep strong roots, such as torpedo grass, or with many tensile, branching roots, such as Florida betony, can easily grow through mulch and thrive unless every piece of root is extracted from the soil. (At least you can eat Florida betony's weird white tubers—they add a radishy crunch to your salads.) In short, though mulch provides physical and light barriers that suppress the sprouting of weed seeds in the soil, it's not fool-proof. Depending on the situation, you can increase the efficacy of mulch as a weed suppressant by placing semipermeable barriers beneath it, as discussed in detail in chapter 3.

After mulching, ongoing weed-control is usually minimal. Once a year, lightly rake the top of the mulch to remove small weeds and loosen the surface. Depending upon what type of mulch you used, you may need to add some more, maybe an inch or so at each cleanup. Let the leaves that fall from your trees add to the mulch.

In beds where there is significant planting and transplanting activity (as in a vegetable plot), use a mulch that hangs together, such as hay, straw, or pine needles so that you can easily remove it to do more composting and planting. A thick layer of four inches does a good job of keeping down the weeds.

If your goal is to restore the native woodland habitat characteristic of your part of the state, add a one or two-inch layer of mulch on the land every other year or so until the trees and other plants shed enough mulch to mimic a native forest. The best materials for mulch here are shredded tree trimmings, leaves, or pine needles. Weed removal in this case is limited to the invasive non-natives that might sprout. Get them while they are small. Manual pulling or digging is the best method.

Non-natives Have Invaded Florida

Invasive exotic or non-native plants are pests because they displace native plants and habitats over vast regions of our state—weeds of the worst kind. Landscape managers, whether their properties are large or small, can play a significant role in reducing exotics. The first step is to identify what is growing on your property. Remove the invasive non-natives as soon as you can but also on an ongoing basis. This may not be easy. Your removal efforts will be compounded by the type, size, and number of invasive plants on your property and by how much damage they have already done.

To eradicate woody invasives, such as Brazilian pepper, Chinese tallow tree, and Australian pine, either saw them down or girdle their trunks. Girdling is the removal of a strip of bark all the way around a trunk. With tough plants, you'll need to spray a strong herbicide on the wood underneath. The tree may not die until the next season, and you may have to repeat the process. The advantage of this method is that the snags that are left behind can provide good habitat for woodpeckers and other wildlife. Use girdling only if the tree is not going to do damage when it falls. As an alternative, top the tree at a height of eight to ten feet. Spray the exposed wood on the top with herbicide and also treat new sucker growth around the base. When the tree is dead, plant native vines at its base to cover it.

Bugs will invade the deadwood and your wildlife will thank you. You can also use this shortened snag to support bird or bat houses. When you remove a tree, consider replacing it with a good native that will take its place within your property's ecosystem.

For invasive vines, such as air potato or climbing fern, pull or dig up the roots at the base of wherever they're growing and pull as many of the vines out of the branches as possible. For air potato, harvest the loose tubers or "potatoes," which will start new invaders. In fact, whether the invasive is a tree, shrub, perennial, groundcover, or vine, it's a good idea to remove the fruit in order to slow down the plant's spread from new seedlings. For creeping invasives, whether they spread on top of the ground or by underground stems, pull out as much as you can and then monitor the area for several years. Even a little bit of leftover root can start a new plant and a whole new infestation.

If your property includes a lake or abuts a body of water, chances are good that it's infested with aquatic invasives. Monitor your shoreline and manually remove as much hydrilla or as many water hyacinths as you can. They make excellent compost. Gather as many little pieces as you can, because each one can start a new plant. Depending on the situation, certain methods of aquatic weed removal—those involving herbicides or biological agents and those involving removal of *native* aquatic plants— will require permission from the Florida Fish and Wildlife Conservation Commission, the Department of Environmental Protection, or both.

Using Pesticides

Sustainable management of landscape pests and problems means that your first line of defense will involve IPM—the manipulation of cultural practices in the plant environment and sometimes the use of biological control agents. You may encounter some pest problems so extreme that more aggressive controls are necessary. In these cases, pesticides should be your last resort. Before applying any pesticide treatment in your landscape, consult your local extension agent. He or she can help you identify the problem and determine the most effective, least harmful chemical solution for your locale. Some pesticides, for example, work best when applied at specific stages in the life cycle of a weed or insect—usually the early stages of development. This is the kind of information your extension agent can provide.

If use of a pesticide is called for, select the one that is most pest specific, least toxic to nontarget organisms, and least persistent in the environment. Just because a chemical is derived from a biological source doesn't mean that it's safer than artificially produced chemicals. Read the labels of all pesticides completely and thoroughly. Spot treat instead of applying blanket or wall-to-wall treatments.

Bt (*Bacillus thuringiensis*) is a bacterium that can be formulated to target specific insects. Bt causes digestive failure in the insect and does not persist in the landscape. Bt can be designed to target caterpillars for a few days, while another strain of Bt targets mosquitoes. Use Bt with caution; even though it is not supposed to be toxic to animals apart from the targeted species, it upsets natural balances between predator and prey.

Neem oil, which repels foliage feeders and fungi, breaks down within a few days of application, but it's somewhat toxic to fish. Soaps and oils, insecticidal or fungicidal, can damage plants if applied when plants are water stressed, when temperatures exceed 90 degrees, or when high humidity prevents rapid drying. Some plants are sensitive to oil sprays. Test the substance on one leaf before making a wide application.

Herbicides are sometimes required to kill off persistent invasive plants—very large infestations and overly hardy single species that simply refuse to die. Don't apply herbicides, though, until after the majority of the offensive plant population has been physically removed. Use just a little directed herbicide on the new growth—this will usually kill the roots or tubers of the target plant without affecting surrounding vegetation.

Develop a Tolerance for Sharing Your Landscape with Pests

We may need to give up some of our old ideas about maintaining the perfectly groomed landscape and become willing to tolerate a certain amount of insect harm. Healthy, naturally fertilized, and sensibly watered plants growing in soil alive with microbes can sustain some damage without too much ill effect. Plus, a naturally balanced ecosystem is much less likely to suffer from severe pest infestations than a chemically managed environment.

Resources

Web Sites

The University of Florida's IFAS extension offers two Web sites on IPM: http://ipm.ifas.ufl.edu and http://schoolipm.ifas.ufl.edu.

The National Science Foundation offers an IPM Web site: http://cipm.ncsu.edu.

The Southern IPM Center is maintained by the University of North Carolina: http://www.sripmc.org.

Visit IFAS' Center for Aquatic and Invasive Plants for help identifying and controlling non-native invasive plants: http://plants.ifas.ufl.edu.

The Florida Exotic Pest Plant Council maintains a list of plants that are invasive in Florida: http://www.fleppc.org.

Clemson University's extension service Web site has an extensive collection of pest control articles: http://hgic.clemson.edu.

The Florida Fish and Wildlife Conservation Commission provides information on wild hogs and other Florida animals that might become nuisances: http://myfwc.com/critters.

Water and Irrigation

Florida, legendary for its sunshine, is also famous for its water. With average annual rainfall ranging from 39 to 64 inches and an abundance of natural lakes, rivers, springs, wetlands, swamps, and lagoons, Florida gives the appearance of an endless water supply. But there is a problem in paradise. As the state's human population increases, along with demand for more and more water, our groundwater and aquifers are being strained. We are using too much water and wasting much of it. Especially wasteful is the use of an estimated 50 percent of Florida's precious potable water on lawns. More sustainable water management practices are needed now. Gardeners and landscape managers need to be part of an immediate and statewide water conservation movement and adopt waterwise landscaping strategies. These and other measures can reduce some of the strain on Florida's water resources and on all that depends upon them.

The Floridan and Other Aquifers

The Floridan Aquifer system underlies all of Florida and parts of Georgia, Alabama, and South Carolina. It is our principal artesian aquifer and is the largest, oldest, and deepest aquifer in the southeastern United States. Unlike water in surficial aquifers (those closer to the surface), groundwater in the Floridan Aquifer is mostly contained under pressure by a confin-

A Waterwise Landscape Is Sustainable

Designing a landscape so that it does not demand such a large portion of our freshwater reserves will ease some of the strain on Florida's precious water supply.

Smart use of irrigation systems and developing alternate water sources for irrigation such as harvested rainwater and gray water will further reduce the depletion of our freshwater supply.

ing bed of impermeable sediments and rock—often limestone. When the water pressure is great enough, water breaks to the surface and a spring flows. Florida has many remarkable springs, especially in the northern and west central parts of the state. Their water temperature and volume are usually constant throughout the seasons.

Surficial aquifers, water-laden shallow beds of shells and sand, lie less than 100 feet underground. There are several of these shallower aquifers across the state, and in most places they are separated from the Floridan Aquifer by a bed of soil or rock. The groundwater in these aquifers moves continuously from areas of moisture to drier areas and may join with other waters. They are recharged locally, and the water table fluctuates in response to drought or rainfall. Seasonal temperature and volume of flow from these water table springs or groundwater ponds varies significantly. These shallow aquifers are also more likely to be affected by pollution at the surface.

More than 90 percent of Florida's drinking water comes from either the Floridan Aquifer system or the surficial aquifers. Water is drawn either from individual wells or municipal well systems. People have found, and studies have shown, that if too much water is drawn from our aquifers, salt water can intrude in response to the decreased pressure. Sinkholes form when lack of underlying pressure causes weakness at the ground surface, which collapses into the open cavity below. While sinkholes form in natural environments, more occur when aquifers are not well charged with water. To help the state maintain its water supplies, Florida's five water management districts monitor water quality and availability from wells, sinkhole formations, surface waters, and other holding areas and also consider applications for new developments in terms of their potential water usage. Because of Florida's ever-growing human population and its apparently quenchless water demands, this is no easy task.

Drought

Drought is a fact of life even though Florida receives a good amount of rain on average. The exact definition of drought is hard to pin down, though. A meteorologist might define a drought with statistics that indicate a significantly lower than average rainfall over a season or two. A farmer or gardener would define drought by the loss of plants that, given average rainfall, would normally survive or by the extra irrigation needed to keep them alive. The hydrologists at your local water management district, in fact, define drought by the lowered ground- and surface water tables.

If you haven't already lived through one, you will know when your region is experiencing a serious drought by the extra irrigation needed to keep your landscape plants from wilting, by the lower levels of local groundwater ponds, and by the occurrence of more wildfires than normal. In response, your water management district will probably restrict water use just when you could use the water more.

Install a rain gauge to monitor rainfall on your property; reports from centralized weather stations don't reflect your specific precipitation. Florida's weather patterns and storms produce rain patterns that vary greatly across a region. Coordinate your watering schedule with the rainfall so that your landscape receives only the amount it needs. If Mother Nature supplies adequate rainfall over a two-week period, then most of your landscape should not be irrigated during that time. The exceptions might be vegetable beds, fruit trees during certain seasons, container gardens, and newly planted trees and shrubs. To water these, use harvested rainwater from your rain barrels or cistern whenever possible.

A rain gauge helps to coordinate your irrigation schedule with the rainfall so your landscape receives only the amount it needs. In Florida rainfall is highly local.

Drought Proofing Your Landscape

Installing a desert landscape is probably too extreme, and it certainly wouldn't represent the spectrum of native landscapes Mother Nature has created here in Florida. Instead, there are sustainable actions you can take to prepare your landscape for drought and water conservation. Plant for the microclimates on your property and create irrigation-free zones. In Florida's heat, even "full-sun" plants may appreciate some afternoon shade to reduce their need for extra irrigation. On the other hand, some heat-loving succulents like yucca and prickly pear thrive near pavement, hot rocks, and western exposures with reflected heat. Adjust your watering routine to the least amount possible to promote good plant growth.

Whether it's the dry or the wet season, follow any announced water restrictions or limitations. Watering in the early morning works best: because there's usually less wind and less heat from the sun before 10:00 a.m., evaporation is reduced and less water is wasted. Plus, plants that dry off thoroughly during the day aren't as susceptible to fungal infection. As a rule of thumb, irrigate less often and only when needed, but when you do irrigate, water deeply. For a drought-resistant landscape, water once a week during the growing season to provide the equivalent of roughly one inch of rain in combination with the natural rainfall. This will train your plants to grow their roots deeper into the soil to search out the water. Frequent light waterings promote shallow root growth, leaving plants unprepared to weather drought or periods of restricted watering. Surface soil dries more quickly than deep soil—this is true even for sandy soils. Change your watering routine gradually to give your plants time to adjust as their roots grow deeper. This may take several months or even the whole dry season to accomplish. Some of your plants probably won't tolerate these new conditions: find a fitting microclimate for them or send them to your compost pile.

Rather than overuse water resources, it's often better to replace plants that have high water requirements with drought-tolerant plants: native perennials, bunching grasses, and selected shrubs and trees. Group plants with similar irrigation needs together, so if extra irrigation is necessary, only those plants that need the water will receive it. A few fussy plants should not dictate the irrigation for rest of your landscape. In fact, if you've started to replace the non-native plants in your landscape with natives, those natives may not do well in a highly irrigated environment. The most sustainable gardens are ones that thrive with no additional watering after an initial adjustment period.

Do mulch your beds, but make sure that the top layer of mulch stays loose so that water from irrigation and rain can soak in. Some types of mulch tend to form a crusty top layer as they dry. At the start of the dry season, lightly rake the top layer of mulch and, if needed, add a little more to keep the thickness at an ideal three inches. Pay special attention around trees and shrubs. When too much mulch is piled around trees, it may actually shed water, preventing it from soaking into the soil. Mulch should not lean against trees or any other plants in the landscape.

In addition to mulching, add compost and other organic materials to your soil on a regular basis. Whether your soil is sandy, clayey, or gravely, the nutrients and important soil microbes in your compost will improve the soil and keep its ecosystem in good shape. Added to clayey soil, compost and humus increase air spaces and reduce the clay's compaction. In sandy and gravely soils, compost increases water-holding capacity. It's a good idea to apply compost to all your beds, especially around trees and shrubs, before the dry season gets started. Remove the top layer of mulch; add the compost, placing heavier concentrations at and just outside the drip line of your trees and shrubs; then replace the mulch. With its improved water absorption, the loose mulch will insulate the soil from the heat and increase its water-holding capacity.

Weeds compete with your desirable plants for water; so get rid of them. Before the dry season begins, you might also want to thin and prune back your woody plants and perennials. With less vegetation to support, more water will be available to them. Leave enough density to maintain optimal screening and habitat, but give the plants some breathing room. Except for dormant woody plants in northern Florida, the dry season is not normally a good time to transplant—wait for the rains.

Best Practices during Drought

Don't fertilize, over water, or otherwise stimulate plants to grow: growth surges aren't sustainable during a drought. Let your plants return to a semidormant or maintenance stage. Trim back weaker growth to reduce the vegetation load. Move your container plants into more shaded areas to reduce their need for water. Healthy plants are more resistant to disease and water stress than weak ones, so it's most sustainable to provide your plants with the best conditions you possibly can.

Reduce the amount of lawn in your landscape, especially where it isn't growing well. The turfgrass you *do* decide to keep should be mowed less often and at the highest level recommended for that particular species. During its cool-weather, or other slow-growth periods, mow your lawn only as needed: it may not need mowing for months.

During a severe drought, especially when strict water restrictions are in force, your plants may become stressed and face greater risk of attack from insects and other pests. If you find infestations, treat them using IPM methods (see chapter 9), but go easy on soapy water solutions because soaps can damage thirsty plants. Hand water your stressed specimens first. Once they regain their turgidity, work on picking off the offending bugs or wiping off the fungal coatings.

If parts of a plant are hopelessly infested or have been wilted past resurrection, carefully trim off the affected parts and be careful to dispose of them as sealed trash to reduce chances of reinfestation. Rubbing your saw or lopper blades with alcohol will reduce the spread of disease. If a diseased plant is beyond help, pull it up and consign it to the trash (not the compost pile) before its infestation spreads more widely across your landscape.

If a plant wilts in the afternoon on a hot, sunny day, that may be its normal reaction, but if it is still droopy early the next morning, you probably need to irrigate. If the soil is moist, the plant may be a goner.

When you do get rain during a drought, you'll be happy to have a good rain harvesting system to augment your irrigation supply. But a couple of storms will not end the drought. Enough rain needs to fall over the course

Water Movement in Plants

Our hearts actively pump blood around our bodies to deliver the sugars, oxygen, and other vital elements we need to live. Plants rely on a passive process, called "transpiration," to move water and nutrients through their tissues. In addition to transporting nutrients, plants use water for photosynthesis, for keeping their cells turgid, and for air conditioning: as water evaporates it cools the leaf surface by ten to fifteen degrees Fahrenheit. When a plant lacks sufficient water, its cells become flaccid and the plant wilts. A healthy plant's living tissues are 75 to 90 percent water.

For every ounce of water used in photosynthesis, 300 to 500 ounces evaporate into the air. A mature oak tree can transpire 40,000 gallons per year and, as a result of the accompanying evaporation, it can be as much as 20 degrees Fahrenheit cooler in a forested landscape than out in the sun. Healthy green plants transport water from the ground to the atmosphere, and water vapor in the atmosphere feeds the weather systems so rain falls back to the ground again. It's all part of the hydrological (water) cycle: the more biomass (volume of living material) we have in our landscapes, the more water is transpired; the more air is cooled, the more rain we receive.

of the wet and dry seasons for the aquifers and groundwater to begin to recover. There is a delay between rainfall and actual recharge. It can take weeks or even months for rainwater working its way through the soil to reach groundwater level. Sandy soil, of course, has a faster recharge rate than clay.

So that you can repeat your drought-proofing successes, make note of which plants do well during a drought and which ones fare poorly. The next time a drought comes along (and it will), you and your landscape will be better prepared.

Saving Water

Water is a precious resource and must be conserved. Many of us are generally aware of some of the common conservation ideas for daily living such as taking shorter showers and turning off the water while brushing teeth. While all the many ways to save water are important, here are some ideas specifically for the gardener.

- Harvest rainwater from roofs and other impervious surfaces. Use it for all your manual (and maybe automated) irrigation needs. There are many other ways to put this extra water source to work for you. Use it to prerinse root vegetables from your garden, rinse off muddy garden tools (and the muddy gardener), to make compost extract, and to wet your compost piles. Harvested rainwater can also be used for washing your vehicles and topping off your pool. See more details and uses in chapter 11.
- Put a bucket under the faucet as you're waiting for hot water in the shower or bath to catch what would ordinarily be wasted water for watering your plants. Let the water sit for a day before you use to let the chlorine dissipate.
  When you rinse your vegetables, muddy tools, gloves, or dirty hands, put a basin or a bucket under the flow of water and use the basin water on your compost pile or to water container gardens.
- If you use a hose for watering, use a nozzle that shuts off while you are on your way to area that needs the extra irrigation.

- Adjust your irrigation spray pattern so it doesn't water the street, sidewalk, driveway, or other impervious surfaces. Water only during the active growing season and follow all restrictions.
- Don't spray water to clean your driveway or sidewalks. Use a broom or rake instead.
- Install a coldwater outside shower. Gardening and other outside physical activity in Florida's heat will make you hot and sweaty. Instead of tracking mud and sweat through the house to the bath-

SHOWER HEAD AFFIXED TO A SERIES OF PVC PIPES WITH AN ON-OFF VALVE

OUTSIDE SPIGOT WITH "Y" FIXTURE - ONE TO HOSE & SHOWER

AN OUTSIDE SHOWER SAVES WATER

If you use a cold-water outside shower after gardening, you'll cool off quickly, save water, and keep the house cleaner. Using a Y-fixture on a standard outside faucet provides one connection to the shower and one to a hose.

room, build a shower near an outside spigot. Install a Y-connection if you need to use the spigot for other uses. Outdoor showers are sustainable because:

- you won't waste water while waiting for hot water to work through the pipes—there won't be any;
- you'll be less likely to linger in a cold shower, although it does feel good after vigorous activity on a warm day. Also, if you're thoroughly cooled down when you go inside, you won't feel the need to lower the temperature on your air conditioner;
- the inside shower won't need to be cleaned as often. This saves water and reduces the use of water and chemicals in your septic or sewer system;
- nearby plants get an extra watering on a regular basis. You'll be creating a damp microclimate.

Each water-saving idea may not seem like much, but if all Floridians worked just a little harder at conserving water, together we could make a huge impact on our water consumption and actually ease the strain on our aquifers.

Irrigation

Getting the necessary amounts of water to your plants can be as simple as using a watering can or garden hose or as complex as installing and maintaining highly automated sprinkler and drip irrigation systems. Most of us, especially those interested in sustainable gardening and water conservation, use some combination of manual and automated watering. Automated systems can be quite effective in saving water if we use some common sense. Unfortunately, automated systems are one of the reasons our lawns and gardens are over watered. Too many folks think "automated" means "set it, and forget it." You can and should use automated systems, but good water-use practices require careful planning, observation, and human intervention. Sustainable and best management practices *will* reduce water usage by coordinating it with real needs, but such coordination requires the human touch.

Whatever the design of an irrigation system, the frequency and duration of irrigation should be adjusted during rainy periods so that the sum of precipitation and irrigation totals no more than one inch per week during the growing season. During the dry season, reduce this amount as deciduous woody plants and lawns go dormant, depending on your region. This strategy makes perfect sense for the central to northern regions of the state, where the dry season and the cool season correspond. Even in tropical South Florida, though, you should still be able to reduce irrigation rates during the normal dry season months, especially if you've used mostly native plant species in your landscape.

Use your rain gauge to determine how much rain you receive within a set time period—maybe two weeks. Keep a record and coordinate your irrigation times accordingly. In order to accomplish this, you will also need to calibrate your irrigation patterns so you know how long it takes to apply one inch of water. This is a straightforward exercise if your irrigation system uses spray sprinklers that shoot water into the air across the landscape. Place vertical-sided containers, and maybe your rain gauge, in various random spots throughout out the region within range of one particular device such as an individual sprinkler head. Then turn on the system for 15 minutes and measure your amounts. If the water measures one third of an inch on average, then a 45-minute session will irrigate to one inch.

Drip or soaker systems are more difficult to gauge. The rule of thumb is that you get the equivalent of an inch of rainwater from a one-gallon-per-hour emitter with an hour's run time. The distance between emitters is a big variable, though. You may have to let the plants tell you how much water they need.

Water Sources

The first consideration for an irrigation system is the water source. If you are subject to a permitting process where you live, you may be required to use the lowest quality of water available. Potable water provided by municipalities is treated for human consumption and should only be used as a last resort for irrigation. Further, if you have a water softener system, don't use the water that goes through it on any plants—the salts could kill them.

There are several nonpotable, lower quality water sources that are suitable for landscape irrigation. They are listed here from most to least sustainable.

Gray water: This water is collected from sink and shower drains and all water-using appliances in a building (except those linked to sewage or "black water") and is retained in a storage tank. It can be used for irrigation and other functions that don't require a potable water source, such as flushing toilets and supplying outside faucets. Many new housing developments are now planned with gray water systems. Installing a gray water system is definitely a sustainable choice, because it reuses water and reduces strain on sewer and septic systems. Because gray water is the lowest water quality source, it is the preferable source. If you have a gray water system, minimize your use of soap and detergents and use the least caustic cleaning products so you don't poison your plants.

Harvested rainwater: This works as a total irrigation source only if you have a large roof area compared to the size of your landscape or if you have a normal roof area combined with stormwater collection from ground-level impervious surfaces. For harvested rainwater to meet all your irrigation needs, even through a drought, you will probably require a fairly large cistern. Do the math before you install a permanent system. You can harvest 300 gallons of water from a one-inch rainfall on a 500–square foot surface regardless of its slope. (See chapter 11 for details.) On a smaller scale, harvested rainwater collected in rain barrels can supplement other water systems or provide enough water for a soaker hose through a vegetable garden or some other high moisture landscape feature. Some systems add excess harvested rainwater to the gray water cisterns, which will further dilute any soapiness.

Surface water: If your property backs up to or includes a body of fresh (or almost fresh) water with a fairly reliable water level such as a lake, pond, stormwater retention pond, river, or canal, this surface water can become your source for irrigation. A pump will drive a system like this. If you use nutrient-rich lake or pond water, then you really won't need to add any fertilizer to your general landscape areas, including your lawn, because you're fertilizing with every watering.

Shallow well water: A well into a surficial aquifer or groundwater does put a load on the groundwater, but it is more sustainable than a deep well to the Floridan Aquifer, which should be reserved only for drinking water.

Irrigation Design Considerations

Whether you use manual irrigation methods or have an inground automated system, the irrigation needs for different parts of your landscape vary and each section should be treated appropriately. Your vegetable plot will require more irrigation than a restored woodland, and your container gardens will need watering more often than your lawn. As much as possible, divide your landscape into like zones and tailor the irrigation system to best suit each zone. A drip system is a good choice for watering your trees, shrubs, containers, and general landscape mulched beds. A spray system works well for lawn areas, and microspray systems are ideal for raised beds.

An important consideration in the design of a system is to water only the landscape—not the driveways, parking lots, or buildings. The reason for this is primarily to conserve water but secondarily—because so much of Florida's groundwater contains iron—to prevent well-water spray from leaving reddish stains on buildings and other surfaces. These stains are difficult, if not impossible, to wash off and may even reduce your property value. Create a system that sprays away from buildings and other impervious surfaces.

A wide range of irrigation systems is available to property owners and land managers: the hose and sprinkler; the garden cart with built-in water tank and sprayer; tree watering bags that slowly drip water out around newly planted trees; the do-it-yourself drip system with tubing and emitters on a timer; and the sophisticated and somewhat expensive inground computerized system. The most suitable system depends upon your budget and your landscape—both its size and character. It also depends upon people and their energy and dedication to the care of the land. Permanent irrigation systems are not usually required or desired for small spaces or for native habitats, but a temporary drip system, such as the tree watering bag, can be useful when new trees or shrubs have been planted.

Rain Sensors

All permanent irrigation systems are required by a 1991 Florida law to have an automatic shut-off device or rain sensor. This device hooks into your timer or controller, which turns off the irrigation once a certain amount of rain falls. The rain sensor needs to be mounted in the open where the rainfall is unobstructed and where the irrigation sprinklers will not hit it. Rain sensors operate by one of two methods for measuring rainfall. The first uses a straight-sided dish to weigh the rainwater. The main disadvantage of this method is that it will weigh anything that gets into the dish, from fallen debris to a tree frog enjoying a bath. The second and most commonly used method uses a device fitted with absorbent pads or disks. When enough rainwater is absorbed, the pads expand and shut off a pressure switch. The amount of rain required for shutoff is usually set by rotating the disks or by choosing notch settings.

Of course, if you are around when rain is forecast, you can turn off the irrigation system yourself. The shut-off devices really pay off when you are away or in the event of a rainfall event you aren't aware of. We all sometimes miss those overnight rains that fall when we are sound asleep: if your irrigation timer is set to start at five in the morning, the rain sensor will step in where you can't and turn the irrigation off. While such devices are important aids in conserving water, they are not a substitute for your attention and intervention.

Inground, Computerized Sprayer Systems

Though there are different brands and models, inground, automatic sprayer irrigation is a pressurized system with a pump that is set to turn on when there is a drop in its internal pressure. When the computer opens a valve for a zone to be watered, this lowers the pressure and the pump turns on, which activates the sprayers in that zone. Some pop up in response to the water pressure, while others are stationary. They spray either in a settable rotating pattern or in a constant spray. When the computer closes the valve, the sprayers shut off and sink back into the ground. Individual zones can be programmed for various lengths of time and may use different types of removable sprayer fittings depending on the need. Some sprayers are mounted on top of permanent poles for more height. These can be useful for delivering water to plants in large areas where densely planted or tall trees and shrubs would obstruct the spray at ground level. Don't use the pole mounts in mowed areas, though, because they'll make mowing more difficult.

Normally installed by a professional or specialist, computerized inground systems are widely used in residential and commercial properties in Florida. The biggest advantage of this kind of system is that once it's installed and calibrated, it's easy to use. Ongoing maintenance is limited to checking the spray nozzles once every season and checking for leaks by watching the pressure gauge on the pump when the system is not turned on. On the minus side, automated inground systems are too easy to use. People give using them little or no thought, so over watering is common. These systems have two other disadvantages as well: a lot of water evaporates from the shooting spray, and the spray wets plant foliage, creating a favorable environment for fungal growth. To counter these drawbacks, use your sprayer system in the early morning hours, before the temperature rises and when the winds are normally lowest. This reduces the amount of water lost to evaporation and it allows the leaves to dry out during the day to discourage the fungi.

Drip Systems

A drip irrigation system is one in which water is applied to the soil by soaker hoses, porous pipes, or tubes with emitters. Florida's agriculture industry leads the nation in the use of drip systems. Drip systems have a number of advantages. First, little water is lost to evaporation. Second, no trenching is necessary to set up a drip system. Next, because water is delivered to the root zone, foliage stays dry and conditions for fungal diseases are diminished. Fourth, because the ground surface outside the root zone isn't irrigated, weed numbers are reduced. Finally, property owners can design and install their own drip systems using soaker hoses or kits. A drip system is necessary wherever plastic sheeting is used between garden rows.

The simplest of the drip systems is a soaker hose—usually a flat section of hose with many tiny holes along its length. Soaker hoses can be used with any water source that has a standard outdoor water spigot. Usually, you'll want to run a regular garden hose from the spigot to the plant area and connect that to the soaker hose, which you will arrange around the plants to be watered. If you use a soaker hose with a rain barrel, remember to turn it off or your whole 55 gallons could be drained in one drip session. To prevent this problem, you can insert a mechanical timer at the spigot. Remember, too, that since water from a rain barrel is gravity fed, the higher the rain barrel sits above the area to be watered, the more water you'll use because of the increased pressure.

Another simple drip system is a plastic bag or other container with pinholes in the bottom that you fill with water. The water seeps slowly into the soil near a newly planted tree or into a container garden. Bag systems are useful for those times when you'll be away and unable to water by hand each day.

Many kits and parts for more extensive drip systems are available at retail stores. The system can be designed for one set of circumstances and then reconfigured to better serve a change in the landscape or as a temporary setup for newly planted trees and shrubs. No special tools are required, and if you accidentally cut a line, you can repair it with a connector or a "goof plug." Except for lawns, almost any type of landscape can be serviced by a drip system—including containers. Depending on their size, containers are usually set up with spur hoses that have two or three emitters emptying into the pot.

Normally drip system tubes are laid on the soil around the landscape and pinned down with U-shaped staples. Install enough emitters so that at least 50 percent of the area around a small tree's drip line is watered. In a vegetable bed, emitters should be located along a row or planting area so that all the root zones are covered. Most people cover the tubing with mulch to hide the system after testing for leaks and making sure all the emitters are working.

In addition to tubing and emitters, you will need a backflow stop, which prevents contamination of the main water supply, a pressure regulator (this is a low pressure system), and a filter to trap particles from your water supply and prevent clogging of the system. Normally you'd have a timer: some can be programmed like the computer in a sprayer system; others are simple mechanical timers that you set when you turn on the water.

The low-pressure attribute of drip systems makes them susceptible to clogging from soil leaking into the tubes and from buildup of hard water salts and slime from fungi. Regular flushing of the system is necessary to address this problem, and the tubes need to be periodically uncovered and checked for leaks. Because you can't see how it's working, regularly scheduled maintenance is crucial to a drip system's effectiveness.

Manual Systems

Even if you have an automated irrigation system, you'll still need a manual method to augment the irrigation for new seedlings and newly transplanted plants—especially trees and shrubs, vegetables, and the like. Hooking up a hose to a faucet for hand watering a section of a garden or setting up a sprinkler in the yard are traditional watering methods, and getting out in the landscape helps you stay aware of its condition. Since manual systems depend entirely upon your time and energy, the tendency is to under water with the hose nozzle and to over water with a sprinkler.

Hauling watering cans to the outer reaches of your property is good exercise, but if it's too difficult, then maybe your fussy plants out there need to be moved closer. If long-distance watering is a normal situation for you, it might be worthwhile to purchase a watering wagon to reduce the strain. You can fill any type of hauling system from your rain barrels. Additionally, you can set up your rain barrel overflow to fill your watering cans before it flows into a rain garden. It's most sustainable to use a combination of irrigating methods to augment the rains, so your various types of plants and gardens will be supplied with the amount and frequency of water to produce good growth.

Waterwise Landscaping Is Important

Working to use water wisely in the landscape is one of the most sustainable actions you can take. Weaning your plants of their dependence on too much irrigation will take time, but it will make them stronger and prepare them for droughts. As a waterwise gardener, you will be helping to safeguard the future of Florida's water supply.

Resources

Web Sites

Each of the five water management districts has its own regulations, but they've combined resources to put together an 80-page booklet, *Waterwise Florida Landscapes* (2006): http://www.swfwmd.state.fl.us.

Northwest Florida Water Management District: http://www.nwfwmd.state.fl.us.

South Florida Water Management District: http://www.sfwmd.gov.

Southwest Florida Water Management District: http://www.swfwmd.state.fl.us.

St. Johns River Water Management District: http://www.sjrwmd.com.

Suwannee River Water Management District: http://www.srwmd.state.fl.us.

The Florida Department of Environmental Protection offers information on drought and help for dealing with it: http://www.dep.state.fl.us.

Florida's DEP hosts an informative site on the state's extraordinary springs: http://www.floridasprings.org.

For irrigation system articles, installation directions, and products, visit the Urban Farmer Store online: http://www.urbanfarmerstore.com.

The University of Central Florida's Stormwater Management Academy provides detailed information on handling stormwater: http://www.stormwater.ucf.edu.

Books

Christopher, Thomas. *Water-Wise Gardening, America's Backyard Revolution.* New York: Simon & Schuster, 1994.

Cook, Ian. *Waterwise Gardening: Water, Plants and Climate, A Practical Guide.* London: New Holland, 2009.

11

Harvesting Rainwater

Rainwater is a valuable resource, not a waste product. But you'd never guess that here in Florida! The "pipe and pond" treatments so widely used in this state are designed to get rid of water as quickly as possible. Our rainwater is treated like garbage.

Before so much of our state was covered with impervious surfaces, rainwater that was not soaked up by the jungle of plants percolated through the soil and recharged the groundwater and aquifers. Those of us who have helped replace Florida's jungle can make a constructive difference now. Using rain barrels, cisterns, rain gardens, and other water retention features can substantially reduce the first flush of stormwater. This will ease the pressure on community stormwater systems and ultimately help improve the water quality in both our surface waterways and in our groundwater and aquifer formations.

Rain barrels and cisterns catch gutter runoff from roofs and provide a source of chemical-free water. There are many uses for harvested rainwater, but most people use it for watering plants, especially container plants—indoors and out. Mosquitoes are rarely a problem with today's rain barrel systems because screens cover any openings. Unlike our more northerly neighbors, we can use our rain barrels year round—liquid savings for sunny days.

Harvesting Rainwater Is Sustainable

Harvesting rainwater from roofs reduces the volume of the first rush of stormwater into community stormwater systems. Collectively, rain barrels in a community can reduce the necessity for enlarging or redesigning the public stormwater systems. A building with four standard 55-gallon drums will capture more than 200 gallons of rainwater before any of it flows into stormwater systems.

Rainwater is better for plants because it's not chlorinated or artificially softened. You can attach a drip irrigation system to a rain barrel to create a passive watering system for nearby gardens.

Building rain barrels from used syrup or other food-grade containers recycles these plastic objects that might otherwise end up in a landfill.

Harvesting rainwater is not new—it has been practiced from the earliest civilizations down to the present. These days, harvesting is usually accomplished with a series of rain barrels and/or cisterns situated to catch water from roofs and other impervious surfaces via gutters, downspouts, and drains.

Cisterns can store a substantial amount of rainwater—from hundreds to thousands of gallons. When you collect this much water, you can use it to flush your toilets, wash your clothes, or irrigate your landscape. Cisterns are also recommended for firewise landscaping, so that firefighters can have access to an extra cache of local water.

Capturing runoff from ground level impervious surfaces such as driveways, parking lots, or roads is also important. This rainwater can be directed into underground cisterns by a system of French drains and/or bioswales. It can also be directed into rain gardens (shallow gullies or swales planted with deep-rooted plants that tolerate both wet and dry conditions), where much of the water can be absorbed (see chapter 12).

Uses for Rainwater

We know that rainwater is wonderful for plants, but there are many other benefits and uses of this naturally soft water distilled by Mother Nature. Use rainwater

to dampen your compost pile—it won't kill the microbes;

to wash your hair—it won't weigh your hair with hard water residues. (Some of us are old enough to remember this use);

to bathe your pets;

to wash your vehicles (no hard water spots) and to fill their radiators;

to rinse off your garden tools, prerinse your muddy work clothes, and prewash root vegetables from your garden;

to use for your washing machine or to flush toilets, if you collect enough rainwater;

to top off your pool as water evaporates;

to supply a drip irrigation system or a soaker hose to irrigate gardens with high water needs;

to fight wildfires near your house, if you have a high capacity system;

to supply an outside shower. If it's on the sunny side of the building, your shower will be solar heated.

Gauging the Water

Before you design your rain harvesting system, you need to calculate the number of gallons of water you can expect to capture from your roof run-off. To figure out a roof's surface area, measure the length and width of the building—this calculation holds true no matter how steep the slope. Then estimate the fraction of the roof's surface area that is served by each downspout. Use this equation: Gallons = 0.6 × (Inches of Rain) × (Surface Area in Square Feet). The 0.6 is the conversion factor to translate inches of rainfall to gallons. Actually, 0.62333 is possible, but you won't collect every drop of rain—some of it evaporates or is blown off the roof—so 0.6 is a good estimate and it's easier on the brain. For example, if you receive one inch of rain and a gutter system collects rainwater from one fourth of a 2,000-square-foot roof (2,000/4 = 500 square feet), then 300 gallons of water will run through that gutter's downspout (0.6 × 1 inch × 500 square feet = 300 gallons).

The average yearly rainfall in Florida is between 39 and 64 inches, but for our purposes we'll use 50 inches. So on average you'll collect approximately 300 × 50 or 15,000 gallons of water from that one downspout each year. Of course some years you'll get less and some more, but now you'll know approximately how much water you'll be dealing with. Any way you look at it, that's a lot of water. And if you capture it, you don't have to pay for it, and all that water doesn't rush into the community's stormwater system. Usually plants absorb most of the harvested water used in the landscape. The rest will soak into the soil or evaporate as you use it.

Roof Evaluation

In addition to the surface area, you need to consider how your roof type affects rain capture.

- Metal roofs get hot and the first raindrops will evaporate, but other than that a metal roof is probably the most efficient water-harvesting surface. It's smooth, and the vertical channels form protected pathways to keep the rain from blowing off the roof when there is a crosswind. If there are lead-based solders and flashing, the rainwater will not be usable in a potable system, but it will be perfectly usable in the landscape, even your edible garden.
- Tile roofs have a lot of surface area per square foot, but once the rain flows into the channels, it is quite efficient. Tile does not deteriorate and should provide good clean rainwater for the long run.
- Asphalt roofs are rough and reduce water flow slightly. Because asphalt is a petroleum product, asphalt roofs can leach out contaminants in small amounts, and tiny pieces may break off from older roofs. Captured rainwater isn't suitable for a potable water system, but it is generally acceptable for plants, even vegetables.

When you run your rainwater through a fine screen into a rain barrel, the small mineral granules will be filtered out.

- Cedar shake roofs are usually treated with antifungal and anti-mossing herbicides to help them last longer. As a result, rainwater off a new cedar roof isn't going to be good for your plants; an older roof may discharge a reduced herbicide load. If you're concerned about these chemicals, you could run the rainwater through a sand filter to a pond where they will be diluted. You could then use the pond water for irrigation purposes. Left untreated, this water is fine for fighting fires, though.
- Zinc strips are sometimes installed on roofs to help reduce moss and algae growth. With each rain, the strips release zinc leachates in amounts harmful to fish and other wildlife, as well as to your plants. Remove zinc strips before installing a rain barrel or cistern.

To improve the quality of your captured water, you can construct a rain harvesting system with a first flush roof washer to divert dust, pollen, bird poop, and other contaminants away from your main tanks. A roof washer will capture the first few gallons of water in a separate container or in a wide collection tube with a float that stops the water flow once this diversion tube is full. A roof washer is probably not necessary for a system that is harvesting water solely for landscape use, but it may make you feel better about the quality of your water.

If your roof is not suitable for rainwater harvesting, you can install stand-alone rain collection devices. Some look like upside-down umbrellas: arrange them in your landscape as artful shade providers. You can also collect water from a work shed, temporary carport, or other roofed structures.

Rain Barrel Configurations

You can purchase ready-made rain barrels. You can also attend a rain barrel workshop sponsored by one of Florida's county extension offices, where you'll learn how to make a rain barrel and go home with one you made yourself. You can also find detailed directions from various sources and create a rain barrel system that suits your specific needs. There is no one right answer, but any way you harvest rainwater is better than letting it all get away.

Plastic drums (usually 55 gallons) that have contained food products are recommended for rain barrels. Barrels that have previously held certain nonhazardous cleaning products could be used, but they will need a thorough rinsing. Do not use barrels that have been filled with petroleum or toxic chemicals. Finding barrels to use may take some sleuthing, but bottling plants, restaurants, or food processing and import companies often have food-grade barrels left over. If you have a choice, get ones that are opaque, because white or light-colored barrels will let in enough light to allow algae to grow inside. You'll need to clean out the white barrels more often than dark ones—maybe every four or five years. You could paint the barrels, of course, but eventually the paint will peel if the barrel is in a sunny location. You will need to determine the best solution for your situation.

Rain barrels can be set up to work individually or in a series, and your systems can be either closed or open. In a closed system, once the barrel is full, the remainder of the water is diverted back through the downspout. In an open system, once all the barrels fill up with the downspout water, the last overflow hose directs the excess to a landscape area that can absorb the extra water—a rain garden, a pond, or a natural swale in a wooded area. The overflow could also go to a cistern for more storage capacity.

An Open Rain Barrel System

There are various configurations for an open rain barrel system. The first barrel in the system needs a method for accepting rainwater from the downspout. This requires a downspout modification designed to get all of its water into the barrel. For a rain barrel with a screened hole on top, a flexible downspout diverter or elbow rests on the edge of the barrel and empties its water into the hole. The advantage of this method is that the screen keeps the small sticks and leaves that come through the downspout from entering the rain barrel, which also reduces the need for cleaning out the barrel.

One way to create a screened opening is to purchase a small plastic or wire basket (eight or nine inches in diameter works well) with a firm lip around the top. Cover the top of the basket with a metal or fiberglass screen and fold or staple the screening to the rim. Cut a hole in the top of the barrel so the body of the basket just fits inside the hole, but the rim or lip of the basket does not. This basket can sit loosely in the hole or you can screw it in place. Another screening method is to remove most of the barrel top and fasten the screen securely around the outside of the barrel or to the remainder of the top. However you arrange it, the water goes into the barrel but sticks, leaves, and mosquitoes do not.

Install a plastic or metal ¾-inch **hose bibb** (spigot) near the bottom of the barrel so that you can drain it dry. A hose bibb is threaded, so you'll need the correct tool to create the threads in the side of the barrel. Use regular plumbing methods (Teflon tape and silicone sealant) to seal this fixture. There will be significant water pressure when the barrel is full.

The last feature you need to create is an overflow outlet. Excess water can either go into the top of the next barrel in a series or it can empty into the landscape. Flexible, ribbed plastic pipe two inches in diameter can be used for the overflow. Drill or cut a hole near the top of the barrel so that the pipe fits securely into the hole. You can affix it to the barrel, but since there will be very little water pressure, gluing it or securing it in place probably won't be necessary.

Figure out the height of the rain barrel in its final spot near the downspout. It should be elevated on two or more layers of cinderblocks or other stable stand so that the barrel is high enough off the ground to fit a bucket or watering can under the hose bibb. Mount the rain barrels higher if you'll be using them to supply water for a soaker hose or drip system. The barrel should be level or leaning slightly toward the building. Take the time to position the cinderblocks so they won't sink or move with the weight of the water on them. For the best stability lay two blocks side-by-side in one direction, and if you need additional height, lay two more in the opposite direction on top of those, making a square, solid base for each barrel. Some people build a special deck or platform for their barrels. Whatever platform you use, it has to be sturdy—a 50-gallon container will weigh more than 400 pounds when it's full of water.

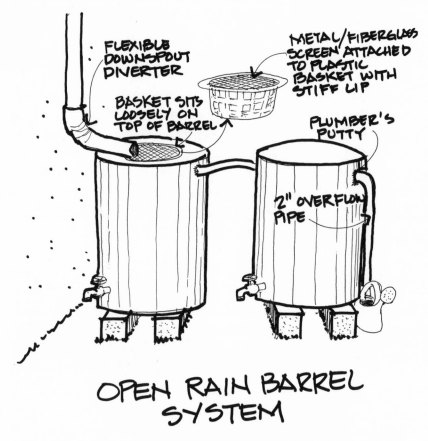

FLEXIBLE DOWNSPOUT DIVERTER

METAL/FIBERGLASS SCREEN ATTACHED TO PLASTIC BASKET WITH STIFF LIP

BASKET SITS LOOSELY ON TOP OF BARREL

PLUMBER'S PUTTY

2" OVERFLOW PIPE

OPEN RAIN BARREL SYSTEM

An open rain barrel system can include a series of barrels with overflow pipes that direct excess water into the next barrel or into the landscape. Collect a few more gallons by placing a watering can under the final outflow. Direct the excess away from buildings and into planned water retention areas.

When the barrel is in place and you have the downspout diverter in hand, saw through the downspout and fit the flexible diverter or elbow over its end so that the other end rests on top edge of the rain barrel and points toward the screened hole. You may need to use a band or hook to stabilize the downspout—attach it to the side of the building.

The next barrel in the series will receive water from the first barrel via the overflow pipe. This barrel will also need the hose bibb near the bottom and its own overflow pipe. Each of the secondary barrels will then have two two-inch holes in their sidewalls on opposite sides of the barrel near the top and one hose bibb near the bottom. When you place a series of barrels next to each other, it's good to plan ahead for sweeping out the leaves that will collect between and behind them. Leave enough room for a broom or rake.

You could connect all the bottom outlets together to one pipe with one hose bibb that drains water from all the barrels at one time. The advantage of this system would be that with only one drainage point you'd have more volume for a drip irrigation system. The disadvantage is that because all the barrels are attached together with a rigid structure, if one needs to be cleaned, you may need to empty all of the barrels. Also, you'll only be able to fill one watering can or bucket at a time.

A Closed Rain Barrel System

Closed systems usually consist of one single barrel located in a restricted site and fitted with a diverter that pushes overflow back into the downspout when the barrel is full. The system is "closed" because there is not a separate overflow outlet—the input and output are through the same pipe. A closed system is suitable only where the downspout water goes through a pipe away from the building to a drainage system or water retention feature such as a pond or a rain garden.

The key feature of a closed system is the diverter. When it rains, the diverter directs the rainwater into the barrel through a pipe (or hose) that is mounted on its side near the bottom. When the barrel fills up, the water backs up through the pipe since there are no air holes or vents in the barrel. As the water collects in the catch basin of the diverter, it reaches the top of the overflow pipe and drains into the downspout. Once the rain stops, the water left in the diverter will slowly drip through the weep holes.

There are commercial diverters available for a closed system, but creating your own is not too difficult. Choose a plastic container that is two or three inches wider than the downspout and at least six inches high to act as your catch basin. Cut away a section of downspout that is an inch or two shorter than the container—if you have an eight-inch-high container, you'll remove six inches of the downspout. You'll need to attach spacers to both parts of the downspout and attach them to the building, because the diverter will sit atop the bottom cut of downspout.

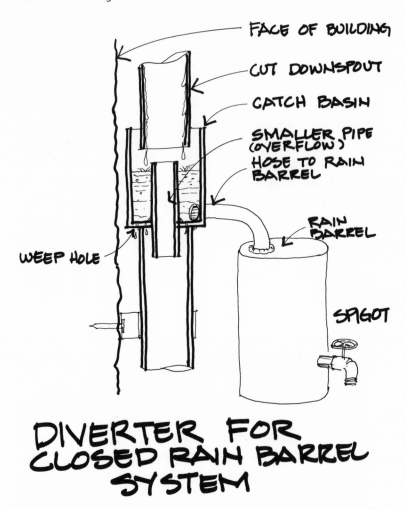

FACE OF BUILDING

CUT DOWNSPOUT

CATCH BASIN

SMALLER PIPE
(OVERFLOW)

HOSE TO RAIN
BARREL

RAIN
BARREL

WEEP HOLE

SPIGOT

DIVERTER FOR CLOSED RAIN BARREL SYSTEM

A closed rain barrel system works best when the downspout is directed into a drainage system. The diverter directs water into the barrel until it is full, then the overflow goes through the downspout.

You'll need to make two holes in the catch basin—one on the side for the pipe fitting that leads to the rain barrel and the other in the bottom to accommodate the overflow pipe. To create a hole for the overflow pipe, trace the outline of the pipe and cut out a hole in the bottom of the container that is just narrower than the outside diameter of the pipe. On the side of the container near the bottom, cut a ¾-inch hole. Also drill three or four weep holes (about ¹⁄₁₆ inch in diameter) in the bottom of the container but not near the center hole. To review: the catch basin will have a two-inch hole plus a few weep holes in the bottom, and it will have a ¾-inch hole on the side, near the bottom.

The overflow pipe is made of two lengths of two-inch pipe that couple at the bottom of the container. (This plumbers' coupling serves to keep the pipe in place with friction.) A four-inch length extends up into the container, and a three-inch length extends below the bottom of the container. Hold the ¾-inch pipe or hose in place with a fitting on the inside of the container. A series of ¾-inch pipes and elbows will go from the diverter through the plastic lid of the barrel. They will not be glued into place but attached with friction flanges. This way, you can lift the diverter from the downspout and twist the pipe assemblage for access to the diverter for cleaning out leaves or pine needles that may collect from the roof. Industrial food-grade barrels will have a ¾-inch fitting on the top into which

This closed rain barrel system diverts downspout water into a series of ¾-inch PVC pipes into the barrel. Once it's full, the water overflows back through the diverter into the downspout.

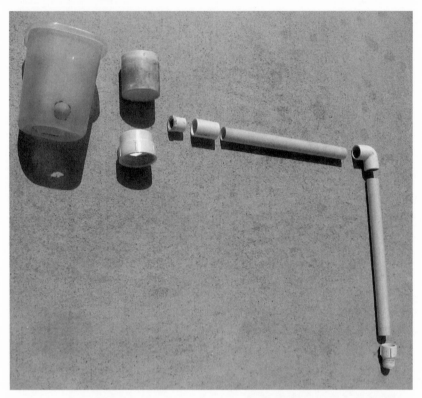

The pieces of the diverter laid out in order: the container with a hole in the bottom and a hole on a side near the bottom, the two-inch pipe fittings that serve as the overflow pipe inside the container, the series of ¾-inch pipes and fittings that direct the water into and out of the barrel.

you can screw your drainage pipes. You could also use hose fittings and a hose for the drainage from the side of the catch basin.

When it rains the water will drain into the ¾-inch pipe and then into the rain barrel. It will burble as air from the barrel is replaced by water. When the barrel is full, the water collects in the bottom of the diverter until it overflows into the overflow pipe and drains into the lower section of downspout. When it stops raining, the water left in the bottom of the diverter will slowly drip through the weep holes.

Depending upon the grade of plastic, the container from which you fashion the diverter will get brittle in Florida's hot sun. You'll probably have to replace it every three years or so. The pipes and fittings will last much longer and can be reused.

Planning for Your Rain Barrel System

Consider the visibility and space available at each downspout and where the runoff goes now. Also consider your need for extra water at that location. Here are two scenarios and possible rain barrel systems that could work for them.

In the first scenario, the downspout is located at an inside corner of a front courtyard garden where it is directed by an 18-inch plastic tray into a garden bed. No water spigot is available. The limited garden area, with no drainage system, floods during heavy rain events. This is a highly visible area with hanging baskets and container gardens in and around the courtyard.

The roof surface area directed to this downspout is 400 square feet for a total of 240 gallons per inch of rainfall. The need for water is high because all those containers and hanging plants need regular watering. Some type of treatment is needed to handle the runoff and to prevent or reduce the flooding.

One possible arrangement would be a double or triple rain barrel system using attractively painted barrels. (If the barrels are painted the same color as the house, they'll appear smaller in this space.) Container gardens set on top of the barrels could help to integrate them into the décor as long as the containers don't block the water flow from the downspout. One or more overflow hoses would connect the barrels, with another overflow hose directed into a decorative watering can. This system would capture approximately 100 to 150 gallons of water, which would significantly decrease the flow into the garden area. A rain garden with an underlying drywell could be installed in the courtyard with the rain barrel overflow directed into it, or a French drain system could absorb the excess water and direct it outside the courtyard.

In deciding whether or not to add a third barrel, consider your need for that extra 50 gallons of water in such a small location. You could start with two barrels and add a third at a later time if you find that you have need for the extra water or if the flooding in the garden is still bothersome. If the downspout in this courtyard were directed through an underground pipe to a pond or wooded area, then a one-barrel closed system would work well for such a small area.

In the second scenario, two downspouts are located in a work area that is out of sight from the street and from most of the landscape. You have, or would like to have, a potting bench and compost bins there, but the fact that there is no running water makes it inconvenient. The surface area of the roof serviced by the downspouts is 1,000 square feet. The downspouts empty onto a cement pad adjacent to the building.

Since this area is not visible and your need for water is great, install a series of rain barrels or a cistern. In order to place the system most conveniently for your needs, you can divert one or both of the downspouts to the catchment barrels. By using flexible downspout extensions, for example, you can even have them meet in the middle of the wall. The overflow from the last barrel will empty onto the cement as the downspouts do now. It would be best to install some type of stormwater retention feature, such as a rain garden, at the edge of the cement pad to absorb the overflow and prevent waste.

Cisterns

For larger rain harvesting needs, cisterns have been used for centuries, especially in rural areas lacking municipal water systems or where wells cannot be drilled. Any way you look at it, if you need the water that falls from the sky, it makes perfect sense to capture as much as you can. If you are collecting water for fighting local wildfires, be sure to label the location of the tank to make it easy for firefighters to find and access.

Various types of tanks can be used as cisterns.

- Galvanized steel is probably the most common cistern material. Off-the-shelf farm tanks are available up to about 3,000 gallons.
- Concrete tanks are generally built on-site using forms, but smaller precast tanks are also available. Use high-strength concrete (7,000 psi) to hold water.

- Ferrocement tanks are made by spraying or plastering a cement mortar over a wire mesh form. Cracks can develop depending upon the thickness of the walls, so some periodic maintenance and repairs will probably be needed.
- Plastic tanks are available in sizes up to several thousand gallons. Some are rigid and others are flexible. They are lightweight, easily moved, and can be used above or below ground. (Tanks designed for underground installation will need more strength and may be more expensive.)
- Durable woods, such as cedar, redwood, or cypress, also can be used for tanks. If properly built, such tanks can last many years. Make sure the cypress comes from a sustainable tree farm.
- A polyethylene liner over a frame provides a low-cost cistern option. Liners for cisterns should be 20 or 30 mils thick to hold water.

For all cisterns, arrange to have durable screening over the top to keep out mosquitoes, children, and debris.

Make the Best Use of Resources: Harvest Your Rainwater

However you accomplish it, harvesting rainwater reduces the consumption of potable water for landscape and other uses. Reducing the flow of rainwater from your property eases the strain on local stormwater systems. Your plants and compost pile will thank you for that chemical-free water, too.

Resources

Web Sites

The University of Florida's IFAS provides many rain barrel resources, as well as announcements of local rain barrel workshops. Search for "rain barrels" on their main Web site: http://www.ifas.ufl.edu.

Southwest Florida Water Management District outlines water conservation programs and provides specific instructions for building and installing rain barrels: http://www.swfwmd.state.fl.us.

For rain barrel parts and kits, visit Aquabarrel online: http://www.aquabarrel. com.

The Arlington Echo Outdoor Education Center in Millersville, Maryland, has good information on how it sells rain barrels to support its programs: http://www. arlingtonecho.net.

The online Rain Barrel Guide provides good information on installing and using rain barrels and provides links to other green gardening sites: http://www. rainbarrelguide.com.

Rain Gardens, Bioswales, and Bog Gardens

Rain gardens (also known as bioretention areas) are designed to absorb and filter stormwater runoff from impervious surfaces, such as roofs, driveways, parking lots, and roadways. Located in natural or constructed low spots where rainwater collects in the landscape, rain gardens are planted with woody and herbaceous plants that tolerate both periodic flooding and extended dry periods. The plants absorb much of the water and the remainder percolates into the soil.

The benefits of rain gardens and bioswales (a sloping version of a rain garden) include a reduction of stormwater runoff and peak flows; integration of stormwater treatment into the landscape; and protection of water quality. They also add value and diversity (and beauty) to commercial and residential landscapes, reduce maintenance costs, and play an important role in low impact development (LID).

Rain gardens create artificial wetlands and provide alternatives to the "pipe and pond" tactics, so widespread in Florida, which dump rainwater as quickly as possible. The Environmental Protection Agency (EPA) has determined that up to 70 percent of the pollution in our surface waters is carried by stormwater runoff. Many studies have shown that the aggregate of nonpoint sources—such as small businesses and homeowners

Rain Gardens Are Sustainable

Building rain gardens is sustainable because stormwater is retained on your property. As a result, silt, nutrients, and pollutants are absorbed and filtered from the water, instead of contaminating nearby lakes and streams. When the stormwater is slowed down in a rain garden it relieves some of the strain on urban and suburban stormwater systems, and more water percolates into groundwater systems. Slowing the flow of stormwater helps to prevent the erosion of your soil. In rural areas, rain gardens may be the only treatment water receives before it's released into waterways.

Rain gardens provide increased diversity of plants and habitats in the landscape and can be incorporated into butterfly gardens and other habitat areas. Once established, rain gardens planted with mostly native plants are easy to care for and provide alternatives to hand-mowed vegetation growing in **swales** and other difficult places in the landscape.

with their lawn care practices, careless use of household chemicals, and roadway runoff—may cause more problems than large industrial polluters. The solution? Slow the flow and filter the stormwater: build some rain gardens.

As developers continue to replace forests, wetlands, and other natural spaces with impervious surfaces, organic materials and pollutants that were formerly absorbed and filtered by forests now wash from streets, parking lots, and lawns directly into local lakes and streams. Stormwater systems are often overloaded and clogged with silt washed from poorly designed landscapes, which can cause local flooding. Rain gardens can help improve the quality of our local waters and the environmental health of our communities by reducing the volume of stormwater leaving our properties. While an individual rain garden may seem insignificant, multiple rain gardens in a community can substantially reduce the stormwater surges and thus improve quality of water in nearby waterways.

Rain gardens may be designed to work in combination with rain barrels, bioswales, or French drains to slow down and manage the water flow. A rain garden may be large or small depending upon the size of the drainage area and whether it serves as an end point for the stormwater or as an intermediate catch basin. An end-point rain garden has the capacity to absorb all the stormwater most of the time. An intermediate rain garden absorbs a portion of the stormwater; the rest is filtered through layers of gravel, sand, and soil before it's gathered in a French drain under the garden and finally released into another water retention area, a stormwater system, or a waterway. An intermediate rain garden can also be configured so that its overflow is directed into a drainage system—either through an elevated drain head or a French drain set to collect water at a high level through the berm wall.

Surplus water exiting from a properly designed rain garden system will have been slowed down and filtered to the extent that it should be free of silt and most water-soluble pollutants. As an added bonus, a rain garden is an easy-to-care-for oasis for birds, frogs, butterflies, bees, and other wildlife.

Locating a Rain Garden

First locate all your underground utilities, including pipes for water, septic system, electricity, natural gas, telephone, cable, sprinkler system, and storm sewers. Stay at least five feet away from any utilities and 20 feet from septic systems—more if you're going to plant trees in the rain garden. Rain gardens should be situated far enough away from buildings to avoid foundation damage: 20 feet if there is a basement and five feet if there's a slab. The overflow and grading should be oriented away from buildings. While you may plant trees in a rain garden, it's usually not a good idea to dig one under an existing full-sized tree: you could compromise the roots, and many trees cannot tolerate the periodic standing water found in rain gardens.

In many parts of Florida, the groundwater is often close to the surface. Before you start anything else, you'll need to know how close the water table is to the surface. Maybe the low spot you thought would be perfect for a rain garden is damp because the groundwater comes to the surface during the rainy season or after a heavy storm. Dig a two-foot-deep hole and let it sit for several hours. If water seeps into the hole, then your groundwater is too close to the surface for an effective rain garden. For the best results, repeat this test several times during both wet and dry periods to avoid a false reading.

When groundwater comes to the surface at a swale on your property, one option is to build a rain garden above that low spot and have the **underflow** or overflow drain there. This way, the rain garden will have captured the silt, nutrients, and pollutants from the stormwater before it reaches the groundwater. You can certainly create a garden in your swale using the same plants that would do well in a rain garden, and it would be ever so much better than filling it and trying to maintain a lawn there. You may even decide to dig a groundwater pond in your low spot to better manage the water and add to the habitat value of your property.

Check for drainage. If the two-foot-deep hole that you dug in the proposed location does not fill with water in an hour or two as described above, then fill the hole to its brim with water. After it drains, fill it again. For a larger rain garden site, you should dig two or three holes to test the whole area during both the wet and dry seasons. If the water lingers in the hole for more than two or three hours, then a drywell or an underflow system in the garden area will facilitate percolation.

Locate the rain garden in a place where it will receive runoff, or could receive runoff with some grading, by removing a piece of curbing or installing a French drain or bioswale. The goal is for the collected stormwater in your rain garden to drain away in less than three days for most rain events.

Sizing a Rain Garden

Determining the needed capacity (the surface area and the depth) of your rain garden will depend on a number of factors. The most critical issue is the watershed or drainage area for the garden. A rain garden collecting stormwater from one quarter of the roof of a small cottage can be much smaller than one receiving the stormwater from a parking lot. If the soil drains quickly, then it can be smaller; if it's a little slow to drain, you'll need to provide more capacity for stormwater.

Calculate the square footage of the impervious surfaces that will empty into the rain garden. For buildings, it doesn't matter whether it's a sloped or flat roof: multiply the length and width of the building and estimate the portion that is collected by the downspout that empties into the rain garden. For impervious driveways and sidewalks, calculate the surface area. Then make a separate surface area calculation for the permeable surfaces—such as lawns, mulched areas, and places covered with pavers—that will drain into the rain garden. These measurements do not have to be precise.

Now estimate how deep your rain garden will be. The depth can be constructed by digging a swale into a level site, by building berms around an area, or by combining these methods. Most residential rain gardens are between five and ten inches deep, depending upon the slope and configuration of the site. (Large rain gardens in commercial landscapes might be several feet deep.) The bottom of the garden should be more or less level, but a berm of soil on the lower edge will catch or contain the water. On a slightly sloping site, the top of that berm should be approximately the same level as the top of the garden. (Steep sites are not suitable for rain gardens.) On a flat site, a berm will be required around the entire garden. More on this below, but for the purpose of sizing the garden or a series of gardens, you'll need to estimate the average depth. If the rain garden will be located in a spot frequented by many people, a shallower rain garden will create less of a hazard and may be more appropriate.

Multiplying factors to determine rain garden size

Rain garden depth	Five inches	Seven inches	Ten inches
Impervious surfaces	0.2 to 0.35	0.15 to 0.25	0.10 to 0.17
Permeable surfaces	0.05 to 0.10	0.035 to 0.08	0.025 to 0.05

Use the table above to help you calculate rain garden size. Multiply the watershed surface area (the source of the runoff water) by one of the decimal factors shown in the second, third, and fourth columns. Use the lower number in the range if your garden area has good drainage. For example, consider a garden that will be seven inches deep, has excellent drainage, and watershed areas include 1,000 square feet of cement driveway, plus

500 square feet of an unmortared brick walkway. For the impervious driveway, multiply 1,000 × 0.15, which is 150, and then for the permeable brick walkway, multiply 500 × 0.035, which is 17.5; now add the two numbers together. Your rain garden should have an area of 167.5 square feet. If this is too large for the area that's available for a rain garden, then plan to make the make garden deeper or install an underdrain or overflow that would run into another rain garden, pond, wooded area, or other water retention feature.

Ideally, the rain garden system should be large enough to absorb most of the runoff generated in the watershed area most of the time. Adjust the rain garden area to get as close as you can to this goal while staying within the space constraints of your site. Florida's heavy rains could quickly fill up your garden, so planning for overflows and underflows is important.

Constructing the Stormwater Feeds

Rain gardens' stated purpose is to absorb the stormwater runoff from some area or feature in the landscape such as a parking lot, driveway, or roof. They also can collect runoff from generally permeable sections of the landscape. Wherever you plan to situate your rain garden or series of rain gardens, create a path to guide the stormwater into the rain garden basin.

If your rain garden will be located to absorb the stormwater from a road, parking lot, or driveway, find the tilt and low spot of that surface. Observe the surface during a rainstorm so you will know where the water collects and arrange to have your rain garden accept the stormwater there. It's generally easiest to build the rain garden right next to the impervious surface, but other configurations sometimes work better. For instance, you could construct a bioswale or French drain along the driveway and have it empty into a rain garden in a lower spot in the landscape.

For large landscapes, commercial properties, or public lands, hiring a design engineer, landscape architect, or other certified professional to design the elevations and flows is a good investment. If you need to remove part of a curb to drain a parking lot or otherwise modify the original flow of the stormwater system, professional oversight will probably be required. Work with your local government to get permits for this work. While the garden is being constructed, you may also have to protect the surrounding areas from erosion with hay bales, compost-filled sleeves, or **biologs** (membrane tubes filled with fiber or rolled fiber mats—the fiber is often made from coconut shells).

Downspouts

When gathering runoff from one or more gutter downspouts, you may need to attach a pipe to the downspout and run it underground for several feet or more before it empties into the top of your rain garden. The underground pipe needs to be long enough to bypass traffic areas around the building and to avoid water damage to the foundation. Install the pipe so there is at least a slight slope away from the building toward the rain garden. Flexible six-inch plastic drainage pipe is a good choice because it's inexpensive, easy to work with, and requires no special tools. This size is large enough to carry the rainwater from one or two downspouts, even during a heavy Florida rainstorm. When the pipe runs under a path, it's a good idea to center a stepping-stone directly over the pipe and support it by firm soil on either side of the pipe, so as people walk on it, their weight is evenly distributed and does not collapse the pipe.

The rush of water coming from the pipe during a downpour could erode the soil in that part of the rain garden, so you probably will want to lay a downspout diverter, some paving stones, or splash rocks to prevent such erosion under the pipe. As the rain garden fills up, you may end up with some backup into the pipe, especially if there's only a slight slope, so it's usually a good idea to drill some holes in the bottom of the pipe as you lay it into its trench or use perforated pipe to prevent water from puddling. You don't want to create a mosquito breeding area.

One or more rain barrels will slow the flow into the garden, especially if the rain barrel water is used on a regular basis. If there's a rain barrel system on the downspout, the last overflow tube can be set up to empty into the underground pipe. This can be arranged so that the smaller overflow hose hangs loosely into the underground pipe or by a more secure connection, which can be fashioned to prevent leaves and animals from entering the pipe.

French Drains

A French drain or blind drain collects water along a stretch of landscape and delivers it to a water retention site. This centuries-old idea of creating a drainage ditch, lining it with tiles, and then filling it with rocks has been updated with the use of permeable, cloth-covered pipe laid in a ditch of rocks. Pipe has the advantage of easier maintenance. When a ditch of rocks fills with silt and sediment, the only way to improve the drainage is to dig out the whole ditch, separate the rocks from the sediment, and reinstall. By design, a cloth-covered pipe will be less prone to siltation, but you can also create an access opening at the head of the pipe to provide a way to clean it. The access opening usually is a ground-level drain head (like a shower drain), which you can remove to insert a plumbers' snake to ream out the whole pipe length.

If you have an impervious road or driveway, you can install a French drain all along its edge to collect stormwater. Dig a trench one or two feet

A French drain, consisting of an end-point drain and cloth-covered permeable pipe, laid next to a cement driveway. The bed is prepared for mulch. Note that the weed barrier cloth protects the pipe from the soil.

from the edge of the surface where stormwater drains—you don't want to get too close or you may undermine the pavement. Depending upon the site, you may need to plan for some demarcation of the pipe so people don't drive over it. You can plant an area of small shrubs, install a fence, or turn the whole area into a mulched garden bed that looks too important to drive on.

Set up the configuration to suit the site; just be sure to build in a slight downward angle toward the rain garden area. The trench should be deep enough to accommodate a layer of coarse, clean gravel, your pipe, and a top layer of mulch. Line the trench with heavy nonwoven weed barrier cloth so that six inches or more lies on top of the soil along either side of the trench. Lay a one- or two-inch bed of gravel on the weed barrier cloth in the bottom of the trench. Use clean, uniform stone for your gravel, not crusher run, which tends to compact. (It uses gravel sizes ranging from the stated particle size all the way down to grit.) You want to have a porous area around the pipe. Place the cloth-covered French drain pipe on that bottom layer of gravel, and then fill with more gravel until you reach the top of the pipe. Fold over the flaps of weed barrier cloth so the cloth forms a complete circle around the gravel and pipe. The weed barrier cloth helps to maintain the integrity of the gravel bed. Cover the cloth with sand and coarse mulch to fill to the surrounding soil level.

Use this permeable pipe configuration along the areas where you want to gather the stormwater. You can attach the permeable pipe to less expensive, plain drainage pipe to span the distance from the driveway area to the top of the rain garden.

Bioswales

A bioswale is a sloping version of a rain garden. It is normally configured as a shallow U-shaped trench with moderate side-to-side curves so that water traveling down the gentle slope will swish one way and then the other. The plants along the edges absorb some of the water, and since the water's movement is slowed, some of it soaks into the soil as well.

You may have seen bioswales arranged to look like dry riverbeds with smoothed river rocks carefully arranged down the center. The river rock arrangements are not sustainable in Florida, because the rocks are not usually found locally and keeping them neat and free of debris and weeds would be a never-ending maintenance chore.

In planning a bioswale, you need to consider the area of the watershed, the configuration of the site, and the angle of the slope. You'll want to divert and retain the stormwater as it makes its way down the slope with a combination of biologs, earthen dams, hay bales, rocks, or other materials that can act as baffles. The goal is not to hold the water as in a retention pond but to slow it down before it exits the site.

Baffles are usually perpendicular to the slope of the swale and angle toward the center of the swale to further slow the water's flow. Most commercially constructed baffles are made with large rocks piled together, but you can also use biologs or hay bales to hold the soil in place and to provide a medium for growing deep-rooted plants. The next baffle farther down the slope should be similarly built along the opposite side from the

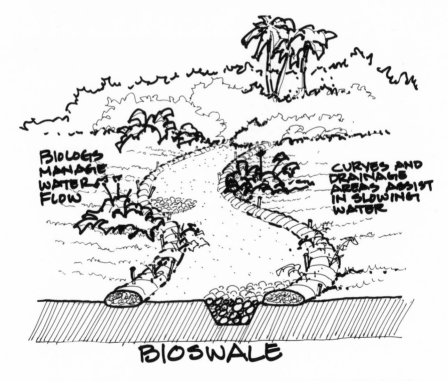

A bioswale can take many forms. This one is lined with biologs and has drywells at each curve to help slow down water. A bioswale is like a sloped rain garden.

first baffle. This way there is not a straight line for water to flow along. In the uphill crook of the baffle and parallel to it, dig a hole a foot or more deep and fill it with one or two grades of clean gravel. This will serve as a drywell to allow the water that's slowed down by the baffle to soak into the ground.

You could pack native soil behind the biologs or hay bales to fill in the baffles and make smooth sloping sides. Install a variety of site-appropriate, deep-rooted perennials, shrubs, and trees at key points along the edges of the swale and around the baffles as well. Keep in mind the adult size of trees and shrubs as you create a layout. After planting, you'll need to irrigate the whole area on a regular basis for several months or more, especially if you've planted in the dry season or if a drought hits your area. Temporary drip irrigation systems are good for handling these situations, if you can arrange it.

Because the water moves through a bioswale, don't mulch it with bark or coarse wood chips or other materials that could float away. Compost or compost blankets (compost that's been processed into mats) will work better as mulch here.

The ground can be graded at the bottom of the bioswale slope, so water pools into a pond fitted with an overflow drain or so the water can be directed to a level rain garden.

Building Rain Gardens

The shape of a rain garden is up to you and it can fit into any pocket of open space. Generally it's good to have the broader dimension perpendicular to the slope of the site to better capture the rainwater, especially if there is not a directed flow from a French drain or downspout. Most folks find that rounded corners create the best, most natural appearance and make for easy mowing if the garden is installed next to a lawn area.

Lay a rope or a hose around the area to be dug out as the center of the rain garden. If there is turfgrass here, dig it out first. Use it to replace dead areas in your lawn, add it to your compost pile, or, even better, turn it upside down to use as the base for the berm that will encircle your rain garden.

Normally the soil that you dig from the center is used to form the berm, but you may also use a biolog or compost-filled sock around the rain garden to provide added structure and stability. Lay the biolog outside of your digging area and stake it in place with untreated wood or straight branches such as watersprouts or suckers that you've pruned from the landscape—depending upon the species, some of these stakes may sprout. In addition to the stability that the biologs add, they also provide a good growing medium for edge plants. If you're using these devices, add some of your newly dug soil or sod to the inside and outside edges to increase the water retentive properties of your berm and to provide a gentle planting slope.

Endpoint Configurations

If the rain garden is to be an end point for the stormwater and you have good drainage, dig the bottom out so that it's level. Dig out the soil to the desired depth plus two inches. Unless the soil is really sandy, loosen the bottom soil with a garden fork or, for a large site, with a tiller. After this step, because you want to maintain the increased porosity of the rain garden bottom, restrict traffic in this area to only what's necessary to finish planting the garden. Smooth out the surface and use a piece of lumber and carpenter's level in various sections of the garden bottom to check for unevenness. Then add two inches of compost and install your plants.

If your soil doesn't offer good drainage, you may wish to dig a drywell somewhere near the center of the garden. The size of the drywell should correspond with the degree of porosity of the soil: sites with poor drainage will require a larger drywell. Fill it with clean gravel or a combination of gravel topped with a layer of sand. If you decide to layer your drywell, separating the layers with nonwoven weed barrier cloth will help to maintain their integrity. Then grade the remainder of the bottom so that it will drain toward the drywell. Only a very slight slope of a couple of degrees will be needed to accomplish this.

Even though this is supposed to be an endpoint, the stormwater will probably overflow the berm during tropical storms. Consider where accidental overflows could be directed. You may wish to modify the slope of the landscape below the rain garden so extra water will head into a wooded area, a lawn, or some other feature that can absorb the occasional inundation. Be sure it won't drain toward a building.

Overflow Drainage

An overflow drainage configuration is not uncommon for retrofitting a rain garden into an existing site, such as a parking lot island or a center drainage area in the landscape. The rain garden will capture the first flush of stormwater and allow at least some of it to percolate into the soil or be absorbed by plants before the garden fills up and the stormwater flows into the drain. The level of the rain garden bottom should be six to twelve or more inches below the drain, but the berms or sides should be three to six inches higher than the drain.

In such sites, you may be working with poor quality subsoil, so you may need more than the two inches of compost as described above. You could place a layer of sandy topsoil under the compost for better drainage and healthier plants. Loosen the soil with a garden fork to increase poros-

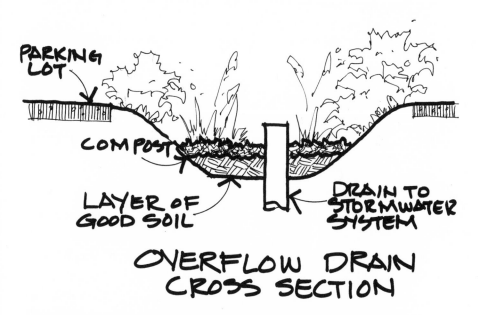

Rain gardens can be retrofitted around parking lot drains. Stormwater flows into the swale first and, if the volume is great enough, overflows into the drain. Silt settles in the garden and water is absorbed by rain-garden plants or soaks into the soil.

ity; for clay or hardpan soil you might want to dig a drywell under the rain garden, so the water left in the garden will drain within three days. Don't use mulch that could float into the drain.

In addition to capture by drywells, the overflow can also be caught by a blind drain and directed to an area with the capacity to safely absorb the extra water. Arrange your garden with two depths: the main part of the garden will be the deeper part, while the shallower section will be located on the side away from the source of the water. The shallow section should be a few inches lower than the berm surrounding the garden. The blind drain is set up just under the surface of the shallow section. When the water level rises, it will flow into the blind drain.

One way to create a blind drain for a situation like this is to dig out a hole under the shallow part of the garden and create a trench for the drainage pipe from the hole to an area lower in the landscape, where the excess water can be absorbed. Line the hole with weed barrier cloth, fill it with clean gravel, and fold the cloth on top of the gravel to keep out the soil and roots. Then cover the end of a drainage pipe with something to screen out the mud (old pantyhose material works well) and butt the end of the pipe up to the cloth-covered gravel. Cover the top of the gravel-filled hole with a thin layer of soil and plant only shallow-rooted ground-cover in this area of the garden. You don't want any plants with aggressive roots to invade the gravel. Cover the drainage pipe with enough soil so people can walk on it without collapsing the pipe. If the area does not allow for that much depth, place stepping-stones directly over the pipe so the pressure is evenly distributed.

Rain Gardens with Underflows

If you're installing a series of rain gardens or if the outflow from the rain garden will be directed into a pond or stormwater system, then an underflow system is most appropriate. An underflow system consists of a French drain installed under the surface of the rain garden. When the rainwater flows into this garden it pools as it is slowed down, drops its sediments, and soaks into the soil to be absorbed by the plants. The excess water is filtered through layers of sand and gravel before it flows into the perforated pipe of the French drain, which directs this filtered water to the next water retention feature.

Start by locating your garden, but before you start digging, determine where the underflow will go and the angle needed to drain to the next water retention feature. If you're building a series of rain gardens, the limitations of the site will probably determine whether it will be easier to start at the bottom and move back up to the first rain garden catch basin or to start at the top and work down. For instance, if the first rain garden is located near a building to catch stormwater from the roof and walkways and the last rain garden one has no size or use limitations, start at the top—you may still have to make more considerations for size, depth, and placement near buildings in full view. On the other hand, if the underflow of the bottom rain garden water will empty into a pond, the size and shape may be dictated by the paths and plantings around the pond area. In this case starting at the bottom rain garden might be more appropriate.

First mark out the dimensions of the rain garden, and then plan for the underflow system. The installation is approximately the same as for the

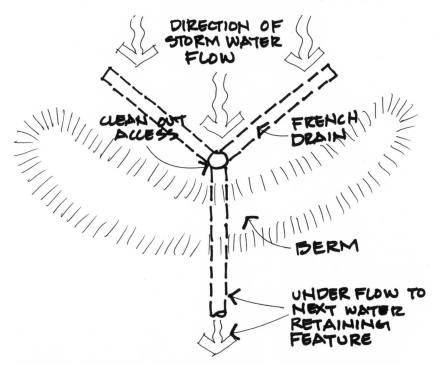

Top view of a rain garden outfitted with a Y-shaped French drain to absorb excess water. Keep large plants away from the French drain.

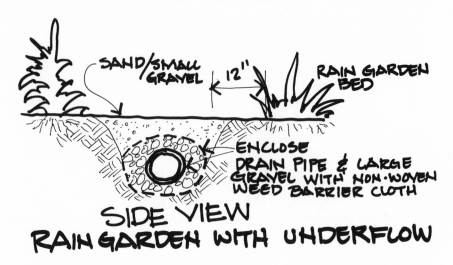

This side view of a rain garden with a French drain shows how stormwater is filtered before it enters the drainpipe.

French drain described earlier in this chapter. The trench for the French drain should be laid out in a pattern appropriate for the size of the rain garden. It might be a wide Y with the two arms running two feet or so above the berm at the lower part of the rain garden. The bottom of the Y, heading to the next water retention feature, could be either permeable or solid drainpipe. If you decide to use a clean-out access unit, locate it in the center of the Y. Unlike the French drain described above, this access point will be solid—not a drain head—since the whole point here is to filter the water.

Dig the whole rain garden bottom to the planned depth plus two inches more, but when creating the berm leave a gap where the underflow drain will be located. This time, the bottom of the bed will not be exactly level but will be graded like the bottom of a shower stall where the bottom slopes slightly (no more than two or three degrees) toward where the French drain pipes are to be installed. Now dig a trench for the drainpipe that is at least twice as wide as the pipe and will allow for at least six inches of sand and gravel to cover the pipe.

Complete the berm over the underflow system, and then finish off the garden as described above with two inches of compost. Plants should be clustered away from the drainage area, especially any shrubs or other plants with aggressive root systems. Trees would not be recommended for this type of rain garden.

Rain Garden Vegetation

When landscaping your rain garden, the challenge is to create a pleasing arrangement of woody and herbaceous plants that are both suitable for the site and look good throughout the year. If the rain garden will be seen from all sides, you might want to plant taller plants in the center and shorter ones around the edges. If tall rain garden plants would block a desirable view, you can use shorter plants with approximately the same height overall.

When selecting plants for your rain gardens, choose those that are appropriate for your planting zone and that can thrive during periods of both inundation and drought. There are different zones of wetness in a rain garden. Typically the centermost or lowest sections of the rain garden will stay wetter longer, while the edges and berms will dry out sooner. Actually the berms will probably be dry enough on a regular basis that you'll only want to use drought-tolerant plants around them.

You'll use mostly perennial and woody plants for greater total biomass, long-term soil stability, and to reduce the ongoing labor. Rain gardens are not a good environment to grow plants from seed, so you'll need to start them elsewhere or purchase seedlings from nurseries. Choose a nursery or supplier that specializes in native plants: this environment offers enough challenges that many fussier imports may not do well here. Using native plants also increases the habitat value of the garden. Never use a plant that is on the exotic invasive list.

Dig a wide hole for each plant. As you remove it from its pot or bag, spread out the roots and pour water in the hole. Firm the soil around the roots and be sure that the plant is set no deeper than it was in its pot—for woody plants you should see the top of the root flare. Create a saucer of soil around each plant to collect water. Since there is a two-inch layer of compost over the surface, no other amendments are necessary. Group the plants in odd numbers and combine a variety of textures in your groupings.

Plant list for rain gardens

Wildflowers and ferns	Trees and shrubs
Black-eyed Susan N, C, S	Bald and pond cypress N, C, S
Blue-eyed grass N, C, S	Buttonbush N, C, S
Cinnamon fern N, C	Cabbage palm N, C, S
Dixie iris N, C, S	Cocoplum C, S
Goldenrod N, C, S	Dahoon holly N, C, S
Meadow beauty N, C, S	Dwarf and saw palmettos N, C, S
Netted chain fern N, C, S	Elderberry N, C, S
Royal fern N, C, S	Inkberry N, C, S
Rushes N, C, S	Red maple N, C
Stokes aster N	River birch N, C
Swamp sunflower N, C	Southern wax myrtle N, C, S
White-topped sedge N, C, S	Sweetbay magnolia N, C, S

Notes: N = North Florida; C = Central Florida; S = South Florida.

For a medium-sized, low-growing garden in a partially sunny location, for example, plant a group of five soft rushes in the bottom of the garden and seven black-eyed Susans up and over the berm nearby. Then on the other side of the garden plant three large cinnamon ferns with five Dixie irises in the bottom and three inkberries up on the berm nearby. In a third area of the rain garden, plant one blue palmetto with seven goldenrods arranged along the berm. This garden will have spiky, ferny, and clumping forms. While some of the plants will die back during the winter months in northern Florida, there should be enough structure throughout the year to keep it interesting.

For a larger rain garden in full sun you could use three southern wax myrtles toward one side and a pond cypress or a sweet bay magnolia on the other. Don't plant them too close together—keep in mind their adult sizes. Between these trees in the bottom of the garden, you could plant three to five saw palmettos. Then, up and over the berm, plant Stokes asters and goldenrods.

Irrigate each day for two or three weeks and gradually taper off to once a week unless a good rain fills up the garden. Keep an eye on your new plants for several months for the best success. Woody plants will need more time to adjust, so be vigilant. If you can, set up a temporary drip irrigation system; otherwise plan on hand watering.

Initial Maintenance

A rain garden should be designed to dry out within three days of filling up. Even after all your planning and calculations, if you find that the water persists for too long, you'll need to take corrective action or you'll have mosquitoes. Take into consideration that your plants will absorb more water as they grow. So if the water is pooling for four days and your plants are just beginning to take hold, it's likely you don't need to do anything more than let your plants mature. If the water pools for six days or more, then it's time to get to work. There are a number of corrective actions you can take. You can expand the size of the garden to accommodate more stormwater, plant more vegetation, dig or expand a drywell under the garden, or combine one or more of these measures. You may even decide to install an underflow drain to another new rain garden. This fine-tuning is to be expected.

All that loosened soil and moist habitat will attract weeds, so be sure to keep after them for the first year or two. Keep in mind that some of these volunteers may be rushes, sedges, or bunching grasses that might actually be good additions to your garden. So until you know, let it grow. Keep the mulch in place as much as possible, but sometimes with flooding and drying, it gets reoriented. Try to keep the foot traffic down in the garden so the soil stays loose.

The plants in a successful rain garden should eventually shade the soil so that, over time, weed growth will be less of a problem. You may decide to rearrange your plantings if you discover that some plants are either doing poorly or doing *too* well. If you treat your rain garden as you would any other garden, it will make you smile—because it's beautiful and also because you will have decreased the stormwater runoff from your site. Mother Nature and Florida's waterways will thank you and all the other rain gardeners.

Bog Gardens

A bog garden is similar to, and may serve some of the same purposes in the landscape as, a rain garden, but it's not supposed to dry up within three days. A bog will hold onto its water for long periods of time and its vegetation is more specialized. This environment often becomes quite acidic and is dominated by sphagnum moss, pitcher plants, sundews, and others.

You would start a bog garden using the same methods as for a rain garden; in fact, you might want to include a bog garden in your rain garden/bioswale system. The main difference would be that for a bog garden you might need to use a liner to help retain the water over the long term. Bog plants are not generally drought tolerant.

The location of a bog garden should include a good reliable source of water; otherwise it won't be sustainable. Your water source could be outflows from rain barrels or an overflow from a pond. Dig a saucer-shaped swale 18 to 20 inches deep in the center and line it with good, thick pond liner. (You could also use one of those preformed plastic pond tubs.) Arrange for an overflow to an appropriate area in your landscape for Florida's rainy season. You can plan for mosquito control with some fish at first, but a bog will eventually create such a thick raft of vegetation and the water will be so acidic that mosquitoes will not find it habitable.

Rain Gardens Absorb Stormwater on Your Property

Rain gardens make great community, church, and school projects because the results are so visible. While the planning and digging creates the structure, the planting and mulching phases are often the more photogenic and newsworthy. Get as much publicity as you can to inspire others to capture their stormwater, too. People get exited when they can see that their efforts are not only beautiful but will also make a significant difference. By installing rain gardens and bioswales throughout the vicinity, your community might not need to expand the stormwater system.

Resources

Web Sites

The Web site for W.A.T.E.R. (Watershed Activities to Encourage Restoration) describes simple, low-cost projects for communities and organizations: http://www.watershedactivities.com.

The Brooklyn Botanic Garden has information and regional plant lists for rain gardens: http://www.bbg.org.

The Low Impact Development Center has a wealth of information and ideas for managing stormwater, including detailed instructions and rain garden designs for sun and shade in the form of a downloadable 32-page booklet: http://www.lowimpactdevelopment.org and http://www.lid-stormwater.net.

The Web site for the City of Portland, Oregon, offers case studies of rain gardens at schools and parks. Search for "rain garden" at http://www.portlandonline.com.

The Center for Watershed Protection has guidelines for rain garden designs: search "rain garden" for publications on residential stewardship. They also have experts available to help design commercial and municipal rain gardens and other systems for handling stormwater: http://www.cwp.org.

The West Michigan Environmental Action Council hosts a handsome and informative rain garden Web site, Rain Gardens of West Michigan: http://www.raingarden.org.

The University of Central Florida's Stormwater Academy has action items for better handling of stormwater: http://www.stormwater.ucf.edu.

Books

Dunnet, Nigel and Andy Cayden. *Rain Gardens: Managing Water Sustainably in the Garden and Designed Landscape.* Portland, Ore.: Timber Press, 2007.

Waterfront Gardening

Dealing with Salt, Sand, Muck, and Erosion

With Florida's more than 1,350 miles of coastline, 50,000 miles of inland and coastal rivers and streams, 700 freshwater springs, and countless lakes and ponds, most of us are not far from water. This is our choice because we love the water, but much of the coastal landscape can be a harsh environment for plants. Many waterfront properties have sandy, nutrient-poor soil. Other areas have heavy clay soil that becomes hard as a rock when it dries. Sand and clay may not be the only challenges.

While sea breezes are one of the charms of coastal living, your plants might not do so well with the constant wind buffeting them and with a possible incursion of brackish water into the groundwater. Too much salt is fatal for many plants. If your property is near a river, lake, or bay, stormwater erosion may wash nutrients from your property into the body of water. Waves or currents may eat away at your shoreline. You may also have poor drainage because of a high water table, or you may be dealing with high nutrient levels in your pond.

The natural shape and habitat of the shoreline are the result of its many years of adaptation to the physical and biological environment. In most residential areas, however, the natural shoreline has been fundamentally

Better Management of Waterfront Landscapes Is Sustainable

Sustainable practices used in caring for waterfront property will improve water quality. Homeowners and property managers can work on this by preventing erosion, decreasing nutrient flow into the water, and increasing wetlands and habitat along waterways.

Restoring shoreline habitat that provides access to and from the water encourages frogs, toads, turtles, shorebirds, and other wildlife. When your waterfront supports a balanced ecosystem, you'll have an abundance of insect-eating predators. This is part of your integrated pest management program.

altered. In such places, property owners and landscape managers can help to restore natural vegetation and shoreline functions. Additionally, a natural shoreline helps preserve "The Real Florida."

Waterfront properties are located along the shorelines of the Atlantic Ocean, the Gulf of Mexico, the Intracoastal Waterway, and the multitudes of rivers, streams, lakes, springs, and ponds that populate Florida. If you don't have waterfront, you can create your own by building a pond. There are obvious charms to being near the water. People are attracted to the simple beauty of the reflections, waves, and the trickling of waterfalls. Easy-to-care-for waterfront plantings can provide color and texture that contrast with the rest of your landscape. Water is a necessary ingredient for building habitat for the birds, butterflies, fish, and other wildlife that are attracted to it, and their presence further enhances your landscape. As a property manager, you'll want to plan for seating, pathways, and other human activities around the waterfront without compromising its integrity or habitat value. There are challenges, additional responsibilities, and possible risks when you own or manage waterfront property.

Managing a Seashore Landscape

There are a limited number of plants that grow well on the beaches and sandy dunes of the Atlantic and Gulf coasts. In order to stabilize the sand to some degree, you'll need to use the old standbys, such as sea oats, beach sunflower, seaside goldenrod, sea grape, cabbage palm, groundsel tree, and other plants native to this harsh environment. Plants that are salt tolerant have a thick leaf cuticle or other type of mechanism that enables them to exude the extra salt they absorb. Most of them also have extensive and aggressive root systems in order to survive in sandy soils. Your extension agent can provide you with lists of good plant choices for the specific environmental conditions in your county.

In preparing a stormwise landscape, planting groups of wind-tolerant trees and shrubs on the windward side of buildings makes a big difference. Wind groves, as described in chapter 6, should be located far enough away from buildings that if one of the trees falls, it won't damage anything. At the same time, the grove should be close enough to disrupt wind currents. In areas where you wish to maintain a view, plan to place the taller trees next to building walls and the shorter trees and shrubs in front of windows and patio areas. Artful placement of a few tall trees within the view will frame your vista with picturesque tree trunks.

On a day-to-day basis, wind groves strategically located in coastal landscapes can buffer stiff breezes and remove some of the salt so that land on the leeward side of the grove has some protection. If you decide to plant vegetables or other "normal" plants in your protected zone, be aware that sooner or later a damaging load of salt will make its way there. Instead of experimenting in this second tier landscape with more vulnerable plants, use salt-tolerant woody plants. Trees and shrubs are long-term investments, and it's more sustainable not to have to replace what you plant.

For gardens on the leeward side of the wind grove, you'll probably find that using raised beds and container gardens works better than trying to amend the sandy soil in the ground. You will have greater control over the soil mixture. Whether you garden in the ground, in raised beds, or in containers, during the dry season it's a good idea to water heavily every two months or so to reduce the salt buildup in your soil. If you can arrange it, water just before or after a rain, so you can multiply Mother Nature's rins-

A Note on Waterfront Regulations

Florida property owners can own the shoreline to the **mean high water** line, but usually the state owns the water. There are federal, state, and local laws and regulations that govern many aspects of shoreline property maintenance, including remodeling, cutting vegetation, and landscaping and building on lands within the shoreline zone—which may be as much as 300 feet from a stream, river, or lake. Before making any changes to your waterfront property, contact the Florida Department of Environmental Protection (DEP), your county zoning office, and your local water management district to obtain information on laws and regulations governing your property.

http://www.dep.state.fl.us.

ing efforts. During the wet season, you typically receive a leaching rain when three inches of rain falls within three days or when four inches of rain falls in a week. Because rainfall is highly local, an accurate rain gauge will provide you with the precipitation totals on your property.

Shoreline Management

While properties fronting moving water, especially waters with wave action, are subject to shoreline erosion, any land can erode as a result of Florida's heavy downpours. Depending on the seriousness of the situation, you may need to take steps to reduce erosion in your landscape. Start by stabilizing your soil—in other words, manage the stormwater on your property. As discussed in chapter 12, water retention systems—often combining rain barrels, bioswales, French drains, rain gardens, bog gardens, and maybe retention ponds—should be constructed to absorb runoff from roofs, driveways, roadways, and other impervious surfaces. When the water is absorbed into the ground, it not only prevents erosion, it also filters out pollutants and silt and recharges the groundwater.

LIVING SHORELINE

T-shaped barriers made from sand, gravel, shells, or biologs and planted with appropriate plants are one way to configure a living shoreline to mimic a natural shoreline and provide much-needed habitat.

The best strategy for protecting the shoreline from erosion will depend upon the potential causes of erosion and the specific nature of the site. If at all possible, avoid bulkheads, seawalls, riprap, groins, and other structures that "harden" the shoreline. When hard or semihard structures replace the natural shoreline, important intertidal habitat is destroyed and the natural ebb and flow of water and sediments is changed. For minor erosion problems, creating a natural buffer zone of shoreline vegetation alone may suffice. A natural solution should be attempted before proceeding to structural solutions. It's more sustainable to preserve habitat with a natural buffer zone, and it's certainly less expensive than installing and maintaining a hard structure.

In cases where ongoing erosion threatens structures, additional action to protect the shoreline is necessary. One alternative to bulkheads involves the creation of living shorelines with biologs or compost-filled socks planted with site-appropriate plants. This option can be used alone or in combination with a second option—the installation of a bar of shells, gravel, or other materials that runs parallel to the shore. This bar will break up the waves and provide habitat for shellfish, and its top can be planted with emergent, deep-rooted plants that can survive the wave action or water flows.

Biologs may also be used to fill or block shorelines that have been undercut by currents or wave action. In such cases, place one or more rows of biologs along the shore and stake them in place with stakes that will take root, such as willow, southern bayberry, or other wetland plants suitable for your location. Use a variety of plant materials to emulate a natural shoreline in your area, so that after a season or two, as the biolog decomposes, there will be a row of native woody plants in place to hold the shoreline. Biologs can also be used as berms for sloping shoreline areas both in and above the littoral zone. If more protection is needed, use a minimum of riprap, but if possible, install it above the mean high water mark to preserve the littoral zone habitat.

Whether or not your shoreline is protected by a hard structure or a living shoreline, maintaining a buffer zone of natural vegetation on the landward side of the littoral zone is an effective way of protecting water quality, coastal habitat, and shoreline stability.

Buffer Zones

In addition to capturing your stormwater, buffer gardens or natural areas next to the shoreline protect the waterway from nutrient runoff, blowing trash, and organic waste such as leaves and lawn clippings. Remove as much turfgrass from the waterfront area as the situation allows. The plants you choose for this area should be low-care and mostly native woody plants and perennials suited for the specific zone and level of salin-

Littoral Zones

Zones of distinct plant communities based on adaptability to water salinity, soil saturation, salt spray, and wind and wave energy determine the character of shorelines. Plant types suitable for the shore also vary depending on elevation, slope, soil type, sunlight, rainfall, and other conditions. The resulting complex of plant communities provides a structure that is defined by and adapted to the dynamic shoreline environment. The four zones defined in relation to water and tide levels can be narrow or wide depending upon the slope of the shoreline:

- Zone one is the area below **mean low water** and is usually submerged. This zone may be naturally unvegetated if there is a lot of wave action or if steep or rocky slopes prevent plant growth. In more protected or still waters, **emergent wetland plants**— those that are rooted on the bottom but grow above the water's surface—will grow in zone one.
- Zone two is the intertidal area between mean low and mean high water. It is submerged at high water levels but is regularly exposed to the air when the water is low. Various wetland species may be appropriate for this zone.
- Zone three is the area between mean high water and the normal limit of storm tides. In this area, the soil is usually exposed, but it is periodically submerged during especially high tides or storm events. Soils are moist, and if the body of water is saline, there may be significant salt content. Grasses and shrubs that are capable of withstanding varying degrees of soil saturation will do well here.

Zones one, two, and three are the littoral zones.

- Zone four is the coastal area above the normal storm tide line. While this area is not regularly flooded, choose plants that can survive consistent winds and salt spray. This is where you'll plant a buffer of natural vegetation. Incorporating a rain garden upland of the buffer will accomplish even more to restore the ecological integrity of the shoreline, because it will absorb the inland runoff and also act as a seasonal wetland.

ity. Observe what grows naturally in areas similar to your site. If existing vegetation (other than turfgrass and invasive non-native plants) is doing well, let it stay. Any buffer is good, but 30 to 50 feet is recommended for the best treatment along the shoreline.

Build pathways to upland areas adjacent to the shoreline to provide access for turtles and amphibians. You can mulch this area as long as the mulch can't possibly wash into the water. But don't use weed barrier cloth under the mulch: it reduces habitat value. Turtles need access to the soil so they can lay their eggs, and toads need places where they can bury themselves during the day to keep cool in summer and to warm up during colder months.

While the buffer area can provide habitat for some wildlife, it can also be designed to keep out other kinds. For instance, if there are geese in the area, a dense stand of sturdy, stickery bushes such as palmettos, blackberries, hollies, mangroves, or wax myrtles might keep them from tromping all over your fragile shoreline, while keeping it open to frogs, turtles, and other animals access to and from the water. Thick buffer vegetation also prevents erosion and stabilizes the shoreline by absorbing wave energy, trapping sediments, slowing stormwater runoff, and moderating the effects of storms and floods.

Softening a Hard Shoreline

Bulkheads and riprap of large rocks create hard shorelines. Too much of Florida's original habitat and vegetative breakwaters has been replaced by hard shoreline structures. In addition to creating buffer areas above the bulkhead, you can also take steps to vegetate all but the most exposed shorelines. Waterside plants soften the shore's exposure to wave action and water flows. In addition to functioning as a kind of bumper to take the brunt of storms, such plants can also absorb nutrients from the water.

Logs Outside a Bulkhead

One of the problems with bulkheads around every inch of a lake or river shoreline is that they leave no access for turtles or other animals. By connecting a tree trunk, a log, or a series of logs to your bulkhead in such a way that turtles can use them for basking and as a path to the land, you can increase the habitat value of that shoreline (see chapter 5). As trees fall into the water from the shore, leave them in place. Yes, it's tempting to neaten up the shoreline, but a downed tree provides a buffer from the wave action and becomes good habitat for fish and other aquatic life— including those basking turtles.

Biologs or Compost Socks

Biologs are often made of coconut fiber or other fibrous material formed into long flexible cylinders. Compost-filled socks are interchangeable with the fiber biologs and are created onsite with a system that blows compost into a tube of biodegradable netting called a "sock." If you're working with a bulkheaded area, the biologs can be installed on the water side of the hard structure. The configuration depends upon the depth of the water and other site factors.

Biologs can be staked into place to help hold a shoreline while new plants get a good start. Select a variety of deep-rooted plants that will be able to survive and thrive on the shoreline once the logs decompose. If you can arrange it, place the logs in contact with the water so that the plants growing inside remain moist.

Fascines and Native Plants

A **fascine** is a bundle of live branches cut from trees or shrubs that root easily, such as viburnum, wax myrtle, or willow. You can plant fascines in or behind the biologs where the soil is still moist most of the time. Fascines eventually root and become functional shrubs. These can be installed inside or outside of a bulkhead or seawall.

Plant native shoreline grasses, sedges, and rushes along the edges, in front of, and behind bulkheads to soften the shoreline, filter stormwater runoff, and provide food and shelter for shorebirds. Choose plant species that are appropriate for the specific substrate.

Mangroves

These wondrous water margin plants, with their own stilts, do so much to protect and enrich Florida's shoreline that they have their own state regulations governing their treatment: be sure you understand your local regulations. There are three official mangrove species: red, black, and white. Because it so often grows in the same habitat, green buttonwood is often considered an unofficial mangrove. Mangroves can grow in either salt water or freshwater.

Black and red mangroves are hardier than the other species, and their range extends from the Florida Keys into northern regions on both of the peninsular coasts. White mangrove and buttonwood are somewhat more tropical. Typically, the red mangrove, the species with the stilt roots (also called "prop roots") grows farthest out in the water, followed by the black and then the white as you move away from the open water. The green buttonwood grows mostly on dry land, but can withstand periodic flooding.

As a group, the mangroves create fabulous habitat for many types of wildlife, absorb the wave action from open waters, and build new land as they hold onto sediment passing by. If your property fronts on a bay, lagoon, or **estuary**, consider mangroves for your waterfront plans. Too many of our native stands have been removed in the development process.

Ponds in Your Landscape

Ponds in Florida yards provide focus for landscapes and wildlife habitat. Ponds range in size from small, preformed tubs set in the ground to large groundwater or spring-fed bodies of water—the benefits vary depending upon the size and site. If a pond is designed well and long-term maintenance is planned for, it can provide great pleasure and good habitat for many years. Larger ponds can serve as stormwater retention areas and may be a source for landscape irrigation. If your property is in a fire-prone zone, a pond of any size is a great addition to a firewise landscape and may even serve as a source of water for firefighters.

Whether they are naturally occurring, part of site development, or added later, ponds will influence the choices you make about general yard use. If there will be a lot of human traffic, including children's activities, in the vicinity of the pond, consider blocking access to the pond for better safety. A fence, a low hedgerow, a berm, or a low wall may be called for in these situations. A pond could be considered an attractive nuisance in legal terms.

Natural Florida ponds are usually located in the lowest points of a landscape and are filled by groundwater or springs. You could construct a pond in a more visible position, but be sure to consider the overflow and drainage with a pond perched higher in the landscape. The normal structure of natural ponds is wide and shallow, which provides a large amount of littoral habitat. The sunlight penetration in the shallow water supports emergent plants and results in increased pond life activity. Natural ponds less than four feet deep are often completely covered with plants, and the natural tendency is for ponds like this to fill up with detritus, silt, and other organic matter, especially if there is a nutrient overload. This is called "**eutrophication**."

In order to interrupt eutrophication, plan for periodic removal of some of the emergent and aquatic plants to maintain open water. In addition to hand removing the plants, you may also wish to dredge parts of the pond to a depth of six feet or more to discourage the emergent plants and to provide better habitat for fish. Ideally no more than one third of the pond should be covered with vegetation. Other important steps to prolong the life of a pond are to reduce the nutrients that flow into it and to remove excess organic matter like leaves and pine needles and the pond muck from the bottom. The best time to scoop out the bottom is at the end of the dry season when the pond is at its lowest level and more of the bottom is exposed. This way you can see more of what you're doing, whether you're hand digging a small pond or working with larger machinery to dredge out a larger pond. After a good dredging and if the incoming nutrients are drastically reduced, the eutrophication process may be slowed enough so that your pond can provide many more years of pleasure without too much work.

While excessive vegetation can cause problems for ponds and lakes, a moderate amount of underwater vegetation provides aeration of the water as it photosynthesizes. Vegetation also offers good cover and food for fish and snails. Many communities install fountains in their ponds. While shooting water into the air aerates the water, a lot of water is lost through evaporation, so it's probably not the most sustainable way to aerate your pond. To increase the aeration in a more sustainable way, you may wish instead to add a solar-powered filtering system and gentle waterfall to further clean and aerate the water.

Lined or Artificial Ponds

If you'd like a new pond in a sandy substrate with no immediate groundwater to support the water level, you'll probably need to install a liner of some sort unless you're designing a seasonal pond (see below). Here are some thoughts on designing a lined pond.

- Create as big and deep a pond as your space and budget allow. It's much easier to accomplish the digging and laying of plastic, along with the other work, all at one time. Redoing it all later is much more difficult than the initial work.
- The pond should be at least 18 inches deep in the center, but 24 to 36 inches is better. This gives your fish somewhere to hide. Herons and other fishing birds will probably visit your pond, so when you stock the fish, choose lots of small fish that are easily and economically replaced, or select a combination of small fish and a few larger ones that are too big for a heron to swallow.
- Design the pond's edge with sweeping curves to increase the littoral area. This provides more habitat and better planting areas for your interesting shoreline specimens.
- Create a slightly sloping bottom so that all the detritus sinks to one place making it easier to scoop out.
- Incorporate a plant shelf approximately one foot below the water's surface around most of the pond to mimic the littoral zone in a natural waterfront. The shelf should be about a foot wide and sloped slightly toward the pond wall so your pots have plenty of room and will lean toward the wall as their plants get taller.
- Use a quality plastic liner (at least 45 mil) to increase the lifespan of the pond. Follow all the recommendations for its handling and treat it gently.
- If at all possible, use rainwater to fill the pond instead of potable tap water. Inoculate the water with a bucket of water from a natural pond or lake to introduce beneficial microbes. After the pond

is filled, start planting with your potted plants of rushes, irises, sedges, and other emergent plants. Use dark green or black pots to reduce their visibility in the water.

- Cover the top of the soil in each pot with weed barrier cloth held in place by a layer of sand or gravel. This way the soil won't move into the water. Plan to repot your pond plants every couple of years with compost-rich soil. Don't use perlite or vermiculite in the mix because they could float to the surface.

- Let the pond settle with just the plants for a month or two before you introduce fish and snails to the ecosystem. The water may turn green, but that's not unusual. It will balance out, so don't start all over again. Since it's out in the open, frogs, dragonflies, and other beneficial wildlife will find your pond on their own.

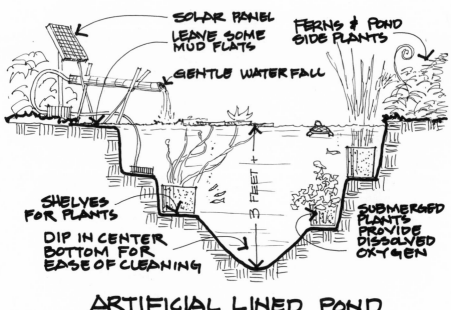

ARTIFICIAL LINED POND

Artificial, lined ponds are commonly used to provide habitat and to create more interest in the landscape. A dip in the center of the pond will collect the detritus and allow for more efficient cleanout.

- Consider a solar-powered pump to circulate water and drive a small, gentle waterfall feature. It will help aerate and filter the water without the installation of an external electrical system.
- Depending upon its size, a lined pond could receive some stormwater runoff, say from one downspout, but water retention is probably not the primary purpose of a small pond like this. Plan for the overflow in case of a heavy rain just as you would for any other water retention feature.

Seasonal Ponds

Because of Florida's typical wet and dry seasons, a common pond type found across much of our flatwoods habitats is the shallow "seasonal" pond—typically two to five feet deep and 30 or more feet across. Standing water recedes in the dry winter months, which often leaves a muddy pond floor. This mud provides moisture required by many amphibians, reptiles, birds, and small mammals.

If you wish to construct a pond to replicate this important habitat, choose an appropriate area where it won't look out of place. Typically this will be a low spot in your landscape or an area in your buffer zone near your shoreline property. The vegetation in this pond will most likely cover its entire area—you don't worry about eutrophication here. This is what a pond that has been through eutrophication would generally look like. It will be a damp meadow for part of the year and a shallow pond during the wet season. You'll probably find that the plants that do well in a rain garden, such as rushes, native irises, and sedges, will also thrive here. In fact, you could consider seasonal ponds a *type* of rain garden, and they do very well as a stormwater retention feature because of their shallow and broad profile. A seasonal pond might be a good use for overflow from bioswales, rain gardens, or rain barrels.

Retention Ponds Are Waterfront, Too

The lowly and ever so common stormwater retention pond can be transformed from an eyesore into an attractive landscape asset. At least one Florida county, Hillsborough, has an adopt-a-pond program where citizens volunteer to care for county retention ponds. To be successful, a project of this kind will need to be a cooperative management effort, and any plan to improve a retention pond will need to include all the neighbors in its vicinity. You'll need to bring in the local government and/or your regional water management district, so use their expertise to help you work out a reasonable plan for your pond.

Before you make any changes, you need to determine the regulations for the pond and whether or not it is designed to be dredged or scraped out on a regular basis. If it is, you'll need to plan for access for heavy machinery on one or two sides of the pond. Even if periodic disruptions of this kind will occur, there are still many ways to improve the pond's health, appearance, and habitat values.

If you can arrange it, have the pond dredged or scraped before you begin any significant work. This way, you'll start with a deeper body of water. Also, you'll know where and how the dredging takes place and can plan for it in the future. In most cases, a retention pond collects stormwater from many sources in its local area, but sometimes its watershed is surprisingly large. In any case, properties closest to the pond are often the largest contributors to the nutrient load, and the owners and managers of these neighboring properties also have the most to gain by the transformation.

The first phase of restoration could have as many as five separate initiatives.

1. Make sure that the neighboring property managers are not using the pond as a dumping place for their yard waste or other trash. If there is trash in and around the pond, hold a "Clean Our Pond" workday. Enlist the aid of neighborhood school kids or youth groups—they may be looking for community service projects. This is a great time to publicize your pond project.

2. Remove non-native invasive plants both from the shoreline and from the water area. Hydrilla, water hyacinths, wild taro, Brazilian pepper, Australian pine, Chinese tallow, torpedo grass, and other exotics need to be removed to make way for more appropriate native species that can provide shoreline stabilization and better habitat. Ask your extension agent for advice on the best ways

to handle the invasives. Keep in mind that those nutrient-rich aquatic plants are great additions to a compost pile.

Depending upon the severity of the non-native plant invasion, the removal effort will need to include careful follow-up. Quite often a simple pulling-out or chopping-down is not enough to wipe out these plants. Tubers or other persistent parts that could renew the infestation may be left behind. As they grow back, pull them again. After three or four removals, the remainder of the plants that grow back may finally need to be treated with an appropriate herbicide.

3. Capture and retain stormwater runoff from roofs, parking lots, driveways, and other impervious surfaces with a combination of rain barrels, rain gardens, and bioswales. This way, by the time stormwater runs into the retention pond, it will have been slowed down, reduced, and filtered.

4. If erosion has eaten away the soil from the sloping sides of the pond, try to find the source of the extra volume of runoff that is causing the problem. This is a part of identifying the sources of water runoff, so you'll need to handle that extra volume of water first. Once rain gardens or other water retention features are in place, then repair the slopes of the pond.

Each situation is different and the best treatment depends upon the slope, the soil type, and more. You might install a rain garden at the top of the slope to capture most of the runoff first. Then a relatively simple fix with a couple of lengths of biologs staked into a wide U-shape could reduce further erosion. You'll need to monitor what happens during a storm to know for sure.

5. Reduce or eliminate fertilization in the vicinity of the pond. Too often ponds receive so many extra nutrients that they have a constant algae bloom. This is not good for the long-term health of the pond's ecosystem. Install plants, such as cattails, that will soak up the nutrients that still make it into the pond. Both actions are necessary.

After you have removed all the trash and the invasive plants in and around the pond and have repaired eroding banks, you can start on the second phase—planting attractive native waterfront perennials and woody plants. This will be similar to the buffer and littoral plantings described above, but a typical retention pond will usually have a larger littoral area and will not have a significant wave problem. During the first phase you should have determined the areas where future dredging may occur. Don't use expensive woody plants there; install only herbaceous plants that are easily replaced, such as rushes, grasses, and sedges.

It will probably take several years to rescue a neglected retention pond, but as a water feature in the community, it does offer a great habitat for native flora and fauna. It can also provide an attractive focal point in both residential neighborhoods and commercial parks. The community-wide effort and increased awareness of the pond may expand beyond this retention pond's watershed. Be sure to take "before," "during," and "after" photographs of the pond and publicize what you've accomplished. Don't forget the educational value of the process of restoring an artificial system to a balanced and vital ecosystem.

Water Quality Issues for Waterfront Residents and Property Managers

Folks who live near water and property managers of waterfront lands can each make a difference in the overall quality of Florida's waterways. Unfortunately people tend to think that their own small actions won't make much difference, but when it comes to saving our water, nothing could be further from the truth. Here are some action items that will help reduce the nutrient and pollutant flow into the water.

- Waterways are not dumps. Keep garden and grass clippings and leaves out of the water and out of the storm drain system. Leave the clippings on the yard or put them in the compost pile. Manage your yard service so they understand that blowing leaves, grass clippings, and other trash into the water is not acceptable. Yard debris will increase the organic load in the water, and as the debris decomposes, bacteria, fungi, and algae will increase. These organisms will deplete oxygen levels in the water, which might cause fish kills.

- It's best to wash your car or truck at a car wash where the water is recycled, but if it's done on residential or commercial properties, park on a permeable surface so the water can soak into the ground. Use the smallest possible amount of the least caustic soap or detergent. Also use the least amount of water: use a bucket with soapy water (from rain barrels) to wash and then quickly rinse with a hose.

- Don't litter. Cigarette butts, plastic bags, and other trash will end up in lakes, ponds, canals, and even all the way down in the Everglades, where they can cause much harm to fish, birds, and other wildlife.

- Check your vehicles regularly for spills and leaking of oils and coolant. If there is a leak, park over a tray to catch the fluids until you can get the problem repaired. Dispose of used oil, coolant, and other pollutants properly—never down the storm drain. Clean up spills with old rags and dispose of them properly at a hazardous waste site.

- Sweep driveways and sidewalks instead of washing them down with water both to conserve water and to avoid washing hazardous substances into the stormwater collection system.

- Construct docks, decks, and other outdoor structures from sustainable recycled plastic composite materials. Don't use pressure-treated lumber because its infused poisonous chemicals could leach into the waterways.

- Pick up pet waste immediately and dispose of it properly—in your toilet, in the trash, or by burying it. It's not recommended for compost.

- Maintain sewage and septic systems.

Septic Tank Maintenance

People living near any body of water have a greater responsibility than other property owners to maintain their septic tanks, otherwise their drainfield runoffs add nutrients directly into our overburdened waterways. Here are some recommendations to help your septic system operate correctly.

- Don't plant trees or shrubbery over a septic tank or its drainfield. Roots can invade the drainfield pipes and reduce the tank's capacity or block the tank's inlet or outlet. Herbaceous plants are fine, and the top of a drainfield is a great place for a dry meadow.
- Don't use your garbage disposal for greasy or fibrous products. In fact, with a few exceptions, most of your kitchen waste can be composted.
- A septic tank should be inspected every three to six years, depending upon the age and type, to see if it is operating properly or if it needs to be pumped out.
- Enzymes, yeast, or bacteria will not repair a failing septic system. If pumping it out doesn't relieve the problems, the septic system will probably need to be replaced or repaired.
- Reduce the strain on your system by flushing your toilet less, and, unless you have a gray water system, don't wash several loads of clothes and run the dishwasher all in a short period of time. Spread the jobs across the week.

Wise Management of Waterfront Properties Is an Investment for the Future

Our waterfront and shoreline properties are valuable in many ways. How we manage them affects the overall health of our waterways. Preserving the quality of our waterways for our children and grandchildren will allow them to experience "The Real Florida."

Resources

Web Sites

Florida's DEP offers zip code–specific information on proper disposal procedures for household hazardous waste: http://www.dep.state.fl.us.

Hillsborough County has an adopt-a-pond program, where residents can sign up to take care of one of the area stormwater retention ponds: http://www.swfwmd.state.fl.us.

Select "Florida" on the U.S. Geological Survey's Water Resources Web site to see detailed information about water resources and their management for our state: http://water.usgs.gov/.

NOAA's habitat Web site has detailed information on living shorelines and other wetlands restoration issues: http://www.habitat.noaa.gov.

Books

Florida's DEP, with the cooperation of the Department of Agriculture and Consumer Services, the Department of Community Affairs, Florida's water management districts, the University of Florida, and private industry partners has produced a 68-page booklet, *Best Management Practices for Protection of Water Resources in Florida*, June 2002. (Available online: http://www.dep.state. fl.us.)

Harrison, Marie. *Gardening in the Coastal South*. Sarasota, Fla.: Pineapple Press, 2003.

Sullivan, Barbara. *Garden Perennials for the Coastal South*. Chapel Hill: University of North Carolina Press, 2002.

Tobe, John D., coordinating ed. *Florida's Wetland Plants: An Identification Manual*. Gainesville: University of Florida, IFAS, and Florida DEP, 1998.

14

Preparing the Landscape for Disasters

Florida is a paradise with its warm weather and abundance of beaches, coral reefs, rivers, clear springs, lakes, parks, preserves, its amazing birds and other wildlife. But sometimes there's trouble in paradise. Hurricanes have rampaged through Florida on a regular basis, greatly affecting the coastal regions that have also attracted the most development. For countless centuries, wildfires have raged across the state, and its wild areas are well adapted to fire, but as development is intermixed with forested areas, more homeowners are concerned that wildfires could threaten their communities.

Prudent design, thoughtful plant selection, and ongoing landscape maintenance may help to reduce damage to buildings, vehicles, other property, and the landscape itself when disaster strikes. There are no guarantees in disasters, of course, but wouldn't you feel better doing what you can to reduce your risk?

Preparing for Disasters Is Sustainable

Preplanning to create a disaster-resistant landscape is sustainable, because this kind of preparation can dramatically reduce chances of injury and damage to property. Having a plan of action to consult before and after a disaster strikes will help organize your actions so that you and your family can make the best use of your time, energy, and money. Preparing your landscape for disaster can save you heartache in both the short and long run.

Hurricanes and Tropical Storms

Hurricanes and tropical storms can cause significant damage in any part of Florida with their one-two punch of high winds and torrential rain. Coastal regions are more vulnerable than inland areas for two reasons.

1. Storm winds have more velocity as they make landfall, weakening once they lose contact with the warm tropical water and move over land. Fast-moving storms have nonetheless caused severe damage further inland.
2. Storm surges and heavy rainfall may cause significant erosion and flooding on properties near beaches, bays, estuaries, and rivers. Surges are usually more severe on the Gulf Coast due to its shallower waters, but heavy rain can cause problems anywhere. Surges and high winds near coastal areas may also drench the landscape with salt-laden water, damaging plants that aren't salt tolerant.

No landscape is totally storm proof. Even normally wind-resistant trees, which have stood for a century or more, might not survive a direct hit from a strong hurricane. Many Floridians learned the hard way, during recent hurricane-filled years, that no part of the state is safe from damage.

Even so, with stormwise preparations and ongoing maintenance, you can reduce the amount of destruction left behind by lower intensity storms or strong ones that graze your immediate community. Your approach will be three-pronged: first, stormwater management; second, ongoing maintenance of trees and landscape; and third, stormwise tree selection.

Stormwater Management

Start by observing where rainwater collects on your property after a heavy rain. If puddles of water remain around bases of trees for more than a day, those trees may be more vulnerable to uprooting in a tropical storm. The exception would be wetland-adapted trees such as bald cypress, sweet bay magnolia, water tupelo, or Carolina willow. Ideally you'll want to create a series of swales or French drains to direct surplus water away from buildings and away from the trees near buildings to a rain garden, bog area, or pond. Rain barrels will fill up quickly in a tropical storm, so you'll need to consider their outflows as well. This is not flood control, but creating a space where excess stormwater can collect and percolate safely into the ground is one way to reduce the likelihood of uprooted trees and to lessen damage to building foundations. Having most of the rainwater percolate through the soil is also much better for the health of our waterways than allowing it to run unimpeded across the surface, sweeping debris and pollution in its path.

Tree Evaluation

It's particularly important to manage trees in areas where they could do the most damage—we'll call this the **damage zone**. A tree close enough to fall on a building, power line, vehicles, or other valuable property is in the damage zone. A plan of action for a tree in this zone would include its identification and evaluation of its health. If it's basically sound but overgrown, develop a pruning plan. If it has major structural problems that cannot be remedied by pruning and/or cabling, it may need to be removed. Trees outside the damage zone are less critical, but reducing the risk of their falling will save time and money in the cleanup after a storm.

If you don't know the species of trees on your property, find out. Ask an experienced gardener, purchase a book on Florida's trees, or take a photo of the whole tree to show to your county's extension agent. Also take with you a clipping of a twig with leaves and, if possible, with flowers or fruit. This will make it easier for the agent to identify the tree. If you have many unknown trees, it's probably a good idea to hire an arborist to evaluate your trees for vulnerability to storm damage. Ask him or her to identify your trees and to provide a written list as part of the process. Do it now—a week before a storm hits is too late.

Various trees react differently to wind pressure. Some fast-growing trees have brittle wood and could snap under pressure from wind. Shallow-rooted trees may not break, but they could inflict even more damage if they uproot and fall over. Thick-crowned trees may be top-heavy and fall over or break. Multiple attached trunks or major branches at narrow angles to the trunk are more likely to split in a high wind. Some trees, such as sweet gums, certain pines, and most palms are flexible and can bend in the wind. Others react to wind pressure by losing their leaves, twigs, and branches—after a storm they may look stripped, but afterward they'll grow new leaves and branches. Highly visible examples of this process in South Florida are the Norfolk Island pines. Habitually taller than the surrounding canopy of trees and buildings, they sometimes snap right off in high winds. After a hurricane the ones left standing often look naked, but new branches sprout from the trunk; sometimes multiple trunks arise from a storm injury.

In chapter 6, we covered evaluation of trees already in your landscape, including suitability for the space, soundness of the trunk, weakness of attached branches, circling of roots, and more. If a tree is basically sound, the most sustainable action is to keep the tree, but you might need to prune it to lighten its crown—topping is never recommended. According to University of Florida professor Dr. Ed Gilman, who has been conducting controlled wind tolerance experiments, corrective pruning is probably more important for a tree's survival during a windstorm than its species. Certified arborists follow the standards defined by the Tree Care Industry Association for pruning methods that reduce the crown, encourage a single dominant trunk, and remove branches with weak attachments.

Although a tree's species may not be the only criterion for its survival, the following non-native trees fell in great numbers during recent hurricane seasons: weeping fig, queen palm, African tulip tree, Australian

pine, camphor tree, Chinaberry, Chinese tallow, eucalyptus, and melaleuca. Even some of our native trees, such as Carolina laurelcherry, laurel
oak, red cedar, sand pine, and water oak, have not fared well in recent
hurricanes. Develop a plan to prune or remove these trees before the next
hurricane strikes. Local tree ordinances may require permission to remove mature trees, so check with county or town officials before taking
action.

Planning for new trees in your landscape should include stormwise
choices: you want to select not only the storm-worthiest species but those
that are most suitable for specific locations and microclimates. Some of
the more wind-resistant trees for all of Florida include bald cypress, cabbage palm, dahoon holly, fringetree, live oak, magnolias, sand live oak,
and tupelo. For southern regions of the state, add buttonwood, Florida
thatch, Geiger tree, gumbo-limbo, mahogany, royal palm, sea grape, silver
palm, shortleaf and strangler figs, strong bark, and stoppers. For northern
Florida, add dogwood, persimmon, river birch, winged elm, and yaupon
holly.

Remember to plan for the eventual size of trees, both of the crown
and root system, in your placement. While estimated dimensions of adult
trees usually include the height and width of the above-ground parts, a
good rule of thumb for estimating the size of the root system is to add 30
percent to the width of the crown. Smaller, wind-resistant trees are useful in the landscape when planted close enough to buildings to shade all
but the north-facing walls. You want them to help reduce your air-conditioning needs, but not to become so large that they could cause damage.
Choose smaller trees for street trees as well, because they won't outgrow
the limited space between the street and sidewalk. Provide plenty of room
for larger trees, such as live oaks, in the landscape so their root systems
can spread out enough to support their large crowns.

Groups of trees usually survive tropical storms better than those growing singly or in rows. A group of five or more wind-tolerant trees could
act as a windscreen or wind grove by interrupting airflow. While a tropical storm's main thrust could come from almost any direction, look at the
paths of past hurricanes and your local conditions to estimate the most
likely direction for future storms. If you have room on your property, lo-

cating a wind grove 20 to 30 feet from the most vulnerable side of a building could reduce the wind damage to both the building and the landscape. A well-designed wind grove might also take the brunt of flying debris.

Ongoing Maintenance

Prudent, ongoing maintenance of your landscape trees, both in and out of the damage zone, consists of thinning their crowns, protecting their trunks, and trimming out diseased and dead wood, coconuts, or other parts that could become missiles in a storm.

According to the pruning standards that guide arborists, the thinning of a tree's crown may take several years, because trimming more than 20 percent of a tree at a time may be too much of a shock for it. Create a pruning plan, and after several years the crown will be well shaped, balanced, and airy—from a distance it shouldn't look pruned. After this initial period of lightening the crown, you may need to retrim every five or so years to keep it in good shape. The frequency of trimming depends upon the species and previous maintenance practices.

It's more important with palms than other trees not to injure the trunks because they cannot heal a gouge. To avoid clipping them with a mower or grass trimmer, get rid of the lawn around them and encircle the base of each tree with a mulched bed at least two feet wide and two or three inches thick. Palms with injuries at the base are more likely to drop in a high wind. Never top a palm because it grows only from the top, and removing its only growth node will kill it. Each year, remove only the dead fronds, old flower stalks, and fruits, especially coconuts—they make it top-heavy and could become missiles in a high wind. Don't prune back any green fronds, even if they droop, because palms have so few leaves that they need them all to maintain vigor.

While stormproofing your trees and controlling excess stormwater are the most important parts of creating a stormwise landscape, there are other considerations and actions that could reduce damage in a storm.

- Choose wind-resistant shrubs, perennials, and groundcovers or ones that will readily grow back if they are knocked down or broken off during a storm. These smaller plants don't cause the damage that trees do, but not having to replace them after a storm saves time and money. In coastal areas, consider using salt-tolerant plants, even if salt spray is not a daily problem.

- Eliminate loose and lightweight gravel on your property. Yes, it's sometimes recommended for waterwise and firewise landscapes, but such gravel could be lofted in a high wind event. The scoop on gravel mulch is found in chapter 3.

- Limit your use of lightweight landscape ornamentation, such as wind chimes, outdoor furniture, birdfeeders, gazing balls, gnomes, and the like. Have only as many as you can easily put away before a storm, otherwise they could become windborne and do damage. Include their removal in your prestorm plan, as described below.

- Choose either heavy containers that won't blow over or lightweight ones that are easy to move or secure for your container gardens. Have a plan for handling your containers during storm season. Maybe you could locate your heaviest containers to the normally leeward side of buildings and use the lightweight containers on the windward side so you can move them with ease before a storm hits. A dolly to move heavy containers will make the job easier—straining the gardener's back is not a sustainable practice.

Develop a Pre-storm Plan for Your Landscape

Before the storm, put away container plants, lawn ornaments, outside furniture, wind chimes, or other items that could blow away or tip over. Some people suggest throwing lawn furniture into your pool, but this is probably not very good for either the pool or the furniture. If a tall containerized plant is too heavy to move easily, lay it down, and if possible strap or tie it in place—don't leave a plant like this for more than a day or two, or it will start to grow vertically. You may want to unstake newly planted trees and shrubs before a storm and just let them blow over. You'll have to replant and restake them afterward, but this is better than letting the high winds break them off at the staking point.

Be careful about hiring guys that come to your door with chainsaws before a storm. If you do hire them, have them cut only dead palm fronds, coconuts, or deadwood in your shade trees and have them either shred or haul the waste away. You don't want those branches or fronds lying around to become airborne in the storm.

These days, we normally have fair warning of approaching storms, but if you'll be out of town during peak hurricane season, it's a good idea to make your landscape storm-ready just in case. If Murphy's Law is working, once you've made all your preparations, there will be no storm while you're away.

After the Storm

Hurricanes don't know how to prune! Even if you've lightened the crowns of your shade trees, you may find many branches torn off or broken at odd angles after a major storm. As soon as practical, trim these broken branches back to just outside of the most logical crotch, as if you were heading it back. Trees will try to put out new leaves and branches at a

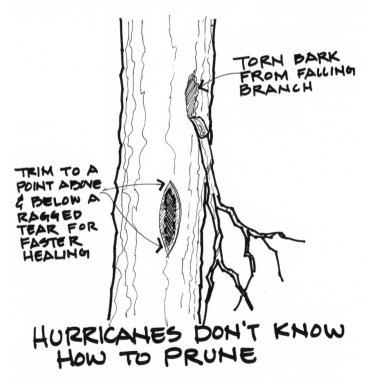

TORN BARK FROM FALLING BRANCH

TRIM TO A POINT ABOVE & BELOW A RAGGED TEAR FOR FASTER HEALING

HURRICANES DON'T KNOW HOW TO PRUNE

If a branch has been torn from a tree, trimming the scar so there are points on the top and bottom will promote easier healing.

wound and a quick pruning will spare them the effort of growing back in an inappropriate way. Trim the edges of torn bark with a sharp knife and create a vertical, almond-shaped wound at the juncture where the branch or limb was torn off. Be careful not to expose any more cambium (the thin layer of living tissue just under the bark) than necessary—this way the tree will be able to heal more quickly. Do not try to rebalance the crown of a tree that has been hurricane pruned. Prune only the storm-damaged branches and let it recover for a year or more before you start to rebalance it.

There may be trees that are too damaged to save. A tree that has lost more than half of its crown or one that has been deeply split should probably be removed. Look for trees with loosened root systems. If a tree has been recently planted or is still small and otherwise healthy, you may be able to tilt it back to a vertical alignment. After you've reburied the roots, treat it like a new transplant with plenty of water while it redevelops its root system.

Salt residue can poison plants that aren't salt tolerant. If a tropical storm includes a saltwater storm surge or if salt-laden winds are not followed by a good rinsing rain, the landscape may suffer. While there's usually *a lot* of clean-up after a storm, rinsing the salt residue from remaining trees and shrubs may be one of the more important and time-sensitive tasks for their long-term survival. Freshwater may not be readily available after a severe storm, so this is a time you'll be grateful to have a rainwater harvesting system filled with gallons of freshwater to use for this task.

Evaluate what has been left standing and what has been knocked down, not only on your own property, but also in your entire neighborhood. You can develop your own localized stormwise ideas with your observations of storm damages in your specific locale.

Wildfires

There is probably a wildfire burning somewhere in Florida as you read this. Much of the state is susceptible to **wildfires**—they are natural occurrences in many of our ecosystems. On average, Florida's 5,500 wildfires burn more than 200,000 acres annually. Fire-adapted areas include forests, scrub areas, grasslands, parks, and even wetlands. As development is pushed into wild areas, the **wildland-urban interface** expands, and more homeowners and other property owners find that wildfires could threaten their property.

Properties that border a large wild area generally have a greater fire risk than those in well-developed suburban or urban neighborhoods, but a fire can happen anywhere. If you're not sure of your risk, ask your local fire department, extension agent, park ranger, or forester about your property's vulnerability to wildfire damage.

First some background. As you know, fires require fuel, oxygen, and heat to burn. There are three types of wildfires. A **surface fire** burns the material above the ground and below the treetops or canopy. Fuel includes leaf litter, mulch, shrubs, vines, and other low-lying objects. A hot surface fire is generally necessary to start or support either a **canopy** or **crown fire,** which burns in the tops of the trees, or a **ground fire**, which burns roots, **duff,** and other organic materials under the surface.

The good news is that firewise landscape design combined with ongoing maintenance could very well save your house and other buildings. Firewise landscapes provide less potential fuel for fires, especially surface fires. Depending upon the size of your property and its possible exposure to wildfires, there are many ways to reduce your risk to a tolerable level. Create a plan of action suitable for your situation.

A firewise landscape is generally organized into three zones. The measurements from buildings offered below are suggestions; customize them to fit your property and your lifestyle.

Maintaining Zones One, Two, and Three

Zone One

Create a 30-foot defensible space around your house and other buildings by removing or isolating the most flammable fuel in this area to provide a firebreak. You should also provide a 16-foot-wide access area and maneuvering room for fire equipment all around buildings. Remember to block access to septic tank and drainfield areas with small shrubs or raised gardens around the edges so heavy trucks don't collapse these underground structures.

Here are some suggestions for creating and maintaining zone one, your most important firebreak.

- Maintain a mowed yard. Choose a grass, clover, or other mowable groundcover that is well suited to your soil. Irrigate it so these mowed plants develop deep roots. In a fire-prone region, dried grass is a fuel for surface fires, so regular mowing and a computerized irrigation system may be more important here than elsewhere. Consider the expense of installing and maintaining this infrastructure as an investment in property protection—your own insurance policy.

- Remove flammable fences or other structures that could provide a direct fire link to buildings. Remove dead trees, dead limbs, and brush piles.

- Move woodpiles and compost piles to an area outside of zone one—more than 30 feet away from buildings. While composting is an important and sustainable way to recycle garden waste and other vegetable matter, your compost pile needs to be located away from buildings because it is fuel. You might want to use three-sided, dry-stacked cinderblock or cement block walls to contain your compost piles, with the open side facing away from your house. The cinder blocks could act as a firebreak. Keeping the compost consistently moist will not only hasten its decomposition, but will also make it less likely to burn.

- Under mature trees, remove tall shrubs, vines, Spanish moss, or anything that could act as **ladder fuel** for a surface fire to climb up into the canopy. You should pay particular attention to poison ivy, Brazilian pepper, and poisonwood trees—eliminate them from all zones because if they burn, urushiol, the toxin that causes skin rash, is carried in the smoke and could cause severe reactions for anyone who breathes it. The lungs and eyes are most vulnerable to internal or systemic inflammation from urushiol-laden smoke.

- Trim the branches of mature trees so that the lowest ones are at least ten feet from the ground; on smaller trees, remove lower branches to the first third of the tree's height. Prune branches so that they are at least ten feet away from any building and 15 feet away from rooftops. This process may take two or three years, because removing more than 20 percent of a tree at a time can damage it. It may take several years to train saplings into their most firewise (and stormwise) forms.

If you have a mature live oak tree with large, low-growing branches in zone one, you may not need to remove these important branches unless it's to provide fire equipment access or space between it and buildings. Live oaks are fire (and wind) resistant; you'll need to prune only the tertiary branches to reduce their crowns. Remove Spanish moss to ten feet from the ground—about as high as you can reach with a rake.

- If there are mature pine trees or other conifers, such as bald cypress, in this zone, trim the branches to 20 feet from the ground and remove enough conifers so the crowns are ten to fifteen feet apart. Remove most small conifers, and don't choose new decorative conifers for your landscape. (It's probably still a good idea to nurture a few choice native pine and cypress saplings to renew your forested areas.)

- Planting areas should be widely separated from each other to provide breaks in the potential fuel for a fire. Use the least flammable trees, shrubs, and herbaceous plants for new plantings in your landscape. (See the list of most and least flammable plants below.)

- Remove leaf litter, pine needles, and other flammable items from the ground and from roofs and gutters regularly. When danger of fire is high, monthly removal is not too often.

- Within six feet of buildings (maybe we should call this zone 1-A):
  - use bricks or other nonflammable stone or cement pavers to cover the soil. Any type of vegetative mulch could burn even if it is damp, so don't use it here. Use a weed-retarding cloth under the pavers and slant them away from the foundation. Heavy stones can be used for hardscape elements, such as pond edges, dry streambeds, and succulents-only gardens. Don't use gravel as a mulch.

- pavers are a better firewise choice for outside living areas than wooden decks. If there's a significant slope away from the building, it's safer to build up the level with dirt and cement or stone blocks. The open space under a flammable deck provides a pathway for fire. If you decide not to replace your wooden decks, treat them with fire retardant and use metal grating to skirt the undersides. Make sure that leaves and other flammable debris cannot blow under the deck.
- remove tall shrubs, vines, trellises, or other flammable objects, especially from under eaves. They could serve as ladder fuel to elevate a surface fire into the attic space.

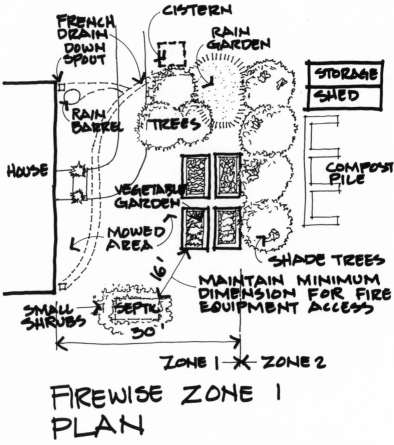

Firewise landscaping can save your house. Zone 1 extends at least 30 feet from buildings and along driveways. Be sure to leave 16 feet of access for fire equipment.

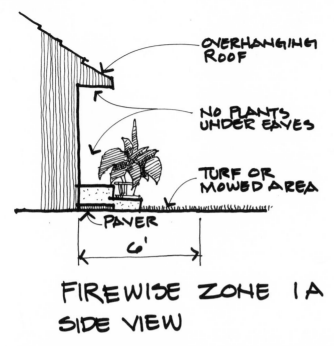

FIREWISE ZONE 1A SIDE VIEW

Zone 1A is six feet from buildings. Remove shrubbery from this area. Use pavers and mulch around buildings and keep the area irrigated and mowed. Containers should be moved inside buildings or outside of Zone 1 when fire threatens and when you're away during the fire season.

Zone Two

This zone extends from 30 feet to 60 feet from buildings, starting just at the outer boundary of zone one. Moderate thinning and fuel reduction should break the continuity of fuel available for a wildfire. Remove all poison ivy and most dead plant material. In this zone it is probably all right to leave some of the standing deadwood for its wildlife value, but remove any ladder fuel around snags. Remove ladder fuels from under mature trees—particularly conifers. Clear out some vegetation between trees and plantings. If an access road or driveway runs through this zone, treat it as zone one and thin back to 15 feet on either side.

Zone Three

Starting just outside the boundary of zone two, this zone extends from 60 to 100 feet from buildings. Zone three marks the transition to the wild areas in your landscape, and its maintenance should include removal of poison ivy and ladder fuels under conifers and dead wood.

If these outside zones and the areas beyond are included in community common lands, management and fuel reduction need to be coordinated for the whole neighborhood. If these areas are public or private lands, work with the property managers to coordinate fuel reduction efforts. Prescribed burns may be part of the plan, so be tolerant of, and grateful for, these efforts. An unmanaged property in a fire-prone locale could put the whole area at risk.

Once you've cleared away fuel, your landscape doesn't have to look like a desert or a moonscape. It should look more like a lovely, open forest with live oaks, magnolias, and other high-moisture broadleaf trees closest to the buildings. There are a number of firewise landscaping projects that might increase your enjoyment of the land.

Collect rainwater from your roofs and other impermeable surfaces such as driveways and patios. Divert some of the downspout water into rain barrel systems for watering your plants. You might then take the rest of the runoff and collect it in a cistern for firefighting—a 2,500-gallon tank is a good size, but a larger tank might be necessary if you use the water for irrigation as well. A gray water collection tank can serve the same purpose or the gray water can be collected in the same tank as the rainwater. Label the water source clearly so that firefighters can easily spot it, and provide access to it for a large hose. If the top is open, install a screened cover to keep out mosquitoes and small children. Plan for a spillover from the cistern into a low area on your lot or into a pond. You should check with your local authorities to find out if there are regulations for cisterns.

A pond, water garden, rain garden, or bog garden can be a good addition to a firewise landscape: the water-rich plants supported by these wet environments are not as flammable as others and the water itself could provide a firebreak. Because you need to plan for the 16-foot fire equipment access, the cistern and water features should either be located close to buildings or toward the far edge of zone one and away from septic systems. A large pond could substitute for a cistern and could be used for fire fighting around your property—a typical fire hose uses a ¼-acre-foot of water over five hours. Mosquitoes shouldn't be a problem in a pond

Fire-prone plants to be removed from zone one and reduced in zone two:

- Remove small palms and palmettos (native or non-native). Mature cabbage palms and other native palms with trunks six feet tall or more can be spared as long as the browned fronds and boots are removed on a regular basis. They are adapted to fire and survive as long as their growing tips are not destroyed.
- Remove red cedar, arborvitae, and other ornamental conifers. Remove wax myrtle, hollies, and groundsel trees.
- Don't use ornamental grasses, because their decorative stalks are highly flammable.
- Cut down vines growing up trees or buildings, particularly greenbriar and poison ivy—these serve as ladder fuel.
- For the sake of Florida's ecosystems and because they are flammable, remove noxious non-natives, such as Australian pine, eucalyptus, melaleuca, and Chinese tallow trees.

Install less flammable and more fire-tolerant plants recommended for use in zones one and two: beautyberry, coontie, dogwood, ferns, fringetree, hophornbeam, magnolia, oaks, persimmon, redbud, red maple, soapberry, sparkleberry, sweetgum, viburnum, white geiger, wild azalea, wild plum, and winged elm.

because fish, dragonfly larvae, and other predators will control them. Vegetable gardens can also be added to a mostly sunny spot in zone one.

You may wish to use containers for your close-to-the-house landscaping for color and variety. Fireproof containers like ceramics, terra cotta, and cement are probably your best choices. If a fire approaches, you can move your plants into a building or outside of zone one. You might not have much notice to prepare for an advancing fire and moving dozens and dozens of containers can be tedious, so keep both their sizes and numbers manageable. If you travel during fire season, store containers in a building or outside of zone one—maybe near the compost area.

Before and After a Fire

If a fire is headed in your direction, have a plan and rehearse it with the whole family so that everyone knows what to do if communication is cut off. Turn on your sprinkler system to soak the whole yard, and, as recommended in firewise literature, water your roof as well. Remove debris inside zone one. Then be ready to evacuate as directed.

Fires have occurred throughout Florida on a regular basis for millennia and natural areas are adapted to and may even require fire to thrive. On undeveloped land, no action is recommended after a fire. In areas where we humans live and work, we just feel better when we clean up the mess.

If the fire was a quick surface fire, the roots of grasses and shrubs may be viable and will start to sprout within a week or two. If this is the case, just rake away the ashes and debris, water remaining plants, and remove charred, dead wood so it doesn't become fuel for the next fire. Those ashes will be a good addition to your compost pile. Mature trees will usually survive a quick fire.

If the fire was hotter and longer lasting, the soil may have been overheated. Dig several inches into the soil in an area near where perennials or shrubs were growing. If the small roots are white and turgid, they are probably viable. In this case leave things alone and wait to see what grows back. If the small roots are blackened or mushy or if the soil is dry and hot, it has probably been cooked. You'll need to develop a plan for seeding or resodding the yard area and starting to replant the gardens. Start with inexpensive annuals to fill in the gaps while you wait to see what will grow back. If a waterway is nearby, pay special attention to erosion control after a fire. Replace burned out shrubs and perennials with natives that are both fire resistant and fire tolerant.

While There Are No Guarantees, Planning for Disaster Can Make a Significant Difference

To develop both a stormwise and firewise landscape, assess your risks for each type of disaster and make the best compromises in managing the landscape to reduce your chances of damage or injury to an acceptable level. There is no one answer or solution—it's up to you.

Resources

Web Sites

Florida's Division of Forestry provides information on forest management and wildfire prevention and suppression: http://www.fl-dof.com.

The University of Florida's IFAS extension offers excellent information on pre- and post-storm tree care, along with the comparative wind resistance of different tree species: http://treesandhurricanes.ifas.ufl.edu.

Universal Fire Shield sells fire-retardant products and has a distribution center in Lakeland: http://www.firechemicals.com.

The Florida Division of Emergency Management offers guidelines for storm-proofing your property and for coping with Florida wildfires: http://www.florida disaster.org/.

The Web site of the Tree Care Industry Association (TIA), formerly the National Association of Arborists, provides comprehensive information on tree care and tree safety: http://www.tcia.org.

For wildfire mitigation contacts and information on fire prevention in Florida, visit the Florida Department of Agriculture and Consumer Affairs' Wildland Fire Web site: http://www.fl-dof.com/wildfire/firewise_contacts.html.

Books

Florida Department of Community Affairs (DCA). *Wildfire Mitigation in Florida: Land Use Planning Strategies and Best Development Practices.* Tallahassee, Fla.: Florida DCA, Division of Community Planning Publications, 2004. (This and other documents are available for download under publications at http://www.interfacesouth.org.)

Glossary

Acidity: The acidity of the soil determines the rates of uptake of various nutrients from the soil. Soil acidity is measured on the pH scale of 1 to 14, where pH is short for the "potential of hydrogen." Seven is neutral. Substances measuring below seven are acidic, while those that measure above seven are alkaline. When you test your soil, the acidity is one of the measurements. Most plants do best at a near neutral state, but some thrive in the extreme acid soils found in bogs, while others have adapted to the extreme alkaline soils like the limestone substrate found in the Keys.

Actinomycetes: A filamentous soil bacterium that provides that wonderful "good earthy" soil smell. Actinomycetes were formerly classified as a fungus because of their long strands and spore formation, but since they have no nuclei, they were demoted to bacteria. Actinomycetes facilitate the breakdown of the toughest organic materials, such as cellulose (found in cell walls of plants) and chitin (found in insect exoskeletons and fungi cell walls). A gram of soil can contain one hundred million individuals.

Aerobic: A condition in which air or oxygen is present. If your compost piles and your ponds are aerobic, they hold enough oxygen to support organisms that require oxygen for respiration. They also smell sweet, not sour. See **anaerobic**.

Algae (sing. alga): Primitive **photosynthetic** plants that lack true stems or leaves. Many algae are single-celled microscopic, green plants that can live in a variety of habitats, including soil and water. Several hundred thousand algae can live in one gram of soil as long as it's near the surface where they can receive light for photosynthesis. Red and brown algae are more complex multicelled organisms, such as seaweeds. Algae can also survive in a symbiotic relationship with **fungi** to form lichen.

Alien: See **non-native**.

Allelopathic: Some plants release chemicals into the soil that have beneficial or harmful effects on other plants—these are called "allelopathic." Plants can inhibit the growth or reproduction of competing plant species. Black walnut is a prime example of allelopathy: the tree produces the chemical juglone, which suppresses the growth of trees, shrubs, and vegetation. Other allelopathic trees include Australian pine, sycamore, eucalyptus, and hackberry.

Anaerobic: A condition in which there is no air or oxygen. This may describe a process such as fermentation, or it may used to describe a microbe that can function without air. If your compost pile becomes anaerobic, it will have an unpleasant or sour odor. As described in chapter 3, turn your compost pile and work in dry materials to introduce more air if it smells sour. See **aerobic**.

Angiosperm: Flowering, fruit-bearing plants. The seeds of these plants develop within an enclosed ovary. See **gymnosperms**.

Arborist: A certified tree specialist. This is not the same as some guy with a chainsaw who knocks on your door during hurricane season. To find or verify an arborist in your area, see the Tree Care Industry Association Web site: http://www.tcia.org.

Bacteria: Pervasive, one-celled organisms that play an important role in decomposing organic materials. One gram of soil may contain 200,000 types of bacteria and billions of individuals. Special bacteria (*Rhizobia*) form a symbiotic relationship with the plant roots of legumes (and some other plants) whereby the bacteria fix the nitrogen from the atmosphere, which supplies a usable form of nitrogen to the plant.

Beneficials: The living creatures or organisms—including bacteria, fungi, larvae, insects, birds, bats, and so on—that prey on those that damage crops and other desirable plants. Encouraging the beneficials is an important part of your integrated pest management (IPM) program as described in chapter 9.

Biolog: Long rolls of organic material used for erosion control. Usually they are staked in place and planted with plants that will grow on the shoreline as the logs decompose. The material most often used for biologs is **coconut coir**, but there are also large biodegradable sleeves or socks available that can be filled onsite with compost.

Biomass: The amount of living matter, in the form of organisms, present in a particular habitat, usually expressed as weight-per-unit area or as the carbon, nitrogen, or caloric content per unit area. It can also mean the weight of plant materials and animal waste that can be used for fuel.

Boots: The hard, wedge-shaped leafbases that persist on the trunks of some palm trees—particularly cabbage palms—after the fronds have fallen off. Palm boots provide habitat and food sources for many different plants and animals, including orchids, ferns, bromeliads, strangler figs, birds, lizards, and even small mammals.

Branch collar: An area of growth tissue in the bark that forms around branches at their juncture with another limb or the tree trunk. On most trees it looks like a few wrinkles in the bark, but on some it may be a slight swelling. When pruning, prune inside of the branch collar so the tree may heal. See chapter 6 for more details and illustrations.

Bt (*Bacillus thuringiensis*): A naturally occurring bacterium common in soils that can infect and kill insects by paralyzing their digestive systems. Various strains of Bt have been developed for controlling specific insects, such as leaf-eating caterpillars, black flies, and mosquitoes. At present, Bt is the only "microbial insecticide" in widespread use and is favored by organic farmers because it is not a general poison and it degrades quickly.

Caliper inch: Nursery tree size is measured by caliper inch. This is the diameter of the trunk at 12 inches above the top of the root-ball. If this measurement is less than four inches, measure at six inches instead. Established trees are measured at four and one half feet from the ground—a measurement referred to as DBH (Diameter Breast Height).

Cambium: The slimy greenish layer of growing wood just under the bark of a tree (except for palms). The cambium carries the sugars from the leaves down to the roots and back. It is the growth of this layer of wood that creates annual rings. If a tree is girdled—slicing the bark around the entire trunk—the cambium cannot function and the tree will die.

Canopy: The tops of the trees in a forest. A dense canopy blocks all direct sunlight from the forest floor. A thin or broken canopy allows sunlight and supports a more diverse variety of plants and animals.

Canopy fire or **crown fire**: A fire in the treetops, burning both live and dead fuel. It is normally supported by hot **surface fire** and often presents a wall of flames from the ground to the tops of the trees. Canopy fires are the most dangerous and destructive.

Carbon-offset companies: These nonprofit or for-profit organizations accept payments from individuals and companies to counterbalance their release of carbon—mostly carbon dioxide (CO_2)—in their day-to-day living or business operations. You can be carbon neutral if you have the carbon you release offset by the projects of the carbon-offset companies. The money is used to plant trees in open land, cover land-fills to reduce methane (CH_4) emissions, and develop renewable energy and other sustainable projects. Critics of this movement say that people and companies need to change their behavior and not just be able to pay money to assuage their guilt.

Carbon sink: A carbon sink occurs when carbon is absorbed and held or sequestered. A tree becomes a temporary carbon sink because it absorbs carbon dioxide as part of its photosynthesis. The sugars, which contain carbon and become woody tissues, tie up the carbon until that wood rots or burns and the carbon is returned back into the atmosphere. A young and growing forest will be a carbon sink, but a mature forest becomes carbon-neutral as the older trees fall and decay. Artificial carbon sinks can be accomplished by chemically locking up carbon dioxide and storing it an underground reservoir—this is sometimes mandated for smoke stacks of coal-fired power plants.

Climax community: A stage in ecological development in which a community of organisms, especially plants, is stable and capable of perpetuating itself. With no outside disturbances, a climax community will not be succeeded by a different set of plants—it will have reached an equilibrium.

Coconut coir: Coir (pronounced core) is the name of the layer in the coconut shell from which it is extracted. Sold in compressed bricks, it expands many times its size when hydrated, will absorb up to eight times its weight in water, and is easy to rewet. With an acidity close to neutral, coir serves as a more sustainable alternative for **peat moss** in your potting soil mix and for humus in your soil. Coconut coir is also available in mat form for lining hanging planters and as **biologs** to control water flows and prevent erosion.

Conifer: A tree or shrub with cones instead of flowers, such as pines, junipers, and cypresses. Most conifers are resinous and burn readily. Botanically they are called "**gymnosperms**," meaning naked seeds. True flowering plants are called "**angiosperms**."

Cotyledon: The first leaves to emerge from a seed that were preformed inside the seed. If there are two leaves, the plant is a **dicot**. If there's one leaf, it's a **monocot**. Only true flowering plants or **angiosperms** have these cotyledons.

Crotch dropping: A pruning practice for reducing the canopy of trees or shrubs where a main branch is cut back to a convenient crotch at the point where a side branch or a side bud occurs and is facing in the direction suitable for more growth. Chapter 6 has more information on pruning.

Crusher run gravel: (Sometimes called "crush and run.") A class of gravel from a stone crusher that includes stones ranging in size from the stated maximum down to grit: 1.5-inch crusher run will include some rocks that size, but most of the material will be smaller. It's generally less expensive than clean gravel because it's not run through a sieve to size the gravel.

Cultivar: A plant that has been developed for the horticultural trade by hybridization, selective breeding, or by taking advantage of accidents of nature. Cultivars don't always breed true with open-pollinated seed and are often reproduced asexually by cuttings or divisions.

Damage zone: (A term created for this book.) A tree close enough to fall on a building, power line, vehicle, or other valuable property is in the damage zone. It's roughly equal to the height of the tree.

Dead zones: See **nutrient cycle**.

Desiccation: The process of a plant's losing water through overheating and/or strong winds causing too much **transpiration**. Wilting is usually the first symptom of desiccation.

Detritus: A combination of dead plants and animals, plus their waste products, in various states of decay. Detritus is naturally found in the leaf litter on the forest floor and in the bottoms of ponds, lakes, and other waterways. Various animals, bacteria, and fungi feed on detritus and contribute to the decomposition. See **eutrophication**.

Diatomaceous earth: Crushed sedimentary rock composed of skeletons of diatoms—hard-shelled aquatic algae. The individual pieces are sharp and will penetrate soft bodies of crawlers such as caterpillars, worms, or slugs. This is a physical pesticide and does not differentiate between pests and beneficials. Handle with care: wear gloves and don't breathe any of the dust.

Dicot or **dicotyledonous**: An angiosperm or flowering plant that has two **cotyledon** leaves preformed in the seed. When it sprouts, these two seed leaves are the first two leaves. The first true leaves normally look much different than the cotyledons.

Drip line: The area around a tree or shrub defined by where water would drip to the ground from its outermost branches. The area inside this ring is known as the drip zone. The root zone usually extends at least 30 percent beyond drip line on a healthy, well-established tree.

Duff: Partially decayed organic matter under the leaf litter in a forest or under mulch in a garden.

Earthworms: These segmented worms eat their way through the soil (a third of their body weight per day), creating tunnels, and leaving behind their wastes, euphemistically called "castings." Earthworms aerate the soil and break down the humus. They respire through their skin and prefer damp, rich soil, seeking out the best areas, such as under wet leaves or in your compost pile. Worms can even live in water for a few weeks. Earthworms are hermaphrodites, each having both female and male reproductive organs. If you accidentally cut an earthworm in half, only the front part has a chance of living.

Ecology: The study of the relationship of organisms to each other and to their environment. The organisms and their environment are known as an ecosystem. (When people say that they are taking an action for the good of the ecology, they are misusing the term unless they are funding a school.)

Ecosystem: A complex interrelationship of organisms (plants, animals, fungi, and bacteria) in the substrate where they live and die.

Ecotone: The transition area between two types of environments. For instance, the area between a meadow and a forest produces an ecotone where exposure to direct sunlight causes the trees along the edge of the forest to produce many more branches. Understory shrubs and herbaceous plants grow along this corridor. Ecotones support a greater than usual diversity of both plant and animals.

Emergent wetland plants: Plants that grow from the bottom of a body of water and emerge to the surface. Examples include water lilies, spatterdocks, and some rushes and sedges.

Epiphyte: Epiphytes, also known as air plants, absorb moisture and nutrients from the air rather than soil. Generally, they use another plant for support, but do not invade its tissues and rob it of nutrients. Examples include several orchid species, bromeliads, resurrection ferns, and Spanish moss.

Ergonomics: The study of the design and use of equipment, tools, and machines related to human safety, comfort, and convenience. An ergonomically correct tool is one designed to increase the efficiency and comfort of the person who uses it.

Estuary: A coastal body of water with one or more freshwater rivers or streams flowing into it and with a free connection to an open sea. The mixture of freshwater and tidal saltwater provides essential habitat for many species of plants and animals.

Eutrophication or **eutrophy**: A process whereby nutrient-rich lakes, estuaries, or slow-moving streams fill up with **detritus** and eventually become marshes or swamps.

Evaporation: The process of a liquid's changing from liquid to gas: water becomes water vapor, for instance.

Exotic: See **non-native**.

Fascine: A bunch of greenwood cuttings stuck and rooted in damp soil to stabilize wet areas. Cuttings are made from easily rootable species so that a fascine will become a multibranched shrub.

Fix nitrogen: See **nitrogen fixing**.

French drain: A trench filled with rocks, gravel, sand, or other permeable media constructed to absorb and direct water to a distant point. Sometimes the trench is lined with tiles. Modern French drains usually include a porous, cloth-covered pipe for faster drainage and longer effectiveness. French drains are also known as blind drains because the water enters through percolation, not open channels, and the drains themselves are most often not noticeable.

French drains have nothing to do with France or French engineering, but are named after Henry French, a judge and farmer in Concord, Massachusetts, who wrote the book, *Farm Drainage, The Principles, Processes, and Effects of Draining Land with Stones, Wood, Plows, and Open Ditches and Especially with Tiles Including Tables of Rain-Fall, Evaporation, Filtration, Evacuation, Capacity of Pipes; Cost and Number to the Acre, of Tiles, Etc, Etc.* Published in 1859, his book with the really long title was quite successful, and the judge was well known in the area for designing drainage systems—French drains.

Fungi (sing. fungus): Soil fungi are composed of long filaments called "hyphae" (sing. hyphus). Usually hyphae are white or translucent. One gram of soil may contain as many as 100,000 fungi with hyphae, which if strung together would measure 16 feet in length. A collective network of hyphal cells is called a "mycelium." When hyphae from two individuals meet, they can form a fruiting body that produces spores. Some of these structures we know as mushrooms, toadstools, earthstars, slime molds, or those obnoxious, smelly stinkhorn fungi.

Fungi used to be classified as plants but now have their own kingdom. Soil fungi do best in a damp environment. Most are saprophytes that feed on dead organic materials, but some are carnivorous and ensnare nematodes or other soil organisms. Some also invade and reside in plants or animals, such as the fungi that cause fusarium wilts, rusts, and molds on our vegetable crops.

With stinkhorn fungi, the fruiting bodies arise from an egg-like sack. One type has a phallic shape with its tip smeared in a brown slime that smells like feces. The other form is the octopus stinkhorn with red or orange legs that arc up from the ground to form a kind of spongy cage. The slime lines the inside surface of the legs and smells like carrion.

Not all fungi that invade plants are bad, though. Fungi play an important role in composting and will break down dead materials. A specialized fungus called "mycorrhizae" invades tree root cells and aids in transfer of soil nutrients and water into the plant. In some cases the fungal hyphae will extend the roots' absorptive system tenfold or more. In turn, the tree supplies sugars to the fungus.

Green manure: A fast-growing cover crop planted during a fallow period for a particular bed. When it's time to plant the next crop, the cover crop is plowed into the soil. Legumes are favorites for this purpose, because they **fix nitrogen** in their root nodules, thanks to their symbiotic bacteria, and can enrich the soil more than other plants.

Ground fire: A fire that burns below the ground, fueled by organic material such as roots, muck, **duff**, or peat. The two other fire levels are **surface fires** and **canopy fires**.

Gymnosperm: Plants with seeds not enclosed in an ovary. These plants include ginkgoes, conifers (such as pines, cypress, and juniper), plus cycads (such as sago or our native coontie).

Hardening-off: A procedure used to better prepare seedlings for life in the ground. It's the process of acclimating plants to the outdoors. When seedlings are grown in a protected environment, introducing them slowly to elements like wind, intense sun, and less frequent irrigation increases their transplant success. This practice is normally associated with cool-weather climates, but it's also a good idea for Florida gardeners.

Hardiness zones or **planting zones**: In 1990 the USDA issued a map of the United States showing the boundaries of its lowest temperatures. This map is meant to be used as a guideline for selecting plants that will tolerate the coldest temperatures expected in an area. Florida's zones on the USDA map range from 8a in the cooler parts of the panhandle to zone 11 in Florida's Keys. The Arbor Day Foundation (http://www.arborday.org) updated this map in 2006 with more recent weather data. It shows that Florida's zones have shifted northward. The American Horticultural Society (http://www.ahs.org) also issued a map of the United States showing the number of days that are 86 degrees Fahrenheit or higher. Heat might be an important limiting factor in Florida, but as yet, heat tolerance is not widely listed in plant descriptions.

Hardscape: This refers to inanimate or permanent non-plant items in the landscape, such as rocks, benches, stone or cement pavers, walls, fences, arbors, bridges over waterways, birdbaths, trellises, and other items. See **softscape**.

Hat-racking: The process of chopping all the branches of a tree or shrub at the same height. Some trees, such as crape myrtles, are subjected to this poor pruning technique each year. This practice weakens the tree and should be replaced by wiser pruning methods. Utility companies are often forced to top trees because property owners didn't look up when they planted them or think about their eventual size.

Hose bibb: A horizontal faucet with male or female threads on the inlet side and male hose threads on the spout, which is usually angled downward. A hose bibb is usually installed at the bottom of a rain barrel and often referred to as a spigot.

Hyphae: See **fungus**.

Invasive: A plant or animal imported from other regions of the world (hence exotic, as in "exotic invasive") that has escaped from cultivation to invade and outcompete native plants or animals, adversely altering their habitats. Although native plants may be rambunctious multipliers and take over habitats, they are not, by definition, invasive. The Florida Exotic Pest Plant Council maintains two lists of Florida's most destructive exotic invasives on its Web site, http://www.fleppc. org. Category I plants are the most invasive: they have already altered native plant communities by displacing native species, changing community structures or ecological functions, or hybridizing with natives. This damage is ongoing. Category II plants are invasive but have not yet altered Florida plant communities to the extent demonstrated by Category I species. Some of these species may be ranked into Category I in the future.

IPM (Integrated Pest Management): A set of sustainable strategies to control pests in your landscape. See chapter 9.

Ladder fuel: Brush piles or flammable plants such as tall shrubs or vines under trees that provide a ladder for **surface fire** to climb into treetops or the forest canopy.

Limbing up: A pruning practice whereby the lower limbs of trees are trimmed back a little over several years until they are trimmed back to the trunk. This is appropriate for areas where the low branches interfere with human or vehicular traffic and also in a firewise landscape to reduce **ladder fuels**.

Littoral: The transition between water and terrestrial habitats. See chapter 13.

Living Shoreline: A combination of tough native species, such as grasses, rushes, and/or shrubs, planted along the shoreline or on barriers or berms of rock, gravel, and/or sand. Living shorelines allow water flow around the vegetation, while the shoreline is protected from wave action. The scale of a living shoreline can be large or small and configured in various ways depending upon the situation.

Mean high water (MHW) and **mean low water (MLW)**: The average height of all high (or low) waters recorded at a particular point or station over 19 years. (This measurement therefore excludes seasonal variations.) While MHW usually refers to tidal waters, it is also applied to other bodies of water in Florida, where the MHW line is often the determining factor in land ownership.

Microclimates: The different and discrete growing conditions that occur in small or large areas (including your property) and dependent upon factors such as amount of seasonal sunlight, drainage conditions, nutrients availability, competition (among roots), soil pH (including acidity altering elements such as alkaline cement or limestone), and proximity to heat-retaining **hardscape**, such as foundations, large rocks, or paved surfaces. Make sure your plants are well suited for their microclimates.

Monocot or **monocotyledonous**: An angiosperm or flowering plant that has one cotyledon leaf preformed in the seed. When it sprouts, this seed leaf emerges first. Monocots include grasses, irises, rushes, and sedges. See **dicot**.

Monoculture: A situation where only one type of plant grows in an area. Usually, a monoculture is artificially created—a St. Augustine lawn or a ficus hedge, for example. Invasive exotics can create monocultures when they crowd out native plants in an area. On the other hand, monocultures can occur naturally, as in the saw grass prairie of the Everglades.

Mycelium: See **fungi**.

Mycorrhizae: See **fungi**.

Native: A native plant is one that grew in Florida before the onset of colonization by Europeans. See **non-native**.

Nematodes: Microscopic roundworms found in soil or water. Some are harmful, such as the infamous root-knot nematode, but most are beneficial and play a significant role in the ecosystem of a healthy soil. In addition to plants, nematodes may feed on bacteria, spores, fungi, each other, or animals such as insect larvae. One gram of healthy soil can contain several hundred nematodes.

Nitrogen-fixation or **nitrogen fixing**: Seventy-eight percent of our atmosphere is composed of nitrogen gas. Plants require nitrogen to grow, but they can't make use of nitrogen gas directly. Nitrogen-fixing soil bacteria produce ammonia products, and other soil bacteria that decompose plant and animal products produce it, too. Legumes and some woody plants, like wax myrtle, harbor symbiotic bacteria in their roots that process the nitrogen gas into ammonia. Nitrogen (N_2) + hydrogen ($8H_2$) $\rightarrow$ ammonia ($2NH_3$) + hydrogen (H_2).

Non-native: Plants or animals that have been imported from a different region. A generally accepted guideline for a Florida non-native plant is one that did not occur here before the European colonization. See **native**.

Non-point-source contamination: A form of pollution, non-point-source contamination comes from many diffuse sources: fertilizers and pesticides from agricultural and residential lands, nutrients from pet and livestock wastes, as well as human wastes from faulty septic systems. As runoff moves over impervious surfaces and over the ground, it dissolves natural and man-made contaminants and transports them to streams, rivers, wetlands, lakes, and groundwater. Aggregated non-point-source contamination is the leading and most widespread cause of water quality degradation. See **point-source contamination**.

Nutrient cycle: Generally speaking, a nutrient cycle is the path taken by any life-essential substance (like nitrogen or oxygen) as it moves through different physical and biological environments—from soil to plant, for example, or from plant to air. The nutrient cycle for a natural pond, lake, or slow-moving river starts with plants (simple, one-celled algae to more advanced multicelled flowering plants, such as eel grass) and their ability to **photosynthesize**. Drawing energy from sunlight, this process uses carbon dioxide (CO_2) and water (H_2O) to form sugar ($C_6H_{12}O_6$) and oxygen gas (O_2). During photosynthesis, oxygen dissolves in the water, where it becomes available to aquatic plants, animals, and bacteria that all require it for respiration. **Respiration** is the chemical process—opposite to photosynthesis—whereby plants and animals take in oxygen and break down sugar needed for life energy and release water and carbon dioxide as byproducts.

Animals eat plants and other animals and produce waste products as they live and die. The waste products, dead plants, and dead animals sink to the bottom of the water body to form muck. This muck, called "**detritus**," breaks down with the help of bacteria and bottom feeders to produce nutrients. The more nutrients there are and the more available they become, the faster aquatic plants, especially the algae, grow. This may be okay during the day when photosynthesis produces enough oxygen to support the larger **biomass** of plants and animals, but it is not okay at night when no oxygen is produced. When the biomass becomes too large for the dissolved oxygen supply, plants and animals die. As their bodies decompose, there is a surge of bacterial activity that uses up even more oxygen. Eventually, nothing (except anaerobic organisms) can live in such waters, called "dead zones."

Organic: The chemical definition of "organic" is a compound that includes carbon. With very few exceptions, anything that's alive or has been alive is made up of organic materials, because most life on our planet depends in some way on carbon-based sugars formed during **photosynthesis**.

J. I. Rodale formulated a newer meaning of the term in the 1940s, when he started writing about farming without using artificial chemicals. The materials he used for fertilizer and pesticides were made entirely from plants and animals—organic entities. Organic farmers now have a rigorous process to become certified.

Osmosis: The process whereby water moves from a region of high water concentration through a semipermeable membrane, such as a cell membrane or cell wall, to a region of low water concentration. Osmosis is the process that allows water in the soil to move into plants' roots.

Peat moss: Partially decomposed **sphagnum moss**. Peat moss takes centuries to form in a bog environment and is acidic and sterile when mined: the pH ranges from 3.5 to 4.5. Harvesting peat is not a sustainable practice. Use compost instead of peat moss in your gardening: it has more nutrients, is not inherently acidic, doesn't dry out as much, and adds beneficial microbes to the soil. Plus you can make new compost from waste material in a month or two instead of the centuries needed to create peat moss.

Petiole: A leaf stalk or the part of the leaf that attaches the leaf blade to the stem or trunk. If the leaf stalk (petiole) grows part or all the way around the stem, then it's referred to as "sheathing" or "clasping."

pH: See **acidity**.

Photosynthesis: The chemical process (in green plants) that, with the aid of radiant energy from the sun, combines carbon dioxide (CO_2) and water (H_2O) to form sugar ($C_6H_{12}O_6$) and oxygen gas (O_2). For most vascular plants, the water involved in photosynthesis is supplied by **transpiration** and the carbon dioxide is available from the air. **Respiration** is the opposite chemical process.

Point-source contamination: Discharge of pollutants or nutrients from power plants, factories, and sewer treatment plants that is easily identified and regulated. The greater problem is **non-point-source contamination**, which is not as easily identified or regulated.

Respiration: The chemical process by which plants and animals obtain life energy. Inhaled oxygen (O_2) reacts with sugar ($C_6H_{12}O_6$) to produce energy, while releasing water (H_2O) and carbon dioxide (CO_2) as byproducts. Respiration takes place within individual cells. **Photosynthesis** is the opposite chemical process.

Root-bound: A term used to describe the condition that occurs when a plant's roots grow to exceed the limits of the container it is planted in. In such cases, the dense network of tightly packed roots almost entirely replaces the soil in its planter, sometimes circling the root-ball inside the pot or growing through the pot's drainage holes in search of more soil.

Root pruning: The process of cutting the surface roots of trees and shrubs with a shovel in a circle around the plant. This is usually an appropriate preparatory action for plants that are to be transplanted, so that they have time to adjust to fewer roots. More details in chapter 2.

Softscape: The ever-changing plant materials in the landscape. Softscape is comprised of the dynamic features of the landscape. See **hardscape.**

Stinkhorn fungi: See **fungus.**

Stomata (sing. stomate): Openings or pores in a leaf surface that allow water to escape through **transpiration** and air to flow into the leaf tissues to supply carbon dioxide for **photosynthesis**. Most leaves are arranged with their stomata on the bottom surface, away from direct sun and water. These pores stay open as long as the guard cells, a pair of kidney-shaped cells located on either side of the opening, are turgid and filled with water. When there is water stress caused by high temperatures or general drought conditions, the guard cells become flaccid and the pore closes.

Succession: The gradual process of ecosystem development brought about by changes in community composition and the production of a climax characteristic of a particular geographic region and soil type. A fallow field in Florida can become a pine forest or a forest dominated by oaks, for instance. Fire will alter this process, and a new succession will begin.

Sucker: A vigorous shoot growing vertically, often from the soil or low spot on the tree trunk. Also see **watersprout.**

Surface fire: A fire confined to the area above the ground and below the treetops or **canopy.** Fuel for surface fires includes leaf litter, mulch, shrubs, and other low-lying objects. A hot surface fire is generally necessary to start or support a **canopy fire** or a **ground fire**.

Swale: A naturally occurring or constructed low spot in the landscape where precipitation can collect.

Symbiotic: Term describing a mutually beneficial relationship between two separate organisms. As an example, lichens consist of fungi and an algae living together. The fungi use the sugars produced by the algae during **photosynthesis,** and the algae are protected from desiccation by the fungus. Legumes and a few other types of plants provide sugar for bacteria in their roots that **fix nitrogen** from the air. Some trees host a mycorrhizae fungus in their roots that help absorb more water and nutrients.

Thatch: A layer of dead stems and roots of grass and other plants that accumulates near the soil surface in a lawn. Some thatch helps protect the roots, but excessive thatch (more than half an inch) prevents moisture, oxygen, and nutrients from penetrating the soil. "Florida thatch" is a type of palm.

Tilth: A description of soil structure including ease of tilling with a plow, seedbed quality, ease of seedling emergence, and deep root penetration. A soil with good tilth is rich in organic material with both good porosity and the ability to hold water. A handful of soil should have many different sized, but mostly rounded particles. The particles of soil should withstand gentle pressure, but should break apart easily. Such soil is neither too sandy nor too clayey.

Transpiration: The passive process of **evaporation** of water from a vascular plant, mostly through its pores or **stomata** on its leaves. Water is absorbed from soil into the roots and is sucked through the vessels by the loss of water from the leaves. The rate of transpiration is determined by the amount of water in the soil, the humidity, temperature, and whether the plant's **stomata** are open or closed. Less than one percent of the water pumped through the plant is actually absorbed into the plant's tissues or used in **photosynthesis**. Transpiration cools the plant's tissues and the surrounding air. A full-sized oak tree pumps 400,000 gallons of water per year.

Turgid: The state of being firm and filled with fluids; the opposite of the state of being flaccid or wilted.

Underflow: When constructing a large rain garden, you can install a perforated pipe or **French drain** system under layers of mulch, sand, and gravel in the floor of the garden so that any water reaching this pipe will have been filtered before it's released into the next water retention feature. The released water is the underflow, and a rain garden is one with an underflow design.

Vermiculite: Derived from rocks containing large crystals of the minerals biotite and iron-bearing phlogopite, also known as mica. These rocks are mined then heated to produce the worm-like strands that are broken into smaller flaked pieces to produce the moisture-holding medium, vermiculite, often added to commercial potting mixes. Wear a facemask when handling this material to protect your lungs from the fine dust it produces when dry.

Watersprout: A vigorous, vertical branch growing from a more horizontal tree branch. It's generally a good idea to prune back watersprouts because they may weaken the whole tree structure making it more prone to wind damage. Also, they tend to grow into the center of the crown where they may cross other branches, reduce airflow, and block light penetration, all of which can promote fungal growth. Also see **sucker**.

Wildfire: An unwanted fire. In the natural, unpeopled environment, they are part of the natural cycle. On average, Florida's 5,500 wildfires impact more than 200,000 acres annually. Controlled burns are one way to reduce damage from wildfires.

Wildland-Urban interface: Areas where development, commercial or private, is next to private or public wildlands—forests, parks, scrub, or other vacant land. There are three types of wildland-urban interface: (1) "boundary," where wildlands border a large area of development on one or two sides; (2) "intermix," where developed land is interspersed in an otherwise uninterrupted wild area; and (3) "island" or "occluded," where urban or suburban areas surround wild undeveloped land.

Wind grove: Five or more wind-resistant trees grouped together in a naturalized arrangement to shield buildings or landscape features from prevalent winds and flying debris. This is usually most effective with a compatible variety of trees and shrubs underplanted with mulched, shade-loving perennials and annuals.

Plant List

This list provides general information on the plants mentioned in this book. It is not intended to be a complete or recommended list for all of Florida. It is organized alphabetically by the common name used in the text, followed by other useful data so that each entry looks generally like this:

Common name (Latin binomial) (zone range). Native or non-native. Height if woody. Plant description.

Only Florida's hardiness or planting zones are listed, using the USDA 1990 hardiness map. Plant heights given indicate the high number of a range: from 15' to 30' is listed as 30'.

Richard P. Wunderlin and Bruce F. Hansen provide the authority for scientific name, range, and the Florida native status in their book, *Guide to the Vascular Plants of Florida* and the associated Web site, http://www. plantatlas.usf.edu.

Florida Exotic Pest Plant Council's Web site, http://www.fleppc.org, provides the authority for the invasiveness of a species as of 2007. Category I is most invasive and has already damaged Florida's ecosystems. Category II is regionally invasive and has the potential to become more invasive. These lists will change in the future.

African tulip tree (*Spathodea campanulata*) (10b–11). Non-native, from Africa. 60' tall. Evergreen tropical tree. Attractive flowers and large compound leaves. Not wind resistant. Not recommended.

Asters (*Symphyotrichum* spp.) (8–11). There are numerous asters native to Florida. Most are herbaceous perennials and some are annuals. Cultivars are available. Most bloom from late summer to fall and work well in meadow areas. Recommended. Stokes aster (*Stokesia laevis*) belongs to a different genus and has showier flowers and extended blooming times. Highly recommend.

Australian pine (*Casuarina equisetifolia*) (9–11). Non-native, from Australia. 100' tall. Evergreen. Category I invasive exotic. Neither a pine nor a conifer but a flowering tree with yellow flowers, the Australian pine's tiny leaves grow along needle-like twiglets and the fruit looks a little like a pinecone. Though it grows in poor soils and is salt tolerant, it is not wind resistant. Neither is it tolerant of fire, but it can recolonize a fire site. This tree has been most ecologically damaging along southern coasts where it has crowded out and suppressed native plants with its allelopathic chemicals. By crowding out the plants that native animals depend on, the Australian pine has damaged habitats for crocodiles, loggerhead turtles, gopher tortoises, and other wildlife. If you have it, remove it, and kill all its suckers and seedlings.

Azalea (*Rhododendron* spp.) There are thousands of azalea cultivars. Most of the evergreen species have parent stock from Asia. Some cultivars have been bred to bloom twice a year, while others may break bloom dormancy in the fall in Florida because of temperature fluctuations when the day length is the same as their spring blooming time. As a group, Asian azaleas don't do well in the tropics. If you already have these cultivars in your landscape, go ahead and keep them going. But if you're purchasing new shrubs, consider using native azaleas for moist acidic spots to create a great understory:

Florida flame azalea (*R. austrinum*) (8). Native. 10' tall. Deciduous shrub. Showy yellow flowers in the spring.

Swamp azalea (*R. viscosum*) (8–9). Native. 15' tall. Deciduous shrub. White flowers. This is our most widespread wild azalea—in Florida, it occurs naturally from the Panhandle down to Lake Okeechobee.

Wild azalea or **Pinkster azalea** (*R. canescens*) (8–9). Native. 15' tall. Deciduous shrub. Pale pink flowers.

Bald cypress (*Taxodium distichum*) (8–10). Native. 100' tall. One of the few deciduous conifers. Slow to moderate growth. Wind resistant with deep roots. Flammable, but fire resistant—trim away low branches for firewise landscaping. Drought tolerant. This long-lived tree is wetlands adapted and while it is a good choice for large rain gardens and the edges of waterways, it will also grow in drier areas. Highly recommended in all but the most fire-prone areas. Do not plant near mowed areas: cypress knees—vertical root protrusions that may aid in aeration in moist soils—are hazardous for pedestrians and for lawnmowers. Pond cypress (*T. ascendens*) is a somewhat smaller native tree with features similar to *Taxodium distichum* and is also highly recommended.

Bean (*Phaseolus* spp.) (8–11). Native, or non-native from Central America. Vining or bushing growth habits. These legumes form root nodules that, with a symbiotic bacterium, fix nitrogen from the air into a usable nutrient for the bean plant. Nitrogen-rich fertilizer or composted manure in the soil will probably result in more vegetative growth and fewer beans.

Beautyberry (*Callicarpa americana*) (8–11). Native. 8' tall. Deciduous shrub. Full sun or partial shade. Drought tolerant—does best in well-drained soil. This excellent shrub, with unbelievably purple berries (favored by many birds), has graceful arched branches, but may be pruned if it outgrows its space. Highly recommended.

Blackberry (*Rubus* spp.) (8–11). Native. Deciduous perennial. Several blackberry species are native to Florida and if you've developed a native meadow on your property, you probably have some already. Their normal pattern of growth is to produce canes one year that produce flowers and fruit in the following year. Blackberries form brambly thickets that provide excellent habitat and form effective barriers. If you are adding blackberries to your edible garden, cultivars for Florida produce bigger more reliable berries, usually during May and June. Species that run along the ground are called "dewberries." Recommended for wildlife habitat and for eating.

Black-eyed Susan (*Rudbeckia hirta*) (8–10). Native. Herbaceous perennial. Full sun or partial shade. Widespread throughout Florida except the

Keys. Its showy, reliable blooms attract butterflies and other pollinators. Tolerates drought and neglect. Highly recommended for sunny rain gardens, meadows, and for your picking garden. There are a few, uncommon species found in Florida and there are many cultivars.

Blueberries (*Vaccinium* spp.) Native to eastern North America. Woody shrub. The acidic woods and swamps of Florida are populated with at least eight wild blueberry species—sparkleberries, rabbiteye blueberries, deerberries, and southern highbush blueberries. No area of the state lacks wild blueberries, except where soil pH is above 6.0. Excellent wildlife habitat, blueberry species are recommended for habitat restoration, as well as for your edible garden. Be sure any cultivar you purchase is suited to Florida—New Jersey has fine blueberries, but those Jersey blueberries don't do well here.

Blue-eyed grass (*Sisyrinchium angustifolium*) (8–11). Native. An herbaceous perennial in the iris family, with small blue to purple flowers and grass-like leaves. Tolerates damp and dry conditions. A good addition to rain gardens or along pond margins as long as the lawnmowers or yard workers don't mow it down thinking it's just grass. You may even find it in your lawn once you stop the herbicides and stop mowing during turfgrass dormancy.

Brazilian pepper (*Schinus terebinthifolius*) (9–11). Non-native, from South America. 40' tall. Evergreen. Category I invasive exotic. A shrubby, multistemmed tree, Brazilian pepper is one of the most aggressive of the invasive, nonindigenous plants in Florida. It has been found as far north as St. Augustine, but it has caused the most damage farther south. It can regenerate from the smallest twigs or pieces of root, so if you have it, it may take a number of tries before you kill it. Millions of dollars have been spent trying to eradicate it from the Everglades and elsewhere in South Florida. Its foliage and wood contain the same toxin as poison ivy, so handle with care and don't burn it.

Broccoli. See **Cabbage**.

Bromeliads. Various genera in the pineapple family. Some are epiphytes, while others are terrestrial. Some have spectacular, long-lasting blooms. The epiphytes are often sold attached to a piece of wood designed to be strapped to a tree, fence, or lattice. They make a great addition to a small gardening space because they don't require much care. After blooming, they typically die back leaving a ring of offshoots or pups: each of these may be grown as a separate plant.

Buttonbush (*Cephalanthus occidentalis*) (8–11). Native. 10' tall. Deciduous shrub with arching branches that grows in sun or partial shade. Attracts butterflies and tolerates wet soils. Good addition for wildlife habitat, rain gardens, and pond margins. Recommended.

Buttonwood (*Conocarpus erectus*) (9b–11). Native. 60' tall. Wind resistant, slow-growing evergreen tree. A small mangrove-like tree or shrub, button-wood is limited to coastal areas where it grows in full sun or partial shade at the edges of fresh, brackish, or saltwater marshes. It can withstand the rigors of urban settings and makes a durable street or parking lot tree. A great addition to a rain garden, wetland, or pond's edge. Recommended.

Cabbage (*Brassica oleracea*). Non-native. The wild mustard, which has given rise to a dozen crops, is native to the Mediterranean coastal region. Annuals, the cabbage-based or cole crops include broccoli, Brussels sprouts, kale, cauliflower, collards, kohlrabi, and more. Cabbages have also been bred for winter color in the flower garden. All of these are cool-weather crops in Florida and should be planted in late fall or winter for the best results.

Camphor tree (*Cinnamomum camphora*) (8–9). Non-native, from China and Japan. 70' tall. Evergreen. Category I invasive exotic. The camphor tree's shiny, dark green foliage is aromatic—it smells like camphor when crushed and was the source of camphor until manufactured products replaced it. Because it is so stinky, few pests will eat it. Remove it from your landscape, or new camphor trees will soon be popping up all over your yard.

Cardinal flower (*Lobelia cardinalis*) (8–9). Native. 3' tall. Perennial with showy red flowers. Tolerates wet soils and is recommended for damp sites. Use it in a rain garden, but only if the site doesn't dry out, because cardinal flower isn't drought tolerant. Attracts hummingbirds and butterflies.

Carolina laurelcherry (*Prunus caroliniana*) (8–10a). Native. 40' tall. Evergreen tree that grows best in sun or partial shade and in rich neutral to acidic soils. Not wind resistant as a specimen tree. The fast-growing Carolina laurelcherry is recommended for areas away from buildings. Use in a hedgerow. It's a good screening tree when planted in groups and makes excellent wildlife habitat.

Carolina willow (*Salix caroliniana*) (8–10). Native. 60' tall. Deciduous tree or shrub. Adapted to wetlands, but tolerates drier terrains to some degree. Branches stuck in damp ground often root. Not wind, drought, or salt tolerant. Recommended for bank stabilization. Host plant for viceroy butterfly. Black willow (*S. nigra*) grows well in northern Florida and has similar characteristics to *S. caroliniana*.

Chinaberry (*Melia azedarach*) (8–11). Non-native, from China and Southeast Asia. 50' tall. Category II invasive exotic. A small, deciduous, fast-growing tree, it is prone to wind damage. Its fruits are poisonous to humans and livestock, but not to the birds that spread the seeds everywhere. Introduced as an ornamental in the mid-1800s. Not recommended.

Chinese tallow or **popcorn tree** (*Sapium sebiferum*) (8–10). Non-native, from China. 80' tall. Category I invasive exotic. This deciduous tree, introduced into the United States from China by Benjamin Franklin in 1776, is now located in many counties throughout Florida. Once widely planted for its fall color and fast growth, the Chinese tallow tree is not wind resistant. It crowds out native species and causes habitat loss. Not recommended. Remove it from your property.

Citrus (*Citrus* spp.) (8b–10). Non-native, from Asia. 20' tall. This popular evergreen and shrubby tree does best in full sun and a dry location—don't use mulch. In northern sections of Florida be sure to purchase species that are cold hardy to the minimum temperatures in your zone. Recommended for your edible garden.

Clover (*Trifolium* spp.) Most species are non-natives from Europe and grow mainly in central and northern Florida. Clover is a legume and can fix nitrogen. It is often used as a green manure to grow between planting times for crops. It can also be used as a lawn—it tolerates drought, traffic, and poor soils. Clover doesn't need to be mowed often and it attracts pollinators, which is part of your IPM strategies. Recommended instead of, or in addition to, grass in the lawn.

Cocoplum (*Chrysobalanus icaco*) (10–11). Native. 30' tall. This evergreen shrubby tree grows well in many soils from sand to mud. Drought tolerant. Edible fruit. Highly recommended for screening, beach stabilization, rain gardens, and for its wildlife value.

Coontie (*Zamia pumila*) (8b–11). Native. 3' tall. This evergreen perennial is a cycad but looks like a cross between a palmetto and a fern. Cycads are a primitive, nonflowering group of plants. Large male and female cones of clustered seeds arise from the same plant. Another common name for this plant is "Seminole bread"—the Seminole Indians ground its tuberous roots to make flour. Coontie provides an easy-care, long-lived, drought-resistant groundcover. Host plant for the rare Atala butterfly. Highly recommended. A somewhat larger relative of the coontie, the cardboard palm (*Z. furfuracea*), a non-native from Mexico, has similar attributes, but with coarser foliage and a somewhat narrower growing range, 9b–11.

Coral honeysuckle (*Lonicera sempervirens*) (8–10). Native. This drought-tolerant vine attracts butterflies and hummingbirds with its long, dark orange, tubular flowers. Other birds eat its orange berries. You can grow this in a container or in the ground, and it will put on quite a show. (It's not invasive like its relative from Japan [*L. japonica*].) Recommended for its showiness and wildlife habitat value.

Crape myrtle (*Lagerstroemia indica*) (8–10a). Non-native, from India. 30' tall. Deciduous tree. Wind resistant. Widely planted in all but the south-

ernmost regions of the state for its showy summer flowers, long blooming cycle, and mottled bark. It's routinely mutilated with ugly hat-racking
pruning. Though the spelling is different, the word "crape" in the tree's
common name refers to its finely wrinkled flowers, which suggest the
texture of "crepe," the fabric. Not recommended because crape myrtles are
already so widely planted.

Crinum lily or **string lily** (*Crinum americana*) (8–11). Native. Bulbaceous
perennial. The drought-tolerant crinum lily prefers well-drained, rich soil
and partial shade to full sun. There are many crinum cultivars as well as
non-native crinums available to suit a variety of tastes and styles. All are
useful in a sustainable landscape because they require so little care.

Cucumber (*Cucumis sativus*). Non-native, from Asia. An annual vining
vegetable crop that's been a staple in edible gardens for centuries. For best
results, plant in full sun and provide a trellised device.

Dog fennel (*Eupatorium capillifolium*) (8–11). Native. This herbaceous
perennial can grow to 12' once established. Though usually considered
a weed, dog fennel needs no care and attracts butterflies, bees, and birds
with its tiny florets. You probably won't find it at nurseries or plant sales,
but if dog fennel grows in your meadow area, keep a few plants for its
wildlife habitat value. Other plants in this genus include the interestingly
named boneset, Joe Pye weed, thoroughwort, horehound, Yankee weed,
and justice weed. All are valuable in your meadow areas.

Dogwood (*Cornus florida*) (8–9). Native. 30' tall. Deciduous tree with
showy bracts around its flowers. In the wild, dogwood usually occurs as
an understory tree in the wild, but it can tolerate full sun. Wind resistant and somewhat drought tolerant, dogwood has shallow roots that are
sensitive to traffic and fill. It is plagued by several diseases. If you have
dogwoods in your landscape already, keep those that are in good health,
but if you are looking to plant anew, there are flowering trees with fewer
problems to choose from.

Dollarweed or **pennywort** (*Hydrocotyle* spp.) (8–11). Native. Herbaceous perennial. There are several species of pennywort native to Florida, and all are normally considered weeds. They grow in your lawn, into your ponds, and into flowerbeds. Once they get started they are hard to get rid of because of their long runners (stolons). Dollar weed is an effective aerator plant for ponds.

Elderberry (*Sambucus canadensis*) (8–11). Native. 15′ tall. Deciduous in northern Florida but mostly evergreen in central and southern regions, elderberry is a dense vase-shaped shrub that forms thickets. It grows in acid or alkaline soils, tolerates salt spray, and though best suited to moist soils, also withstands drought. The flattish white and lacey flower heads followed by dark purple or blue-black berries are attractive in the garden and a good habitat plant for birds. A good choice for a large rain garden or the upper edge of a wetland. Highly recommended.

Eucalyptus (*Eucalyptus* spp.) Non-native, from Australia. The three eucalyptus species found in southern Florida are highly flammable and not wind resistant. Not a recommended landscape plant, but mulch made from its wood works well as for paths because of its allelopathic properties.

Ferns. Various genera, both native and non-native. Shade or partial shade. Some require constant dampness, while others do well in dry meadows. Ferns are often a good choice for rain gardens, pond margins, and wetland areas. Some may do well under trees where you've removed turfgrass. Highly recommended, but remove invasive climbing ferns and tuberous sword ferns.

    Cinnamon fern (*Osmunda cinnamomea*) (8–10). Native. 5′ tall. Deciduous. Bunching fern.

    Netted chain fern (*Woodwardia areolata*) (8–10). Native. 1′ tall. Deciduous. Spreading fern.

    Royal Fern (*Osmunda regalis* var. *spectabilis*) (8–11). Native. 4′ tall. Deciduous. Bunching fern.

Figs (*Ficus* spp.)

Common fig (*F. carica*) (8–10). Non-native, from Mediterranean region. Drought resistant. Grows in partial to full sun and likes cool roots, so mulch well. In northern parts of the state, it will die back with the frost but will resprout. Figs are a good addition to your edible garden.

Shortleaf fig or **wild banyan** (*F. citrifolia*) (10–11). Native. 70' tall. Grows well on limestone substrate in full sun. Drought tolerant. Low salt tolerance. Recommended for Miami and the Keys.

Strangler fig (*F. aurea*) (9–11). Native. 70' tall. Grows on limestone or other soils in full sun or partial shade. Drought tolerant. Wind resistant. Moderately salt tolerant. Often started when a bird deposits a seed in another tree (frequently a cabbage palm or bald cypress), it then grows aerial roots to the ground and, after a number of years, takes over that space engulfing (strangling) the host tree. It can grow from the ground up as well. Recommended for waterwise and storm resistant landscapes.

Weeping fig (*F. benjamina*) (10–11). Non-native, from Asia. 60' tall. This popular house and mall plant has been widely planted in South Florida front yards as hedges and specimen trees. As a stand-alone tree, weeping fig has low wind tolerance because of its enormous crown and shallow roots. It caused widespread damage in recent hurricanes by toppling onto houses, cars, and power lines. If you have one, lighten the crown by pruning, but don't prune all those aerial roots that provide additional anchorage to the ground. Not recommended.

Fringetree (*Chionanthus virginicus*) (8–10). Native. 20' tall. Slow-growing, deciduous tree. The showy white flowers provide outstanding landscape interest, and the berries attract wildlife. Wind and fire resistant, fringetree thrives in well-drained acid soil but tolerates occasional wet feet. Mostly sunny locations produce the best blooms, but fringetree tolerates understory shade. Highly recommended.

Geiger tree (*Cordia* spp.)

Orange Geiger tree (*C. sebestena*) (10–11). Non-native, from the West Indies, but some consider it to be native. 25' tall. Moderate growth rate. Tolerates drought, flooding, salt spray, and is wind resistant. Grows in alkaline or sandy soils in full sun or partial shade. Good as a street tree and good for large containers or raised beds. Beautiful clusters of orange flowers attract hummingbirds. Recommended for southernmost Florida. Called "Geiger tree" by John Audubon because it grew in Captain Geiger's yard on Key West.

White Geiger or **wild olive** (*C. boissieri*) (9–11). Native. 20' tall. Rare in the wild in Florida. Also native to Texas, where it's called the "Texas olive." White Geiger grows well in full sun or partial shade, although it's growth rate is slow. It is wind and fire resistant as well as salt tolerant. This evergreen tree has a distinctive rounded crown and produces white, funnel-shaped flowers. Birds eat the fruit. Highly recommended.

Goldenrod (*Solidago* spp.) (8–11). Native. Herbaceous perennials that spread via underground runners, more than 20 goldenrod species occur across the state except for the Keys. Seaside goldenrod is salt and drought tolerant. Other varieties are similarly drought tolerant, will probably volunteer in your meadows, and need no extra care. A prolific bloomer from late summer into the fall, this plant is a great addition for your butterfly and rain gardens. Despite its reputation, it's not the source of fall allergies—ragweed is. Highly recommended.

Grape (*Vitis* spp.) (8–11). Native and non-native. There are a number of grapes native to Florida, but temperate grapes from France won't do well here. Muscadine grape (*V. rotunifolia*) is most widespread in Florida and can produce good fruit. You will have the best success if the cultivars are grafted onto sturdy rootstock. Recommended for both the edible garden and for wildlife habitat.

Grasses. Many genera and species. Unlike sedges that have triangular stems or rushes that have round stems and no branching leaves, grass blades encircle the round or flattened stem and the stems have nodes. Most people limit their use of grass to turf (as discussed below), but there are many well-behaved, native bunching grasses that work well as specimen plants.

Bahia grass (*Paspalum notatum*) (8–11). Non-native, from Mexico. This heat- and drought-tolerant grass is widely recommended as a more sustainable turfgrass than St. Augustine and other high maintenance lawn grasses. Since it has naturalized and replaced native grasses in many parts of Florida, it is not recommended for meadows or habitat restoration.

Bermuda grass (*Cynodon* spp.) (8–11). Non-native; native to southern Europe, Asia, and Australia, but not Bermuda, where it's invasive. Widely used as a turfgrass. Drought resistant. Because it has escaped from cultivation and can be found throughout the state, Bermuda grass is not recommended for meadows or native habitat restoration.

Blue-eyed grass. Not a grass. See **Blue-eyed grass** on page 288.

Buffalo grass (*Buchloe dactyloides*) (8–11). Non-native, from the Great Plains, Montana through Mexico. This grass has low fertility requirements and grows best in heavy soils and in regions that receive only ten to twenty-five inches of annual rainfall. It is not adapted to irrigated or shaded sites in Florida. Though Buffalo grass requires little mowing to achieve a uniform appearance and is widely touted as a drought-resistant native grass, it is probably not your best choice for turf in most of the state.

Centipede grass (*Eremochloa ophiuroides*) (9–11). Non-native, from China. This turfgrass is widely recommended as a drought-tolerant alternative to thirstier Florida turfgrasses. It does not need and reacts poorly to too much nitrogen-rich fertilizer. Centipede grass isn't well suited to high traffic areas or high pH soils, and it doesn't do well in regions with long, cold winters. Cold-tolerant cultivars are available, however. If you need a low-care lawn, this grass might be a good choice.

Saw grass. See **Sedges.**

Seashore paspalum (*Paspalum vaginatum*) (8–11). Native. Salt and drought tolerant. Tolerates wear. Irrigation water can be somewhat saline, and periodic freshwater flushing is not necessary as it is for other beachside turfgrasses. While it does have limited shade tolerance, this might be a good choice for coastal landscapes.

St. Augustine grass (*Stenotaphrum secundatum*) (8–11). Native. Many cultivars of this most widely used Florida turfgrass are available. St. Augustine lawns hold up to foot traffic, thrive in a wide range of soil types, crowd out weeds when healthy, and have some salt, shade, and drought tolerance. On the other hand, this grass is susceptible to cinch bugs and other pests, as well as to a variety of fungal diseases.

Torpedo grass (*Panicum repens*) (8–11). Non-native, from Australia.

Category I invasive exotic. Torpedo grass forms floating mats at the edges of waterways, but on land, its thick rhizomes, with their pointy ends, are usually buried deep in the soil. It can invade turf areas and garden beds and should be removed. Dig it up with a shovel, because pulling it doesn't usually remove the deep roots with torpedo-shaped points.

Zoysia grasses (*Zoysia* spp.) (8–11). Non-native, from Asia. Several Zoysia species are used for turf. Slow growing and drought tolerant, they are generally thought to require higher maintenance than other turf-grasses. Zoysia grasses will brown in the winter in central and northern parts of the state.

Greenbriar (*Smilax* spp.) (8–11). Native. Woody, prickly vine that can form large tubers. Twelve *Smilax* species occur in Florida, and most are widespread. The vine offers good habitat for wildlife, and birds eat its berries, but most gardeners would rather keep it out of the way because of its thorny tangles. If you want to get rid of it, dig up the tubers—some as big as ten inches across—otherwise it will come back stronger than ever. The tubers of some of the species were once used to make sarsaparilla.

Groundsel tree or **high tide bush** (*Baccharis halimifolia*) (8–11). Native. 16' tall. This shrub or small tree is salt tolerant and easy to care for: it will grow almost anywhere. Because it is highly flammable, groundsel tree is not recommended for fire-prone landscapes, but it is useful for edges of rain gardens and for wildlife cover where other plants won't grow. One of the few woody plants in the daisy family, groundsel tree is dioecious with showy male and female flowers on separate plants. It takes well to severe pruning, but prune in the winter so flowers have a chance to form for the next fall season.

Gumbo-limbo (*Bursera simaruba*) (9b–11). Native. 50' tall. Semideciduous, gumbo-limbo loses its leaves in early spring just before the new leaves appear. Fast growing, but wind resistant, salt and drought tolerant, it grows well in either acidic or alkaline soil. The tree's irregularly shaped branches, massive trunk, and unique peeling red bark make it a great choice for adding interest to your landscape. Its branches root easily—just stick them into the ground. Highly recommended.

Hollies (*Ilex* spp.) Hollies are dioecious with male and female flowers occurring on separate trees. Hollies are generally wind resistant. If you want berries, buy female trees and at least one male if there are no native populations nearby. Excellent for wildlife habitat, providing both dense cover and berries. Recommended.

Dahoon holly (*I. cassine*) (8–11). Native. 30' tall. Evergreen in warmer areas, deciduous in northern areas of the state, the vivid red berries of this holly brighten the winter landscape. Occurring naturally in wet environments, Dahoon hollies can adjust to drier spots but are not drought tolerant and only moderately salt tolerant. They grow in partial sun to deep shade. A good choice for rain gardens and wetlands.

Inkberry or **gallberry** (*I. glabra*) (8–11). Native. 8' tall. Handsome evergreen shrub that occurs naturally in moist areas throughout Florida, except for the Keys. Grows in full sun to understory shade and prefers moist, rich, acidic soil. Its springtime clusters of tiny vanilla-colored flowers are followed by pea-sized purple-black berries that birds like to eat. Though flammable, it resprouts from its roots after burning. A good choice for rain gardens, wetlands, and pond margins. Not recommended for fire-prone areas, but otherwise a good understory shrub. Compact cultivars are available.

Yaupon holly (*I. vomitoria*) (8–10a). Native. 25' tall. This striking evergreen tree with dark green leaves and bright red berries adds life to a winter landscape. It grows rapidly in a variety of landscapes, moist to dry, sunny to shady. Both drought and salt tolerant, it is a good holly for coastal areas and an excellent wildlife habitat tree.

Hophornbeam (*Ostrya virginiana*) (8–9). Native. Medium-sized, slow-growing tree to 50'. Hophornbeam is drought, wind, and fire resistant, tolerates full shade, and adapts to any type of soil, but it doesn't like wet feet or salt. This tree has many points of landscape interest: dark brown, scaly bark; sharply veined, bright green leaves with serrate edges; dangling yellow catkins; and hanging clusters of papery seed sacs that lie, one on top of the other, in multilayered stacks of beige to golden-brown nuts, prized by birds and other wildlife. Highly recommended.

Irises (*Iris* spp.) Native and non-native. Many of the Dutch irises don't do well in Florida, but the natives are great additions to your pond edges and rain gardens. The spiky, flat leaf-blades and vibrant flowers add interesting texture to your garden. Highly recommended.

Dixie iris (*I. hexagona*) (8–11). Native. Deciduous or evergreen. Tolerates wet areas and is good for rain gardens.

Virginia iris (*I. virginica*) (8–9). Native. Deciduous or evergreen. Tolerates wet areas and is good for rain gardens.

Lizard's-tail (*Saururus cernuus*) (8–11). Native. Herbaceous perennial. Grows in damp or wet areas. Its spreading habit makes it a good choice along the margins of ponds or lakes. Not salt tolerant. Heart-shaped leaves and a long, drooping stalk of fine, cream-colored flowers (resembling a tail) make a good show. Recommended.

Loblolly bay (*Gordonia lasianthus*) (8–10). Native. 70' tall. Evergreen tree with a narrow crown. Both the leaves and the flowers resemble sweet bay magnolia, but the backs of its leaves are green, not silvery. Loblolly bay grows slowly on damp sites in full sun to partial shade. It is wind resistant but intolerant of drought and salt. Recommended for wetlands and pond edges.

Magnolias (*Magnolia* spp.) A number of non-native magnolias are grown in Florida as landscape trees, but if you have a choice, select a native.

Southern magnolia (*M. grandiflora*) (8–10). Native. 90' tall. Stately, evergreen tree with large leathery leaves and beautiful, fragrant, large white blossoms. Wind and fire resistant, Southern magnolia grows in full sun or partial shade in moderately acidic soils. Though moderately drought tolerant, it grows best in moist soils. While this tree is probably not a sustainable addition next to a lawn—it drops its leaves constantly and the shallow roots compete with grass—it is highly recommended for nonlawn areas: the edges of meadows and among other trees and shrubs in a woodland setting, where it provides good wildlife habitat.

Sweetbay magnolia (*M. virginiana*) (8–11). Native. 70' tall. Evergreen in southern parts of the state, but may lose its leaves during colder winters in zone 8. Sweetbays need damp or wet acidic soil and are not salt tolerant. They grow in full sun to partial shade and often send up shoots from surface roots to form thickets and screening. The sweetbay's leaves and flowers are smaller than those of the Southern magnolia, and the backs of the leaves are silvery. Highly recommended for rain gardens, pond margins, or freshwater wetland habitat.

Mahogany (*Swietenia mahogani*) (10–11). Native. 75' tall. The semideciduous mahogany loses its leaves in spring just before growing new ones. It grows in sun or partial shade and adapts to most soils, including limestone gravel. Though not salt tolerant, mahogany withstands heavy winds and can handle drought. Widely planted, this tree provides a light shade that allows understory growth. Highly recommended.

Mangroves (various genera). The mangrove ecosystem lies from the shoreline out into shallow waters. Mangrove seeds germinate while still attached to the parent tree. Once germinated, the seedling grows to form a propagule, a weighted seedling that has roots and can photosynthesize. When dropped, it floats away until it lands on a favorable site where it can quickly send out roots. Mangroves are salt tolerant but can also grow in freshwater. A mangrove ecosystem is wind resistant and protects the shoreline from wave and wind damage. Mangrove forests support many types of terrestrial and aquatic wildlife. Highly recommended for shoreline areas within their range.

    Black mangrove (*Avicennia germinans*) (9–11). Native. 65' tall. Occurs in waters shallower than those favored by red mangroves and deeper than those favored by white mangroves. From its roots grow pneumatophores, vertical, straw-like extensions that project above the soil to supply needed oxygen to the roots.

    Buttonwood. Often grouped with the mangroves, because it grows on the landward side of this ecosystem, buttonwood is not a true mangrove. Listed above under B.

    Red mangrove (*Rhizophora mangle*) (9–11). Native. 80' tall. This species grows farthest out in the water. Tangles of prop roots increase the tree's stability and capture rich sediments from the surrounding water.

    White mangrove (*Laguncularia racemosa*) (9b–11). Native. 50' tall. This species usually occurs on the landward side of the other two mangroves and usually lacks the prop roots and root adaptations characteristic of the black and the red species. Like the others, though, white mangrove thrives in a salty or fresh environments and provides habitat and food resources for terrestrial and aquatic wildlife.

Meadow beauty (Rhexia spp.) (8–11). Several species are native to Florida. Herbaceous perennials with showy pink or yellow flowers that spread via short rhizomes. Highly recommended for meadows and rain gardens.

Melaleuca, **paper bark**, or **punktree** (*Melaleuca quinquenervia*) (9b–11). Non-native, from Australia. 65' tall. Category I invasive exotic. This tree has become a noxious invader of Florida's wild spaces from mid-peninsula southward. If you have this pest on your property, remove it. To help defray the enormous cost of its eradication, try to purchase melaleuca mulch for your gardens instead of cypress.

Mexican petunia (*Ruellia tweediana*) (8–10). Non-native, from Mexico and Central America. Herbaceous perennial. Category I invasive exotic. Don't buy this plant, and rip out what you have. If you see it for sale (even the sterile version), complain to the manager. Use wild petunia (*R. caroliniensis*) or other natives instead.

Milkweeds (*Asclepias* spp.) There are more than 20 milkweeds native to Florida—some are better suited for the northern part of the state, others the south. All are recommended for butterfly gardens and dry meadow habitats. Milkweeds are somewhat poisonous, and the milky sap may irritate the skin. Caterpillars (monarchs and others) eat the milkweeds to become poisonous themselves and therefore less attractive to birds.

Butterfly weed (*A. tuberosa*) (8–11). Native. With its bright orange to yellow-orange flowers, this plant makes a great addition to a sunny, dry butterfly garden and meadow areas. Highly recommended.

Scarlet milkweed (*A. curassavica*) (9–11). Non-native, from South America. Flowers are usually two-toned: red on the bottom, orange on the top. This milkweed has escaped cultivation in central and southern parts of the state. Perhaps because it tolerates more variable conditions, scarlet milkweed is more widely available than the native *A. tuberosa*. While a native is preferable, this species can be a reasonable substitute.

Mints (various genera). Members of the mint family have square stems, opposite leaves, bilateral flowers, and are often aromatic. Various genera make important additions to the herb garden: basil, oregano, thyme, rosemary, sage, bee balm, and diverse mints (peppermint and spearmint, for example). These are native and non-native, but use the natives in your butterfly garden and meadow areas. Some, such as bee balm (*Monarda* spp.) and the mints (*Mentha* spp.), may spread aggressively in the garden.

Morning glories (*Ipomoea* spp.) Native and non-native twining annual vines. Choose one of the dozen natives such as moonflower (*I. alba*), railroad vine (*I. pes-caprae*), or beach morning glory (*I. imperati*) if you need a fast growing, colorful, and no-care flowering vine.

Norfolk Island pine (*Araucaria heterophylla*) (10–11). Non-native, from Norfolk Island east of Australia. 200' tall, but in Florida the height is more limited. Even so, this widely planted tree towers over much of the landscape in South Florida. Not wind tolerant or fire resistant. Not recommended.

Oaks (*Quercus* spp.) Florida oaks range from smaller, scrubby oaks to our majestic live oaks with their signature spreading branches. All provide good habitat.

    Laurel oak (*Q. hemisphaerica*) (8–11) Native. 90' tall. Deciduous. Does best in damp or wet sites—not drought tolerant. Not wind resistant.

    Live oak (*Q. virginiana*) (8–11). Native. 60' tall. Spreading evergreen tree and signature tree of "The South." Salt and drought tolerant, this usually fast-growing tree adapts to many soil types. Exceptional wind resistance—one of the most resilient trees in a hurricane. Grows best in full sun. Can live in excess of 200 years. Good addition for a large site.

    Sand live oak (*Q. geminata*) (8–10). Native. 60' tall. Spreading, mostly evergreen tree. Salt and drought tolerant. Wind resistant. Good addition for a large, dry site. Leaf edges curl downward.

    Turkey oak (*Q. laevis*) (8–10). Native. 30' tall. Deciduous. A smaller oak, good for size-restricted sites. Fast growing. Tolerates drought and infertile, sandy soils.

Water oak (*Q. nigra*) (8–10). Native. 75' tall. Semideciduous—doesn't usually lose its leaves until new spring leaves are ready to grow. Tolerant of many soil types and once established needs no care. Widespread over all but the southernmost regions of the state. Not wind resistant—remove or prune in areas where it could cause damage.

Oleander (*Nerium oleander*) (8–11). Non-native, from the Mediterranean. 20' tall. Evergreen. Poisonous. Some cultivars are hardier than others. Drought tolerant. Larval food for polka-dotted wasp moth.

Palms (various genera). Different from other trees because they don't create annual rings of wood each season. See chapter 6 for a full discussion.

Cabbage palm (*Sabal palmetto*) (8–11). Native. 90' tall. Adapts to many different environments. Drought tolerant, wind resistant, and moderately salt tolerant. Fire adapted—remove boots and dead fronds in fire-prone areas to reduce the ladder fuel around the tree. Offers excellent wildlife habitat, and its fruit is enjoyed by birds and many small mammals. Florida's state tree. Highly recommended.

Florida thatch palm (*Thrinax radiata*) (10–11). Native. 30' tall. Grows best on alkaline soil in full sun or partial shade. High wind resistance. Recommended.

Queen palm (*Syagrus romanzoffiana*) (9b–11). Non-native, from South America. 50' tall. Category II invasive exotic in Central and South Florida. Not wind resistant. Though widely planted, it should be removed. Not recommended.

Royal palm (*Roystonea regia*) (10–11). Native. 100' tall. Wind resistant and drought tolerant. Adapts to a variety of environmental conditions. Often planted along streets to produce a magnificent colonnade effect, but they also work very well in more naturalistic settings. Highly recommended.

Saw palmetto (*Serenoa repens*) (8–11). Native. 15' tall, but usually a shrub with its trunk lying on the ground. Salt and drought tolerant. Thrives in wet soils or dry. Provides habitat and food for many species of Florida wildlife. Flammable, but recovers from fire. Recommended for all but the most fire-prone landscapes.

Silver palm (*Coccothrinax argentata*) (10–11). Native. 20' tall. Wind resistant and tolerant of salt spray. Its silvery, fan-shaped fronds add interest to tropical landscapes. Recommended.

Passion vines (*Pasiflora* spp.) Native and non-native. Range varies by species: some are adapted to northern parts of the state, others to the south. All the passion vines have wonderfully complex and colorful flowers and are great additions to the butterfly garden. The natives are all recommended for their home territories and are important host plants for zebra longwing and gulf fritillary butterflies.

Persimmon (*Diospyros virginiana*) (8–10). Native. 60' tall. Deciduous with interesting bark texture. Dioecious, with male and female flowers on separate trees. If you want fruit, you'll need at least one male tree. Be warned that the fruit can make a mess—plant the females away from walkways and high traffic areas. Highly wind resistant. Adaptable to wet or dry soils—drought tolerant. Fire resistant. Good source of wildlife food. Recommended.

Pines (*Pinus* spp.) Evergreen. Pines are gymnosperms, not true flowering plants. Many do well in Florida and are often the first trees to invade a meadow area. The leaves are needles that are well adapted to drought conditions. Generally recommended because they do well in Florida and because of their wildlife habitat values.

Australian pine. Not a pine. Listed under A.

Longleaf pine (*P. palustris*) (8–9). Native. 120' tall. Evergreen with exceptionally long needles—up to 18' long. Fire adapted. Seedlings grow deep roots for a few years before the trunks really start to grow tall above ground. Often lives in excess of 160 years. Wind resistant. Recommended.

Sand pine (*P. clausa*) (8–10). Native. 80' tall. Short needles up to 3 ½ inches. Not wind resistant and should be removed from areas where they could do damage. Not recommended.

Poison ivy (*Toxicodendron radicans*) (8–11). Native. Woody vine. The leaves and wood contain an oily resin, called "urushiol," which causes an itchy allergic reaction in most people. Don't burn it, because breathing in the smoke can cause a systemic allergic reaction and lung inflammation for the whole neighborhood. Remove from fire-prone landscapes and areas where people may come in contact with it. The berries are a significant source of wildlife food.

Poisonwood tree (*Metopium toxiferum*) (10b–11). Native. 40' tall. In the same family as poison ivy and can cause a skin rash on contact. Has large compound leaves and interesting mottled bark. Important food source for white-crowned pigeons and other birds. Don't burn this tree. If you must dispose of it, add it to your compost, but be aware that the compost may also cause skin irritation for up to a year.

Prickly pear cactus (*Opuntia humifusa*) (8–11). Native. 4' tall. A true cactus, the Prickly pear is highly drought and fire resistant. Salt tolerant—good for coastal landscapes. Adds interesting shape and texture to the landscape. The fruits and pads are edible and are widely eaten in other countries. Besides *Opuntia humifusa*, there are several less widespread native prickly pears in Florida and a few cultivars that have escaped from cultivation. Any of the natives is recommended.

Redbud (*Cercis canadensis*) (8–9a). Native. 25' tall. Deciduous with heart-shaped leaves. A member of the bean family, the redbud's pink flowers sprout in early spring directly from the trunk followed by persistent seedpods. Does best in partial shade. Drought tolerant and fire resistant, but not wind resistant. Adds wildlife habitat value. Recommended as an understory tree.

Red cedar or **Southern cedar** (*Juniperus virginiana*) (8–11). Native. 40' tall. There are two forms of *J. virginiana*: the eastern red cedar is more columnar, while the southern red cedar (sometimes referred to as *J. silicicola*) is wider and more salt tolerant. Both are drought tolerant. Seedlings require full sun to grow. Established trees thrive in a wide variety of soils, but not in frequently saturated areas. Singly grown trees are not wind resistant, but groves show good resiliency. Only mature specimens are fire tolerant. Provides good screening and superior wildlife habitat. Use with care in fire-prone areas, otherwise recommended.

Red Maple (*Acer rubrum*) (8–10). Native. 90' tall. Deciduous. Dioecious, with male and female flowers on separate plants. Occurs naturally along freshwater banks and low spots. Has a shallow spreading root system—use only in large areas and don't try to grow grass within its drip line. Fire resistant, but not drought tolerant. Provides vivid fall color. Recommended for large rain gardens, freshwater wetlands, and riverbanks.

River birch (*Betula nigra*) (8–9b). Native. 70' tall. Deciduous. Often grows in groups in damp areas or along freshwater shorelines. Thrives in full sun, but tolerates partial shade. Wind resistant. Attractive exfoliating bark for year-round interest. Not fire resistant. Recommended for edges of rain gardens and constantly damp areas.

Rushes (several genera—most are native). As opposed to grasses and sedges, rushes have round, solid stems. The flower head often appears to arise from the side of a leaf, not the top. Rushes usually grow in damp soil or right in the water. They may volunteer in your lawn or along pond edges. Recommended for rain gardens and wetland habitats.

Sawgrass. See **Sedges**.

Sea grape (*Coccoloba uvifera*) (9b–11). Native. 50' tall. Evergreen. Tree or shrub depending on conditions and maintenance. Drought tolerant. Wind resistant and salt tolerant, sea grape is an important beachside windscreen plant, sheltering buildings and other parts of the landscape. Can be pruned as a coarse hedge. Under palms or alone as a specimen plant, the sea grape's large, round leaves provide great tropical texture; they drop continuously, though, so don't try to grow grass where they fall. Fruits are borne in long brunches like grapes and provide food for wildlife and juice for jellies. Highly recommended.

Sedges (various genera). As opposed to grasses and rushes, sedges are characterized by a solid, triangular stem: "Sedges have edges." Leaves arise from all three sides of the stem. Some native sedges are good choices as wetland plants, while others are great in a dry meadow.
  Nut sedge (*Cyperus esculentus*) (8–11). Non-native, from Mediterra-

nean region. A troublesome weed, but the tubers are edible and used in some Spanish dishes.

Sawgrass or **Jamaica swamp sawgrass** (*Cladium jamaicense*) (8–11). Native. This sedge is the iconic Everglades plant, celebrated in Marjorie Stoneman Douglas' famous tribute to place, *The Everglades: River of Grass* (1947). (Douglas' book should be required reading for anyone interested in Florida's landscape and history.)

White-topped sedge (*Rhynchospora colorata*) (8–11). Native. 18' tall. This sedge has a showy and star-like white flower head. A great addition to rain gardens and pond margins. Highly recommended.

Soapberry (*Sapindus saponaria*) (10–11). Native. 40' tall. Evergreen. Salt and drought tolerant. Grows best in full sun. Wind resistant and fire resistant. Has showy but poisonous round orange berries, each from about one half to an inch across. Grows in almost any type of soil. Recommended.

Sour grass (*Oxalis corniculata*) (8–11). Native. Herbaceous perennial that looks like a shamrock with yellow flowers. Usually considered a weed. The leaves contain oxalic acid, which gives it its sour taste. There are other species in this genus, both native and non-native, with either yellow or pink flowers.

Spanish moss (*Tillandsia usneoides*) (8–11). Native. Spanish moss is an epiphyte, an air plant that does not invade its host plants—usually trees with more horizontal than vertical branches, such as live oak. In fact, it's not a moss at all, but a flowering plant related to bromeliads and pineapples. Grows best in more humid areas near lakes and pond and provides habitat and nesting material for birds, bats, snakes, and insects. Used in the floral trade today, but formerly used to stuff furniture and mattresses. It can absorb up to ten times its weight in moisture. Flammable when dried: it was a spark igniting Spanish moss–filled mattresses that started the great Jacksonville fire of 1901. The common name, Spanish moss, is derived from an insult French explorers used against their bitter rivals in the New World, the Spaniards. Native Americans called it "tree hair."

Sparkleberry or **farkleberry** (*Vaccinium arboreum*) (8–9). Native. 20' tall. Deciduous shrub or small tree. This tallest and southernmost blueberry provides edible fruit for humans and wildlife alike. Fire resistant and fire tolerant. Highly recommended for both edible gardens and wildlife areas where there is acidic soil. See **blueberry**.

Sphagnum mosses (*Sphagnum* spp.) Native. This long, stringy moss— both living and dead—is used in the floral industry to line wire baskets and make wreaths. It can absorb and retain up to 20 times its weight in water. Sphagnum moss grows on top of sphagnum bogs. Peat moss, on the other hand, is formed in the lower levels of a sphagnum bog after centuries of compression. This is why peat moss is not a sustainable product for your garden.

Squashes (*Cucurbita* spp.) (8–11). Non-native, from Central and South American. The cucurbits are vining vegetables that include summer squash, winter squash, pumpkins, gourds, zucchini squash, and more. Plants have both male and female flowers and need pollinators to set fruit. The flowers are edible, too.

Stoppers. Mostly tropical small evergreen trees. Both non-native and native. The native species listed below are recommended for firewise and stormwise landscapes. All stoppers grow best in soils with some organic material, and most produce new growth with a characteristic reddish-pink color. The fuzzy or puffy flowers, ranging from white to yellow to pinkish, tend to have a pleasant, musky fragrance and attract bees and butterflies. Stoppers also provide wildlife cover and food. Native Americans and early settlers used the plants to make an antidiarrheal treatment, hence the name "stopper." Recommended.

Boxleaf stopper (*Eugenia foetida*) (10–11). Native. 25' tall. Salt tolerant—good additon to a hedgerow for screening in coastal areas.

Redberry stopper (*Eugenia confusa*) (10–11). Native. 40' tall. Likes moist soil: neither salt nor drought tolerant. Striking landscape plant with shiny leaves, pinkish-red new growth, clusters of tiny white flowers, and bright red berries.

Simpson's stopper (*Myrcianthes fragrans*) (9b–11). Native. 30' tall. Salt and drought tolerant, but prefers moist, neutral to alkaline soil. Good coastal tree. Blooms year round.

White stopper (*Eugenia axillaries*) (9–11). Native. 25' tall. Not particularly salt or drought tolerant. Prefers moist, sandy, or alkaline soil. Good thicket or screening tree, with striking white to pale gray bark.

Strong bark (*Bourreria* spp.) (10b–11). Native. *Bourreria* is composed of three endangered species with a range limited to the Keys and Dade County. Slow growing, wind resistant, and drought tolerant. The orange fruits make good wildlife food. Don't dig them from the wild, but if you can find a legitimate source, highly recommended.

Sunflowers (*Helianthus* spp.) Herbaceous. Annual or perennial. Fourteen native species, plus many cultivars and non-natives are available. Crawling or erect. Drought tolerant. Attracts bees and butterflies, and its seeds are eaten by a wide variety of birds. Roots, seeds, and other parts of some species may exude allelopathic chemicals that inhibit grow of plants nearby. When possible choose natives. Recommended.

Annual sunflower (*H. annuus*) (8–11). Non-native, from the Midwest, but highly cultivated in Europe and reintroduced to the U.S. 12' tall. Often planted in the edible garden because of its large seeds.

Beach sunflower (*H. debilis*) (8–10). Native. Salt tolerant groundcover. Highly recommended for dunes and other dry habitats.

Swamp sunflower (H. angustifolius) (8–9). Native. Perennial and tuberous. Tolerates wet and dry soil and is recommended for sunny rain gardens.

Sweet gum (*Liquidambar styraciflua*) (8–10a). Native. 100' tall. Deciduous. Good fall color, even in Florida. Somewhat flexible and has some wind resistance when growing with other trees. Fire tolerant and not highly flammable. Has large, aggressive surface roots that tend to send up suckers. The seeds are enclosed in spiny gumballs that are a nuisance because they persist in the landscape. Recommended for wild areas, including wind groves, well away from paths, buildings, and parking areas.

Tomato (*Solanum lycopersicum*) (8–11). Non-native, from South America. Herbaceous annual. Tomatoes were introduced to the U.S. via Europe. They are members of the Solanaceae family, which also contains crops such as bell peppers, eggplants, tree tomatoes, tomatillo, and potatoes. The family also includes tobacco, deadly nightshade, and the deadly supermarket tomato! Grow in early spring or in the fall, because tomatoes may not make it through Florida's hot summers.

Trumpet creeper (*Campsis radicans*) (8–10). Native. Woody deciduous vine with large tubular orange flowers. Trumpet creeper can get rambunctious and cover whole trees, but it can also be trained and restrained. Drought tolerant. Recommended for wild areas or to cover arbors and pergolas. Hummingbirds love them.

Tulip tree (*Liriodendron tulipifera*) (8–9a). Native. 100' tall. Deciduous. A fast-growing member of the magnolia family. Requires rich damp soil. Neither drought nor wind tolerant; not highly flammable, but not fire tolerant either. If it's already established on your property, a tulip tree makes a great addition to a wooded area, but it's probably not a terrific choice for our hot weather and sandy soils. Sometimes called "yellow poplar" or "tulip poplar" because its clear, soft wood is similar to that of true poplars (*Populus* spp.).

Tupelos (*Nyssa* spp.) Native. Deciduous. Wind resistant. Both species are good choices for riparian conditions, and they are also drought resistant because of their deep roots. The fruits provide food for birds. Branches are normally perpendicular to the trunk, so plant these trees away from buildings. In high traffic areas, prune to raise the crown. Though not highly flammable, they are not fire tolerant and won't grow back after a fire. The word "nyssa" is the name of a water nymph; the tree is so called because the type species, *N. aquatica* or water tupelo, grows in water. Recommended.

 Black tupelo or **black gum** (*N. sylvatica*) (8–9). 80' tall. Scarlet fall color.

 Water tupelo (*N. aquatica*) (8–9a). 60' tall. When growing in water, the base of the trunk is often swollen or buttressed.

Viburnums, possum-haw, or **arrow wood** (*Viburnum* spp.) (8–11). Native, non-native, and cultivars. 12' tall. Multistemmed, vase-shaped shrub. Grows in shade or sun and on wet or dry sites. Viburnums have year-round interest—flowers in the spring, thick foliage in the summer, berries in the fall, and interesting branch structures and bark color in the winter. Viburnums can be propagated by greenwood cuttings stuck in damp soil, so they may be used in fascines to stabilize and revegetate shorelines or banks. Fascines are groups of rootable branches. Recommended for wildlife food and cover and for habitat restoration.

Virginia creeper (*Parthenocissus quinquefolia*) (8–11). Native. Woody deciduous vine that can crawl on the ground or climb structures. Fast growing with good wildlife value, providing cover and food. Reliable fall color—vivid scarlet to tawny orange—in north and central sections of the state. On the down side, Virginia creeper can cover small trees and the tiny adhesive disks it uses for crawling can damage buildings. Recommended for meadows and habitat restoration.

Walnut (*Juglans nigra*) (8a). Native. 120' tall. Deciduous. Pinnately compound leaves have 15–23 leaflets. Roots release an allelopathic chemical that prevents germination of seeds and inhibits growth of plants nearby. While it may be a crop tree in the northernmost sections of the state, it's not usually recommended for the general landscape.

Water hyacinth (*Eichhornia crassipes*) (8–11). Non-native, from South America. Category I invasive exotic. A floating pond ornamental that escaped from cultivation near the banks of St. Johns River in north Florida. Millions of dollars have been spent to remove it from Florida's waterways. It is high in nutrients, and some organic fertilizers are made from water hyacinth slurry. Add these waterweeds to your compost pile to benefit your plantings, and you'll also help control this pest.

Wax myrtle (*Myrica cerifera*) (8–11). Native. 30' tall. Evergreen shrub. Full sun or partial shade. Tolerates wet soil, sandy soil, clay, or limestone gravel. Like a legume, it can fix nitrogen in poor soils with its root nodules. Highly flammable and not resistant to wind, but whether it's burned or broken, it will grow back from its roots. It takes well to pruning and can form a dense hedge or screen. Many types of birds feast on its abundant waxy fruit. Not recommended for fire-prone areas or spots where it could do damage in a windstorm, but this is a great, carefree shrub for a wildlife area or to provide screening away from buildings. Colonists used to boil the fruits of this and its more northern relative, bayberry (*M. pensylvanica*), to render the wax for candles.

Wild garlic or **meadow garlic** (*Allium canadense*) (8–9). Native. Bulbaceous aromatic perennial with long, slender, flattened leaves and rounded clusters of small white to pale lavender flowers atop long stalks. Frequent in lawns, meadows, and roadside ditches. A good addition to your herb garden or meadow areas. Related to onion (*A. cepa*), cultivated garlic (*A. sativum*), chives (*A. schoenoprasum*), and others.

Wild plum (*Prunus Americana*) (8–9a). Native. 20' tall. Deciduous tree or multistemmed shrub. Tolerates wet or dry, acid or alkaline soils. Fire resistant. White spring flowers and edible fruit for humans and beast alike. Branches may be thorny. Recommended for its beauty and easy care and for wildlife food and cover. The Chickasaw plum (P. angustifolia) is another good choice for a native plum.

Wild tamarind (*Lysiloma latisiliquum*) (10b–11). Native. 60' tall. Evergreen, with arching branches, ferny leaves, and fragrant, white, puff-ball flowers in spring and summer. Tolerates any type of soil as long as it's well drained. Salt tolerant, drought resistant, and fire resistant. Prune to promote wind resistance, as it tends to produce codominate trunks. A host and nectar plant for a variety of butterflies and preferred habitat of native tree snails. Recommended for coastal areas.

Wild taro (*Colocasia esculenta*) (8–11). Non-native, from the Pacific islands. Category I invasive exotic. Bulbaceous perennial. This plant has invaded and replaced wetland species in most of the state. It sends out rhizomes with thickened sections that each can become separate plants. Once wild taro has invaded an area, it's not easy to eradicate, but you should try.

Winged elm (*Ulmus alata*) (8–9). Native. 80' tall. Deciduous. Full sun or partial shade. Tolerates wet soil and flooding, but also tolerates drier areas. Wind resistant, with low flammability. The small stems have corky extensions or wings on either side. These trees may be susceptible to Dutch elm disease—that dreaded fungal infection that destroyed so many of our American elms (*U. americana*) a few decades ago. Recommended.

Resources

Web Sites

Florida Exotic Pest Plant Council maintains two lists of Florida's Invasive Plant Species: http://www.fleppc.org.
   Institute for Regional Conservation: http://www.regionalconservation.org.
   Floridata. Online plant encyclopedia. http://www.floridata.com.

Books

Haehle, Robert G. *Native Florida Plants: Low Maintenance Landscaping and Gardening.* Rev. ed. Lanham, Md.: Taylor Trade, 2004.
Nelson, Gil, and David Chiappini. *Florida's Best Native Landscape Plants.* Gainesville: University Press of Florida, 2003.
Nelson, Gil. *The Trees of Florida.* Sarasota: Pineapple Press, 1994.
Osorio, Rufina. *A Gardener's Guide to Florida's Native Plants.* Gainesville: University Press of Florida, 2001.
Wunderlin, Richard P., and Bruce F. Hansen. *Vascular Plants of Florida.* Gainesville: University Press of Florida, 2003. Also see the associated Web site: http://www.plantatlas.usf.edu

Index

Ginny Stibolt writes an online column surveying Florida gardening, which appears in Jacksonville's *Florida Times-Union*, in Floridata.com, an online plant encyclopedia, and on her own Web site, www.transplanted gardener.com. She's also the garden writer for *Vero Beach Magazine*. She has created www.SustainableGardening4Florida.com as a companion site for this book. It includes updated references for each of the chapters and other current topics on sustainable gardening in Florida.